PRAISE FOR *RESONANCE*

"It's great! *Resonance* introduces 'The More,' which is really cool and which no one has ever said before. It's clear, beautifully written, and makes a promise that will keep the reader turning the pages. Outstanding—this is gonna be a good one! I wouldn't change a word."

—STEVEN PRESSFIELD, AUTHOR OF *THE WAR OF ART*

"Our brains are wired for connection, but we've lacked a practical framework for cultivating it. *Resonance* fills that gap. Michael Trainer has written the book I wish existed when I started my research—one that translates decades of neuroscience into lived wisdom. This isn't just theory. It's a road map to authentic connection."

—MATTHEW D. LIEBERMAN, PHD, DIRECTOR OF THE SOCIAL COGNITIVE NEUROSCIENCE LABORATORY AT THE UNIVERSITY OF CALIFORNIA, LOS ANGELES AND AUTHOR OF *SOCIAL: WHY OUR BRAINS ARE WIRED TO CONNECT*

"I've always believed that relationships drive business results. In *Resonance*, Michael Trainer shows us the neuroscience behind that truth, and how to turn human connection into a leadership advantage."

—KEITH FERRAZZI, #1 *NEW YORK TIMES* BESTSELLING AUTHOR OF *NEVER EAT ALONE* AND *WHO'S GOT YOUR BACK*

"*Resonance* reveals why some connections transform us while others leave us unchanged. Essential reading for anyone seeking deeper relationships."

—KATHERINE WOODWARD THOMAS, MFT, *NEW YORK TIMES* BESTSELLING AUTHOR OF *CONSCIOUS UNCOUPLING* AND *CALLING IN "THE ONE"*

"Michael Trainer's *Resonance* makes a compelling case that what we are really craving is not more productivity or self-help but genuine connection. Blending neuroscience with personal story, he shows how resonance is both emotional and biological. It is an inspiring and practical invitation to remember our shared humanity."

—DR. LAURA BERMAN, *NEW YORK TIMES* BESTSELLING AUTHOR AND HOST OF *THE LANGUAGE OF LOVE*

"At Modern Elder Academy, we've learned that wisdom comes from connection, not achievement. *Resonance* reveals why—the neuroscience proves that 'the More' Michael describes is real, measurable, and transformative. This is the book I wish I'd had at 30."

—CHIP CONLEY, COFOUNDER AND EXECUTIVE CHAIRMAN OF MODERN ELDER ACADEMY AND *NEW YORK TIMES* BESTSELLING AUTHOR OF *EMOTIONAL EQUATIONS*

Resonance

The Art and Science of HUMAN CONNECTION

Michael Trainer

BenBella Books, Inc.
Dallas, TX

BenBella Books, Inc.
8080 N. Central Expressway
Suite 1700
Dallas, TX 75206
benbellabooks.com
Send feedback to feedback@benbellabooks.com

BenBella is a federally registered trademark.

Printed in the United States of America
10 9 8 7 6 5 4 3 2 1

Library of Congress Control Number: 2025044595
ISBN 978-1-63774-795-7 (hardcover)
ISBN 978-1-63774-796-4 (electronic)

Editing by Rick Chillot
Copyediting by Scott Calamar
Proofreading by Denise Pangia and Jill Kramer
Text design and composition by Aaron Edmiston
Cover design by Brigid Pearson
Cover image © Adobe Stock / coffeemill
Printed by Lake Book Manufacturing

I dedicate this book to the song that wants to live in all of us.

To all my relations; specifically to my father John, my mother Nancy, my sister Lindsay, my niece Liliana.

To those that have gone before me, and my family yet to come. I sing this song for you.

To the music; thanks for showing us the way home.

Contents

PART 3 **STRIKING THE RIGHT CHORD**

PART 4 **BUILDING YOUR BAND**

PART 5 **SHARING YOUR SONG**

PRELUDE

The Symphony Begins

We are the music makers,
And we are the dreamers of dreams.
ARTHUR O'SHAUGHNESSY

There's a melody that plays within each of us, a unique song composed of our values, passions, and experiences. It's the music of our authentic selves, yearning to be expressed. Yet, too often, this inner music is drowned out by the noise of the world, the clamor of expectations, and the dissonance of superficial connections. We find ourselves playing a tune that doesn't resonate, living lives that feel out of sync with who we truly are.

But what if the key to unlocking your potential, to living a life of profound meaning and joy, lies not in striving for more but in tuning in to the music that already exists—the music within you and the music that emerges in the space between you and others?

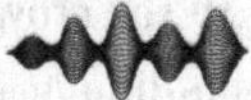

The concert hall fell silent as the conductor raised his baton. A collective breath was held, a moment suspended between what was and what would be. Then, with a graceful downward arc, he released the orchestra into sound—strings and brass, woodwinds and percussion, each instrument adding its unique voice to a harmony far greater than any could create alone.

I sat transfixed, not just hearing the music, but feeling it physically move through me. The Tanglewood performance of Beethoven's Ninth Symphony on that humid summer evening wasn't merely an auditory experience—it was a full-body immersion in something transcendent.

As the familiar notes of the "Ode to Joy" filled the open-air pavilion, I noticed something remarkable happening around me. Strangers seated side by side began to synchronize their breathing. An elderly woman to my right lightly conducted with her fingers. A man across the aisle closed his eyes, his face softening into a smile. We were thousands of individual listeners, yet in that moment, we became something more—a collective presence, breathing together, hearts beating in rhythm with the music.

This was resonance—not just in the physical sense of vibrating strings and air molecules, but in the human sense of souls aligning with something larger than themselves. It's what happens when the boundaries between us momentarily dissolve, revealing a deeper connectedness that was always there, waiting to be awakened.

That night under the stars, as thunder rumbled in the distance threatening rain that never came, I experienced what I've come to call "The More"—that exponential potential that emerges when we connect authentically with something beyond ourselves. This concert wasn't just a beautiful performance; it was a visceral reminder of what's possible when we align our individual songs with others to create a symphony.

The irony wasn't lost on me that Beethoven himself never heard a note of the Ninth Symphony performed. Completely deaf by the time he composed it, Beethoven conducted its premiere in 1824, keeping time to music he could feel but not hear. Legend has it that at the symphony's conclusion, the audience erupted in applause while Beethoven, his back to the crowd, continued conducting. A soloist had to turn him around to see the standing ovation his music had inspired.

Here was a man isolated in silence who nevertheless created one of the most profound expressions of human connection ever composed. He couldn't hear the external resonance his music created, but he felt its truth within himself and trusted that truth enough to share it with the world.

You've likely felt resonance before, even if you didn't have a name for it. It's that electric feeling when you connect with someone on a deep level, that sense of being fully seen, heard, and understood. It's the spark of inspiration that ignites when you find your "band"—the people who share your values and amplify your song. Resonance is the feeling of knowing you are a part of something bigger, something meaningful.

But resonance is not a matter of chance. It's a skill that can be cultivated, a practice that can be honed. And it all begins with a willingness to listen—to the subtle melodies within yourself, to the unspoken needs of others, and to the rhythm of the world around you.

As we begin our journey together through this book, I invite you to consider your own symphony—the unique music that lives within you, waiting to be expressed and shared. And I invite you to consider the spaces between the notes, the relationships that amplify your individual voice into something more powerful than you could ever create alone.

The pages that follow aren't just about building better relationships, though they will certainly help you do that. They're about recognizing that the quality of your connections determines the quality of your life. They're about understanding that resonance isn't just a pleasant addition to an otherwise complete existence; it's the very foundation of a life well lived.

Whether you're seeking deeper connection in your personal relationships, more authentic engagement in your professional life, or a greater sense of belonging in your community, the principles in this book will guide you toward what we all ultimately desire: to be seen, to be heard, to matter, to contribute to something larger than ourselves.

Like Beethoven conducting his masterpiece in silence, you may not always immediately see the impact of the connections you create. But make no mistake—the symphony you compose through your relationships will continue to play long after you've left the stage, reverberating through lives you may never know you've touched.

The world needs your song. Are you ready to play it?

INTRODUCTION

The Symphony of Your Life

Music expresses that which cannot be put into words and that which cannot remain silent.

VICTOR HUGO

The quality of your life is the quality of your relationships.

TONY ROBBINS

It was a crisp autumn evening in New York City. Standing on a stage in Central Park, with the iconic skyline as my backdrop, I watched as Neil Young, Dave Grohl, and Dan Auerbach launched into a blistering rendition of "Rockin' in the Free World." This unforgettable night was about more than just music. It was a powerful demonstration of resonance in action.

Here were world leaders, rock stars, and ordinary citizens, all gathered together with a shared purpose. The energy was electric, the sense of connection palpable. In just nine months our team had built a movement from scratch, culminating in one of the largest syndicated broadcasts in history and generating over $1.3 billion in commitments to fight global poverty.

During my time as co-creator and movement director of Global Citizen, I helped architect what became a movement: a highly effective, hugely scalable model for inspiring belief, creating action, and getting people on your side. We forged meaningful connections at the highest levels and, ultimately, made a real difference in the world. We mobilized millions of people to raise more than $40 billion in commitments set to impact the lives of countless people around the world.

Through this journey, and many others throughout my life and career, I became deeply curious about the power of connection and community. What, specifically, made this undertaking so effective? What was the recipe for our secret sauce? It became clear that music, and the shared experience it creates, was a key ingredient. But more than that, it was the intention behind the music, the intention to connect, to inspire, and to create something bigger than ourselves. This intention, this resonance, is what transformed a simple concert into a global movement.

Life is not a solo performance. It's a complex, ever-evolving composition where the relationships you cultivate serve as the instruments in your personal symphony. Every connection adds a new note, every interaction contributes to the overall harmony. But in today's hyperconnected yet increasingly isolated world, it's easy to lose sight of the melody, to let the noise of superficial interactions drown out the deeper notes of genuine connection.

What if the key to a fulfilling life lies not in the number of connections we have but in the depth of those connections? What if we could learn to cultivate relationships that resonate with our core values, relationships that amplify our joys and support us through challenges? And what if, in creating these resonant connections, we could unlock a potential that goes far beyond what we can achieve alone—a potential for creativity, impact, and fulfillment that is exponentially greater than the sum of its parts?

This is the potential that I call "The More."

This book is your guide to composing such a symphony of resonant relationships. It's a journey into the heart of resonance—that powerful sense of connection and alignment that happens when we truly see, hear, and understand one another. It's the feeling of being in sync, on the same wavelength, vibrating at the same frequency. Resonance is what makes a conversation with a close friend feel like coming home and what can transform a simple gathering into a life-changing event.

THE PROMISE: UNLOCKING THE MORE

Resonance is built on the premise that the quality of our lives, both personally and professionally, is defined by the quality of our relationships. And the quality of our relationships is directly related to our ability to create resonance—to be a stand for connection in a world that often feels disconnected. But this book offers more than just a path to better relationships. It offers a path to unlocking The More, that exponential potential that emerges when we align our relationships with authenticity, purpose, and a shared vision.

The More is the dormant music that wants to live in you—and in the space between you and another person. It's the transcendent potential that's unleashed when you find your "band," the people who resonate with your song and amplify your impact. The More is not about achieving more for the sake of it. It is about achieving more of what truly matters. It is about recognizing that the most resonant note you can play is one of contribution, and that by being a stand for a greater good, you create the conditions for your own unique talents to shine. It's the creative breakthroughs, the amplified impact, the deeper fulfillment that comes from resonant collaboration. It's the 1 + 1 = 11 effect, where the whole is infinitely greater than the sum of its parts.

In my journey exploring human connection across cultures and contexts, I've witnessed a pattern that transcends boundaries: When people experience genuine resonance—that state of synchrony where they feel truly seen, heard, and valued—their capacity for resilience, creativity, and well-being expands exponentially. This isn't just a pleasant social phenomenon; it's a biological imperative wired into our very DNA.

Yet paradoxically, at the very moment when technology has made us more interconnected than ever before, many of us are experiencing unprecedented levels of isolation and loneliness. The US surgeon general has declared loneliness a public health epidemic on par with smoking and obesity. Despite our thousands of digital "friends," many of us hunger for the nourishment that only genuine connection provides.

This book is my response to that hunger—a practical guide to creating the resonant relationships that sustain us through life's challenges and amplify its joys. Drawing on research from neuroscience, psychology, anthropology, and my own field experiences, I'll share a comprehensive framework for building connections that transform not just your relationships but your experience of being alive.

THE FRAMEWORK: SEVEN CORE PRINCIPLES AND INTENTIONAL PRACTICES

At the heart of this approach are seven fundamental principles that I call "the Seven Pillars of Resonant Relationships." Like instruments in an orchestra, each contributes something vital to the symphony of connection. These principles aren't abstract theories but practical approaches I've tested across diverse cultures and contexts. They work because they align with our innate human needs for belonging, meaning, and connection. When applied consistently, they create The More—that exponential expansion of possibility that emerges when we connect authentically with others.

Throughout this book, I'll share stories from my own journey and from the lives of remarkable individuals I've encountered—from musicians who've created transcendent communities through sound to business leaders who've transformed organizational cultures through authentic connection, from families healing generations of conflict to communities bridging seemingly unbridgeable divides.

You'll also find practical tools I call "Resonance Instruments"—exercises, reflections, and practices that help you embody these principles in your daily life. These aren't complicated techniques requiring special expertise; they are accessible approaches anyone can use to create more resonant relationships and help you tune your inner instrument and cultivate resonance in all your interactions. Just as musicians practice scales and exercises regularly to hone their skills, these instruments will help you develop your "resonance muscles," your relational fitness and health, which directly correlate to your capacity for deep listening, empathy, generosity, and authentic connection.

And because music offers perhaps our most accessible experience of resonance, each chapter includes "Resonance Sessions"—explorations of songs and musical stories that illuminate aspects of human connection. These interludes remind us that resonance isn't just a concept to understand intellectually but an experience to feel in our bodies.

This is not a book of networking tricks or psychological hacks. It encourages you to make a fundamental shift in mindset—a shift from seeing relationships as transactional to seeing them as transformational. Achieving resonance requires seeing the world and your interactions in it as an invitation to successfully navigate the space between yourself and others.

My promise is this: If you engage with the ideas in this book not just theoretically but experientially, if you practice these principles consistently in your relationships, you will experience a profound shift in how you connect with others and, ultimately, with yourself. You will begin to unlock The More, discovering that your capacity for impact, joy, and meaning expands exponentially through authentic connection.

The journey ahead won't always be easy. It will ask you to examine your patterns, to risk vulnerability, to practice new ways of being. There will be moments when you'll want to retreat behind familiar walls, when the old patterns of disconnection will call you back like comfortable old clothes.

But the alternative—a life of superficial connection or, worse, of isolation—exacts a far greater cost. Like the twelve-year-old boy I once was, pressing my face into my horse's neck because human connection felt too dangerous, you may have found ways to survive without deep resonance. But survival is not the same as thriving. Protection is not the same as fulfillment.

The world needs your song—your unique gifts, passions, and perspective. But more than that, it needs the music that can only emerge when your song joins with others in a harmony of purpose and possibility. It needs the symphony that you, and only you, can help create.

Prepare to embrace what's beyond the horizon. The symphony of possibility awaits.

PART 1

The Power of Resonance

If you want to go fast, go alone. If you want to go far, go together.

AFRICAN PROVERB

Welcome to the beginning of your journey toward more resonant relationships. In part 1, we'll establish the foundation for everything that follows—exploring what resonance is, why it matters so profoundly in our lives, and how to begin creating it in your relationships.

We'll start by understanding the concept of resonance itself, both as a physical phenomenon and as a metaphor for human connection. You'll discover how genuine connections create The More—that exponential potential that emerges when we align authentically with others.

Next, we'll examine the current crisis of disconnection—the loneliness epidemic that affects so many in our hyperconnected yet emotionally distant world. We'll explore the neuroscience of isolation and connection, understanding how our brains and bodies are literally wired to thrive in relationship with others.

We'll then dive into the first pillar of resonant relationships: being an offering. You'll learn how generosity creates the foundation for all meaningful connections—and how shifting from "What can I get?" to "What can I give?" transforms not just your relationships but your experience of being alive.

Finally, we'll explore how different cultures throughout history have created rituals and practices that foster authentic connection, and how you can adapt these timeless approaches to create your own resonant rhythms in modern life.

By the end of part 1, you'll have a clear understanding of what resonance is, why it matters, and how to begin creating it through generosity and intentional practice. You'll be equipped with practical tools to start transforming your relationships right away, laying the groundwork for the deeper explorations to come in later parts of the book.

Remember, this isn't just reading material—it's an invitation to transformation. I encourage you to engage with the reflection questions, try the practices, and allow yourself to be moved by the stories and music we'll explore together. The most profound insights often come not from intellectual understanding alone but from embodied experience.

Let's begin this journey toward the resonant life you were born to live.

CHAPTER 1

The Heart of Resonance

The measure of a life well lived is in the strength of its connections, not in the scope of its achievements.

UNKNOWN

Close your eyes. Take three deep breaths and allow yourself to fully engage with this reflection:

Think of a moment when you felt completely seen and understood by another person. It might have been during a deep conversation, a shared experience, or even a brief exchange with a stranger that somehow felt significant.

Re-create this moment in your mind's eye. Where were you? Who was with you? What was said or unsaid?

Now, bring your attention to how this moment felt in your body. Perhaps there was warmth in your chest, relaxation in your shoulders, or a sense of expansion. Maybe you experienced a quickening of energy or a profound calm.

This bodily sensation—this felt experience of connection—is your personal signature of resonance. It's the essence of what we'll be exploring together throughout this book.

THE SCIENCE OF HUMAN CONNECTION

The term "resonance" comes from the Latin *resonare*, meaning "to resound" or "to echo." In physics, resonance occurs when a vibrating system or external force drives another system to oscillate with greater amplitude at specific frequencies. When an opera singer hits just the right note to shatter a glass, that's resonance at work.

But resonance is more than just a physical phenomenon. It's a powerful metaphor for understanding human connection. Just as objects can amplify each other's vibrations, people can amplify each other's energy, creativity, and impact when they "vibrate at the same frequency"—when they align around shared values, purposes, and ways of being.

Think about a time when you met someone and immediately felt understood, without having to explain yourself. Or when a conversation with a friend left you feeling more energized than when you began. That's resonance in action.

The science behind these experiences is fascinating. Dr. Daniel Siegel, clinical professor of psychiatry at UCLA, uses the term "interpersonal neurobiology" to describe how our brains literally shape each other through connection. "The mind," he writes, "is an embodied and relational process that regulates the flow of energy and information." When we connect deeply with others, our nervous systems begin to synchronize. Our heart rates align. Our brain waves entrain. We begin, quite literally, to resonate with one another.

This is not mystical thinking but hard science. Researchers at Princeton University used fMRI scanning to observe what happens in people's brains during storytelling. They discovered that when a speaker tells a story and a listener is engaged, their neural patterns begin to couple—their brains start "dancing together." This neural synchrony increases with the listener's comprehension. The better the understanding, the stronger the resonance.

Perhaps the most compelling evidence for the power of resonance comes from the work of psychologist Barbara Fredrickson, who discovered what she calls "positivity resonance." When people share positive emotions in moments of connection, they create an upward spiral of well-being that strengthens not just their relationship but their individual resilience and health. These micromoments of connection literally change our biochemistry, reducing inflammation and improving cardiovascular function.

The science is clear: Resonance isn't just nice to have in human relationships—it's essential to our very survival and thriving.

THE NEUROCHEMISTRY OF CONNECTION

When we experience moments of genuine resonance with others, our brains release a cascade of neurochemicals that fundamentally change our physiology:

Oxytocin, often called the "bonding hormone," increases trust and strengthens social bonds. It's released during positive social interactions, physical touch, and even eye contact.

Dopamine, the "reward chemical," creates feelings of pleasure and reinforces behaviors. When we connect authentically, our brain rewards us with dopamine, making us seek more connection.

Serotonin, which regulates mood, is boosted through social connection, helping explain why isolation often leads to depression.

Endorphins, natural pain relievers, are released during shared laughter and positive social experiences, creating a natural "high" that buffers against stress.

This neurochemical symphony doesn't just make us feel good momentarily—it has profound long-term health benefits, including reduced inflammation, improved immune function, lower blood pressure, and even longer lifespan.

THE SYMPHONY OF THE SEVEN PILLARS

Resonance doesn't happen by accident. Like any art, it requires both understanding and practice. Through years of personal experience, observation, and research, I've identified seven core principles—the Seven Pillars of Resonant Relationships.

Together, they form a comprehensive framework for creating the conditions in which resonance can flourish.

Think of these pillars as tools used to create music, from an intimate duet to a full-blown symphony. Each contributes something vital to the whole, and when all are present, they create something far greater than the sum of their parts:

1. **Be Generous of Time and Energy, Be an Offering (the Hands).** Just as a drummer's hands freely give rhythm that supports the entire band, your generosity creates the foundation upon which all meaningful connection is built.
2. **Listen Deeply and Be Curious (the Ear).** As a great jazz musician listens intently before responding to what's been played, your focused attention creates space for authentic expression and understanding.
3. **Be at Integrity in Word and Action (the Tuning Fork).** A tuning fork provides the precise pitch that brings instruments into harmony; your alignment between values and actions creates trust—the cornerstone of resonance.
4. **Add Value Without Expectation of Return (the Horn).** Like a horn player who contributes a unique voice to the ensemble without dominating it, your authentic contributions enrich others' lives without creating obligation.
5. **Find Uncommon Common Ground (the Strings).** As string instruments create harmony through different notes played simultaneously, your ability to discover unexpected shared territory bridges differences and creates connection.
6. **Create Exponential Opportunities for Connection (the Conductor's Baton).** Just as a conductor brings together individual musicians to create something greater than any could alone, your facilitation of meaningful interactions extends resonance beyond yourself.
7. **Stand for Something Bigger (the Drum).** Like the heartbeat of a drum that unites musicians and audience alike, your alignment with

purpose beyond yourself creates meaning that attracts and inspires others.

While we'll explore these principles sequentially, understand that they're deeply interconnected. Like instruments in an orchestra, they work together to create the symphony of resonant relationships. And like any skill worth mastering, they require practice—intentional, consistent application in our daily lives.

THE UPWARD SPIRAL OF CONNECTION

The process of building resonant relationships follows a natural progression—what I call "the Resonance Spiral." This spiral illustrates how connection creates an upward trajectory that builds upon itself.

It begins with **safety**, the innermost ring. When we feel psychologically safe, we can lower our defenses and allow ourselves to be present. This safety creates the conditions for **vulnerability**, the willingness to show our authentic selves, including our imperfections and uncertainties.

Vulnerability creates opportunities for **recognition**—the experience of being seen and acknowledged for who we truly are. This recognition leads to deeper **attunement** between people, a synchronization of energy and intention.

Attunement produces the harmonic state we call **resonance**, where connection transcends ordinary interaction and creates a sense of alignment and flow. These experiences of resonance build deeper **trust**, creating a foundation for even more meaningful connection.

Ultimately, this process creates **expanded safety**—a broader, deeper sense of security that allows the spiral to continue at increasingly profound levels.

This spiral works in both directions. When safety is broken, we move inward toward self-protection and disconnection. But a single moment of conscious connection can reverse the direction, starting the upward spiral again.

Where are you currently on this spiral in your most important relationships? What one small move could help you spiral outward toward greater resonance?

THE SHADOW SIDE: WHEN CONNECTION BREAKS DOWN

Just as our bodies have built-in systems that reward connection, they also have alarm systems that activate during disconnection. When we experience rejection, exclusion, or chronic isolation, our brains react as if facing physical danger.

The same brain region that processes physical pain—namely, the dorsal anterior cingulate cortex—activates during social rejection. Stress hormones like cortisol flood our system, preparing us for a threat in the short term, but damaging our health when chronically elevated. Inflammatory markers increase, linking loneliness to an increased risk of heart disease, dementia, and premature death. The brain's prefrontal cortex, responsible for complex thinking and decision-making, shows reduced function during social stress.

This biological response explains why disconnection feels so devastating—our bodies interpret it as a survival threat. Understanding this biological reality helps us approach our need for connection not as weakness but as a fundamental human requirement, as essential as food and water.

THE SOUNDS OF SILENCE: MY JOURNEY THROUGH ISOLATION

To truly appreciate the power of resonance, we must also understand its absence. I know this absence intimately.

I was twelve, wandering through narrow cobblestone streets in a small Spanish town on my very first experience alone abroad. The Mediterranean sun beat down as I explored, feeling grown-up and adventurous in my solitude. I remember the golden light, the smell of bread from a nearby bakery, and then—darkness.

What happened next remains fragmented in my memory: rough hands, a face I couldn't clearly see, pain, fear unlike anything I'd known before. I was violently jumped by a gang of more than twenty boys and young men.

A shopkeeper found me and called for help. The physical wounds healed within weeks, leaving only the faintest scars. But something fundamental broke inside me—my sense of safety in the world, my trust in people, my belief that connection was possible.

Back home in Chicago, I retreated into profound isolation. The boy who once raised his hand in class and made friends easily became silent, invisible. At school, already struggling with undiagnosed learning difficulties, I became a target for bullies who sensed my newfound vulnerability like predators sense weakness. Each day became an exercise in disappearing—how to move through the world without being noticed, without being hurt again.

Perhaps you know this place too. Maybe your isolation stems from different wounds—rejection, betrayal, loss, or trauma that taught you people aren't safe. Or perhaps it's more subtle—the slow drift into disconnection that can happen in our hyperconnected yet emotionally distant modern world, where we're endlessly "in touch" yet rarely truly touching. Maybe you've felt the paradox of being surrounded by people yet feeling profoundly alone. Of smiling through dinner parties while screaming inside: *Does anyone actually see me?*

For me, refuge came in an unexpected form—at summer camp, where I found myself drawn to a chestnut mare who had also known trauma. Unlike the unpredictable humans who had hurt me, this horse's intentions were transparent, her presence unconditional. She would stand perfectly still, as if she understood my need for connection. Sometimes she would gently nuzzle my shoulder or exhale softly, her breath warm against my skin.

It was my first experience of resonance—two beings vibrating in harmony—though I wouldn't have called it that then. I only knew that in those moments, the tightness in my chest would ease. The constant vigilance would temporarily subside. I could breathe again.

But resonance with animals, precious as it was, couldn't fill the human-shaped hole in my heart. The loneliness was physical—a constant ache in my chest, a heaviness that made even getting out of bed an act of courage. I developed elaborate strategies to avoid connection, not realizing that in protecting myself from potential pain, I was guaranteeing another kind of suffering.

This is the paradox of isolation: In trying to keep ourselves safe from the vulnerability that connection requires, we inflict a deeper wound—the wound of disconnection. And this wound doesn't just hurt emotionally. It affects us physically, mentally, and spiritually.

Recent research has shown that chronic loneliness increases inflammation throughout the body, weakens immune function, and raises the risk of heart disease and stroke. It impairs cognitive function and accelerates cognitive decline. It's as damaging to our health as smoking fifteen cigarettes a day, and it can be more dangerous than obesity or physical inactivity.

But statistics don't capture the lived experience of loneliness—the way it colors every aspect of existence with a gray wash of meaninglessness, the way it whispers that something is fundamentally wrong with you, the way it convinces you that this emptiness is your permanent state.

My own journey out of isolation was neither quick nor linear. There was no dramatic turning point, no single moment when the walls came tumbling down. Instead, there were pinpricks of light—small moments of connection that pierced the darkness I had wrapped around myself.

The writing teacher who returned my essay with a note: "I see you in these words." The college roommate who sat silently beside me through a panic attack, simply holding my hand. The dance workshop where, for three minutes of improvisation, I completely forgot myself and felt only the music moving through me and the energy of the dancers around me.

Each of these moments became a reference point, a North Star guiding me toward a different way of being. They showed me flashes of what was possible when I lowered my defenses, when I risked being seen. Each one taught me something essential about the nature of resonance and what makes it possible. They were seeds planted in barren soil that, against all odds, began to grow.

RESONANCE ACROSS DIFFERENCES

The power of resonance isn't limited to people who are similar to us or who share our views. In fact, some of the most profound experiences of connection can happen across significant differences.

In 2015, Daryl Davis, a Black musician, and Scott Shepherd, a former KKK leader, formed an unexpected friendship that challenges our assumptions about where resonance is possible.

Their connection began not with agreement but with curiosity. Davis had made it his mission to understand racism by talking directly with KKK members. When they met, Shepherd was still active in white supremacist organizations.

"I gave him the respect of listening to him, and he returned that respect by listening to me," Davis explained in a 2020 interview. This mutual listening—Pillar #2 in our framework—created the conditions for something extraordinary to emerge.

Over time, their conversations led Shepherd to renounce his racist beliefs and leave the KKK. Today, they work together on racial reconciliation projects and consider each other close friends.

Their story illustrates a profound truth about resonance: It doesn't require similarity, agreement, or even shared history. It requires only the willingness to truly see and hear another human being with respect and curiosity.

Is there someone in your life who seems too different for meaningful connection? What might happen if you approached them with genuine curiosity rather than attempting to change their mind?

THE CREATIVE POWER OF DISSONANCE

In music, dissonance refers to a tension or clash resulting from the combination of tones that sound harsh or unpleasant when played together. But dissonance isn't inherently bad—it creates tension that seeks resolution, driving the music forward. Similarly, in relationships, moments of tension and conflict aren't necessarily failures of connection but opportunities for growth and deeper understanding.

The goal isn't to eliminate dissonance but to learn to work with it creatively. Some of my most resonant relationships have emerged from initially dissonant interactions—conversations where worldviews clashed, where misunderstandings created friction, where differences seemed irreconcilable. But by staying in the discomfort with curiosity rather than judgment, by listening for the underlying needs and values beneath someone's positions, by seeking common ground without sacrificing authenticity, dissonance can transform into a richer, more complex harmony.

This is the paradox at the heart of resonant relationships: They require both alignment and difference. Too much sameness and the music becomes monotonous; too much difference without any harmony and it becomes noise. The sweet spot lies in finding the balance—what I call "uncommon common ground"—where our unique notes create a chord more beautiful and complex than any single note could be.

The contrasts between resonance and dissonance aren't rigid categories but points on a spectrum. Resonance involves deep listening, curious questions, authenticity, shared vulnerability, seeking understanding, co-creation, and flow. Dissonance, on the other hand, tends toward defensive listening, rigid statements, posturing, one-sided vulnerability, seeking to be right, competition, and friction.

Every relationship moves between resonance and dissonance. The key is not to avoid dissonance entirely but to move through it toward deeper resonance.

YOUR JOURNEY TO CONNECTION: DEVELOPMENTAL STAGES

As you develop your capacity for creating resonant relationships, you'll likely move through a series of developmental stages:

The journey begins with **awareness**—you start to notice the quality of your connections and the impact of your presence (or lack thereof) on others. You can identify moments of resonance and dissonance after they occur.

From awareness, you move to **intention**—you deliberately prepare for interactions, setting clear intentions for how you want to show up. You make conscious choices about your environment and mindset before engaging with others.

With practice, you develop **presence**—the capacity to remain fully present during interactions, catching yourself when your mind wanders and gently returning to connection. You're able to set aside distractions and agendas.

Presence leads to **attunement**—you become adept at reading subtle cues in others and adjusting your approach accordingly. You can sense when connection is strengthening or weakening and respond appropriately in real time.

Finally, you reach **integration**—creating resonance becomes second nature, not something you do but who you are. Your presence naturally invites others into a state of connection without conscious effort.

Most people begin this journey at awareness or early intention. The practices in this book are designed to help you progress systematically through these stages, developing mastery over time.

Which stage best describes your current capacity for creating resonance? What would moving to the next stage look like in your daily interactions?

STARTING TODAY: FIVE SIXTY-SECOND PRACTICES

While deep resonance develops through consistent practice over time, you can begin creating more connection immediately with these brief interventions:

- **The Full-Body Hello:** When greeting someone, pause for just three seconds longer than usual. Make eye contact, turn your body fully toward them, and silently acknowledge their humanity before speaking. This tiny adjustment signals complete presence.
- **The Curious Question:** Replace "How are you?" with a more specific question like "What's been on your mind today?" or "What's been the highlight of your week so far?" Then listen for what energizes them in their response.
- **The Echo Check:** After someone shares something important, briefly summarize what you heard before responding: "So what I'm hearing is . . . " This simple practice ensures they feel truly understood.
- **The Phone Flip:** Before any meaningful conversation, turn your phone face down or, better yet, put it in another room. This single action dramatically increases your capacity for presence.
- **The Gratitude Moment:** End each interaction with a specific expression

of appreciation: "I really valued hearing your perspective on . . ." This creates a resonant closure that lingers after you part.

Choose just ONE of these practices to focus on tomorrow. Notice what shifts in your interactions when you implement it consistently throughout the day.

THE ART OF ASKING WHAT MATTERS

The quality of our connections often depends on the quality of our questions. Certain types of questions create the conditions for resonance more effectively than others:

- **Questions that invite story** open doors to deeper sharing. "What's a moment from your childhood that shaped who you are today?" or "Can you tell me about a time when you felt truly alive?"
- **Questions that honor experience** focus on subjective experience rather than facts, creating space for emotional truth. "What was that like for you?" or "How did that experience change you?"
- **Questions that explore values** connect to core principles, moving beyond surface positions. "What matters most to you about this situation?" or "When you're at your best, what principles are guiding you?"
- **Questions that create possibility** expand thinking beyond current constraints. "What would become possible if you had all the support you needed?" or "If you knew you couldn't fail, what would you try?"
- **Questions that deepen connection** invite meaningful exchange rather than social script. "What are you learning about yourself lately?" or "Where in your life are you feeling most challenged right now?"

Choose one question from each category that feels most aligned with your authentic curiosity. Commit to asking at least one resonant question in a conversation each day this week, paying close attention to how it shifts the quality of connection.

THE PROMISE OF THE JOURNEY AHEAD

Some years ago, I attended a concert at Ravinia, the open-air music venue outside my hometown of Chicago. A sudden summer storm approached. Lightning flashed in the distance. Thunder rumbled beyond the hills.

The conductor raised his baton anyway, and the first notes of the symphony rose into the darkening sky. As the music swelled, something remarkable happened. The threatening storm seemed to pause, hanging back as if listening. For nearly an hour, the boundary between music and nature, between performers and audience, between strangers sitting side by side on the lawn, dissolved. I felt simultaneously more fully myself and more deeply connected to everything around me than I had in months.

That evening was resonance made visible—thousands of people breathing together, hearts beating in rhythm with the music, creating something larger than any individual could achieve alone.

This is the promise of resonant relationships.

As we continue our exploration in the chapters ahead, we'll dive deeper into each of the seven pillars, examining the science behind them, sharing stories that illustrate their power, and offering practical tools to incorporate them into your life. We'll explore resonance in different contexts—from intimate partnerships to professional collaborations, from family dynamics to community building.

My promise to you is this: If you engage with these ideas not just intellectually but experientially, if you practice these principles consistently, you will experience a profound shift in the quality of your connections and, by extension, in the quality of your life. You will begin to unlock The More—that exponential potential that emerges when we connect authentically and align with purpose.

Here's the transformation that awaits you:

- From seeing relationships as peripheral to recognizing them as central to a fulfilling life
- From unconscious patterns of connection and disconnection to the intentional creation of resonance
- From superficial interactions to meaningful engagement that nourishes your soul

- From isolation as a protection strategy to vulnerability as a pathway to strength
- From transactional relationships to transformational connections that amplify your impact

The journey ahead won't always be easy. It will ask you to examine your patterns, to face your fears, to risk vulnerability, to practice new ways of being. There will be moments when you'll want to retreat behind familiar walls, when the old patterns of disconnection will tempt you to slip back into them like comfortable old clothes.

But the alternative—a life of superficial connection or, worse, of isolation—exacts a far greater cost. Like the twelve-year-old I once was, finding solace with a horse at summer camp because human connection felt too dangerous, you may have found ways to survive without deep resonance. But survival is not the same as thriving. Protection is not the same as fulfillment.

The world needs your song—your unique gifts, passions, and perspective. But more than that, it needs the music that can only emerge when your song joins with others in a harmony of purpose and possibility. It needs the symphony that you, and only you, can help create.

As mentioned, when Beethoven wrote his Ninth Symphony, he was completely deaf. He never heard a note of it performed. And yet, he could feel the resonance of the music within him. He trusted that if he shared his unique song, others would join in harmony.

That trust changed the world.

Are you ready to begin?

FROM INSPIRATION TO INTEGRATION: MAKING RESONANCE REAL

Understanding resonance intellectually is only the first step. Here's a structured process for moving from concept to lived experience:

1. **Select your laboratory relationship.** Choose one specific relationship as your primary focus for applying these principles. The ideal "laboratory relationship" is:
    - Important enough to matter deeply;
    - Safe enough to experiment within;
    - Frequent enough for regular practice;
    - Challenging enough to show meaningful results.
2. **Identify your focus pillar.** While all seven pillars work together, choose one as your initial focus. Which one, if strengthened, would create the most immediate impact in your selected relationship?
3. **Design your minimum viable practice.** Create the smallest possible daily practice that would help you embody this pillar. For example:
    - If focusing on Listening Deeply (Pillar #2), you might practice five minutes of full-attention listening without planning your response.
    - If focusing on Adding Value (Pillar #4), you might identify one small way to contribute to this person's well-being each day.
4. **Create implementation triggers.** Link your new practice to existing habits. For example:
    - "After I pour my morning coffee, I'll text one expression of appreciation to my focus person."
    - "Before each meeting with my colleague, I'll set a specific intention for how I want to show up."
5. **Track and reflect.** Use your Resonance Journal (more details on what this is coming up) to document your practice and its effects. What's shifting in the quality of connection? What challenges are arising?
6. **Expand thoughtfully.** After two weeks of consistent practice with one pillar in one relationship, consider:
    - Deepening your practice of this pillar;
    - Adding a second pillar;
    - Expanding to an additional relationship.

Remember: The goal isn't perfection but progress. Even small shifts in how you show up create ripple effects that transform relationships over time.

Resonance Instrument

THE RESONANCE JOURNAL

Purpose: To create a dedicated space for reflection on your journey toward more resonant relationships

Time Required: 10–15 minutes to set up, then 5–10 minutes daily

Materials: A notebook, journal, or digital document that feels special to you

Practice:

1. **Choose Your Format:** Select a journal format that you enjoy and that fits your lifestyle—whether physical (a beautiful notebook) or digital (a dedicated document or app).
2. **Create Sacred Space:** Designate a specific time and place for your journaling practice—perhaps first thing in the morning with a cup of tea or in the evening as a way to process your day.
3. **Structure Your Journal:** Create sections for different types of reflections:
    - **Daily Reflections:** Space for recording moments of connection and disconnection
    - **Exercise Responses:** Where you'll work through the Resonance Instruments in this book

- **Musical Reflections:** Your thoughts on the songs and musical examples we explore
- **Insights & Questions:** Discoveries and wonderings that arise along the journey

4. **Begin with Intention:** On the first page, write a personal dedication or intention for your Resonance Journal. Why are you embarking on this journey? What do you hope to discover or create?
5. **Make It a Ritual:** Set aside even just a few minutes each day to write. Consistency is more important than length.

Variations:

- **Voice Memos:** If writing isn't your preferred method, consider recording voice reflections.
- **Visual Journal:** Incorporate drawings, photos, or collage elements to express your journey.
- **Shared Practice:** Consider finding a "resonance buddy" with whom you can share insights.

Success Metrics: You'll know this practice is working when:

- You begin noticing patterns in what creates connection and disconnection for you;
- You become more aware of these dynamics in real time during interactions;
- You find yourself naturally making choices that create more resonance.

Common Obstacles:

- "I don't have time." Remember that even three minutes is better than none.

- "I forget to do it." Link it to an existing habit (after brushing teeth, with morning coffee).
- "I don't know what to write." Start with "Today, I felt most connected when . . ." or "I noticed disconnection when . . ."

Real-World Application: Use your journal not just for reflection but as a planning tool. Before important conversations or interactions, write about how you want to show up and which resonance principles you want to embody.

Resonance Instrument

THE RESONANCE JOURNAL

Purpose: To develop awareness of resonance and dissonance in your daily interactions, training your attention to notice what creates connection and disconnection

Time Required: 10 minutes daily

Material: Your Resonance Journal

Practice:

1. Create three columns in your journal:
    - Moments of Resonance
    - Moments of Dissonance
    - Insights and Opportunities
2. Under "Moments of Resonance," record:

- A specific interaction where you felt genuinely connected today;
- What specifically created that connection (Was it deep listening? Shared vulnerability? Finding unexpected common ground?);
- How it felt in your body (What sensations, energy, or emotions did you notice?);
- Which of the seven pillars might have been at play.

3. Under "Moments of Dissonance," record:
- A specific interaction where you felt disconnected today;
- What may have contributed to the disconnect (Distraction? Judgment? Misaligned expectations?);
- How it felt in your body (Tension? Heaviness? Constriction?);
- Which pillar, if present, might have created more resonance?

4. Under "Insights and Opportunities," reflect on:
- What patterns do you notice emerging in your interactions?
- Which relationship could benefit most from more intentional resonance tomorrow?
- Which pillar feels most important for you to practice?

5. Close by setting a specific intention for creating more resonance tomorrow. Make it concrete and actionable: "I will practice deep listening with my colleague during our morning meeting by putting away my phone and asking at least one curious question."

Results to Expect: Within the first week, you'll likely notice patterns in what creates connection and disconnection for you specifically. By the second week, you'll become more aware of these dynamics in real time. By the third week, you'll find yourself naturally making choices that create more resonance throughout your day.

Variations:

- **Resonance Check-ins:** Set three phone reminders throughout the day to pause and notice your current state of connection or disconnection.
- **Paired Practice:** Share your journal insights with a partner who's also working on creating more resonance.
- **Voice Notes:** If writing isn't your preferred mode, record voice reflections instead.

YOUR RESONANCE MOMENT

Take a moment to complete these sentences in your journal:

The most important insight I'm taking from this chapter is:

One specific relationship where I want to create more resonance is:

The first small step I'll take toward creating more resonance is:

The best time for me to take this step is:

CHAPTER 2

The Loneliness Epidemic: A Crisis of Connection

The greatest disease in the West today is not TB or leprosy; it is being unwanted, unloved, and uncared for.

MOTHER TERESA

RESONANCE REFLECTION: THE WEIGHT OF DISCONNECTION

Before we dive deeper into our journey together, I invite you to experience something in your body:

Close your eyes. Take a slow breath in . . . and out.

Now, recall a moment when you felt profoundly alone despite being surrounded by people. Perhaps it was at a gathering where conversations flowed around you but somehow excluded you. Or a family dinner where everyone was physically present but emotionally elsewhere. Or a meeting where your voice went unheard.

Notice where this feeling lives in your body. Is there tightness in your chest? A hollow feeling in your stomach? A constriction in your throat?

Hold this sensation for just ten seconds. This is the physical imprint of disconnection—what millions experience not as a passing moment but as a chronic condition.

Now, take a deep breath and release it. Return to the present moment, knowing that by the end of this chapter, you'll understand both the science behind this feeling and the path beyond it.

We are, at our core, social beings. We crave connection. Our hearts long for it, our minds are wired for it, and our bodies thrive on it. Yet, despite living in a hyperconnected world—a world of instant communication and global networks—a silent epidemic is spreading: loneliness. It's a feeling of isolation, a sense of being adrift in a sea of faces, yet utterly alone. This isn't just a fleeting emotion; it's a pervasive state of being for millions, a crisis of connection that has profound implications for our individual and collective well-being.

JOURNEY MAP: FROM ISOLATION TO CONNECTION

Isolation → (Where most begin)	Awareness → (Recognizing the epidemic)	Understanding → (Learning the science)	Intentionality → (Creating new patterns)	Connection (Creating new connection)

This chapter guides you through these stages, offering insights and practices to move from unconscious isolation to intentional connection. Notice where you currently find yourself on this journey—there's no wrong place to begin.

Resonance Session

THE ALIENATION OF MODERN LIFE

Artist spotlight: The Beatles, "Eleanor Rigby"

If you can, take a moment to play this song before continuing. As you listen, notice how the stark string arrangement and Paul McCartney's melancholy melody evoke the essence of isolation.

In 1966, in the midst of Beatlemania, the Beatles released a song unlike anything in their catalog—a stark, string-driven meditation on loneliness called "Eleanor Rigby." The song emerged from an unusual confluence of elements: a name Paul McCartney spotted on a shop sign in Bristol, the memory of an elderly woman he'd helped with her shopping, and the influence of actress Eleanor Bron.

Producer George Martin suggested the string octet arrangement, creating a sound that eschewed the band's usual guitars and drums for something more classical and somber. The result was revolutionary—a pop song that unflinchingly depicted social isolation through two solitary characters: Eleanor, who "lives in a dream," and Father McKenzie, whose sermon "no one will hear."

The song asks the haunting question, regarding so many lonely people in the world: "Where do they all come from?" This question resonates even more powerfully today, in a world where loneliness has reached epidemic proportions.

Resonance Question: Who are the "Eleanor Rigbys" in your own life—people you observe who seem isolated or disconnected? What might their stories be? How might their lives intersect with yours in ways you haven't considered?

THE SCIENCE OF SEPARATION

The pervasive sense of disconnection so many of us are experiencing these days is not simply a matter of circumstance. It is a reflection of a deeper issue: We are facing an epidemic of loneliness. And while technology offers the illusion of connection, it often leaves us feeling more isolated than ever before.

Sherry Turkle, MIT professor and author of *Alone Together*, has said that loneliness is not the absence of people, it's the absence of connection within the presence of people. The statistics on loneliness are sobering, and they paint a stark picture of the world we live in. A 2020 survey by insurance provider Cigna revealed that a staggering 61 percent of American adults report feeling lonely "always" or "sometimes." This isn't just a problem in the United States; it's a global phenomenon.

And this loneliness isn't evenly distributed. Studies show that individuals from marginalized racial groups often experience higher rates of social isolation. The Cigna study found that 75 percent of Hispanic adults and 68 percent of Black/African American adults reported feeling lonely, compared to 57 percent of white adults. These disparities are often rooted in systemic inequalities, discrimination, and historical trauma that can erode social support networks and create barriers to connection. We are, as the data clearly shows, in the midst of a loneliness epidemic.

Brené Brown, researcher and author, has pointed out that connection is why we're here. We're hardwired to connect with others, she says; it's what gives purpose and meaning to our lives. And so the consequences of this epidemic are severe. Loneliness isn't just an unpleasant feeling, it's a serious health risk. Research has shown that chronic loneliness can shorten your lifespan by as much as fifteen years. It increases your risk of developing heart disease, depression, anxiety, and even dementia.

When we experience social isolation, our bodies react as if they are under threat. The dorsal anterior cingulate cortex—the same brain region that processes physical pain—activates during social rejection. Stress hormones like cortisol surge, inflammation increases, and our immune system is compromised. This biological response isn't a design flaw. It's a survival mechanism. Throughout our evolutionary history, being separated from the group meant danger, and our bodies still respond accordingly.

This explains why loneliness feels so physically uncomfortable. It's not "just in your head." It's a whole-body experience, a biological alarm system signaling that a fundamental need isn't being met. Understanding this can help us approach loneliness with more compassion, both for ourselves and others. It's not a personal failing but a natural response to a genuine human need.

Resonance Question: When did you first recognize isolation as more than just a feeling—as a physical sensation in your body? How does knowing this is a biological response rather than a personal failing change your perspective?

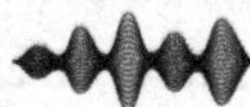

BRIDGE NOTE: THE BIOLOGY OF BELONGING

Our bodies are exquisitely tuned to our social environment, responding to connection and disconnection at the cellular level.

Neurochemical Response:

- Oxytocin, the trust-strengthening "bonding hormone" that's released during positive social interactions.
- Dopamine, the "reward chemical," creates feelings of pleasure and reinforces behaviors. When we connect authentically, our brain rewards us with dopamine, making us seek more connection.
- Cortisol, a stress hormone, increases during isolation, triggering inflammation and weakening immune function.

Physical Manifestations:

- Heart rate variability decreases during isolation, indicating autonomic nervous system stress.
- Inflammatory markers increase, linking loneliness to increased risk of heart disease, dementia, and premature death.
- Blood pressure rises in response to social threats, just as it does to physical danger.

This biological reality explains why connection feels so essential—it literally keeps us alive. Our need for others isn't weakness; it's written into our DNA.

MYTH/REALITY: UNDERSTANDING LONELINESS

Myth: Loneliness means there's something wrong with you.

Reality: Loneliness is a normal signal—like hunger or thirst—that a basic human need isn't being met.

Myth: Introverts don't get lonely; extroverts always do.

Reality: Personality type affects how we connect, not whether we need connection. Introverts and extroverts both require meaningful relationships, just in different quantities and contexts.

Myth: Having many friends or followers prevents loneliness.

Reality: The quality of connections matters more than quantity. One deeply resonant relationship provides more protection against loneliness than dozens of superficial ones.

Myth: Technology is the primary cause of our disconnection.

Reality: Technology is a tool that can either enhance or hinder connection, depending on how we use it. The root causes of the loneliness epidemic are more complex, including community fragmentation, increased mobility, and cultural shifts toward individualism.

The Evolutionary Perspective

But what is it about loneliness that makes it so dangerous? The answer lies, in part, in our evolutionary history. Humans are inherently social creatures. We evolved to live in groups, to cooperate, and to depend on each other for survival.

Anthropologist Robin Dunbar suggests that our brains are structured to handle a limited number of meaningful relationships, with a cognitive limit of around 150 stable social connections. This concept, often referred to as "Dunbar's number," proposes that our social capacity is rooted in our evolutionary past, where we lived in small, tightly knit groups.

Dunbar further suggests that this number breaks down into layers of increasing intimacy, with the innermost layer consisting of about five people (our closest relationships), then expanding to include layers of approximately fifteen, fifty, and one hundred fifty. This inherent limitation to the size of our social circles compels us to be intentional about where we invest our time and energy.

Journalist Sebastian Junger, in his book *Tribe: On Homecoming and Belonging*, takes this idea further, exploring the profound human need for community and belonging. He argues that modern society, with its emphasis on individualism and material wealth, has eroded our sense of tribal connection, leading to increased rates of depression, anxiety, and social isolation.

Junger draws on examples from tribal societies and close-knit communities to illustrate how shared hardship, collective purpose, and strong social bonds create a sense of belonging and well-being that is often missing in modern life. He posits that this erosion of tribal connections is a major contributing factor to the loneliness epidemic we face today.

We don't heal in isolation, but in community.

S. KELLEY HARRELL

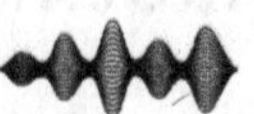

BRIDGE NOTE: THE DIGITAL PARADOX

Technology presents us with a profound paradox: The tools that promise connection often deliver isolation instead. Consider these realities:

The Illusion of Connection: We can have hundreds of "friends" online yet feel profoundly alone. Social media often shows curated highlights of others' lives, creating comparison and inadequacy. And digital interactions lack the nonverbal cues that build trust and intimacy.

The Attention Divide: The average person checks their phone ninety-six times daily—once every ten minutes! Even the presence of a phone on a table measurably reduces connection and empathy between people. Our divided attention signals to others that they are not worth our full presence.

But it is possible to reclaim technology for true connection. We can create tech-free zones and times in our homes and in our lives, practicing "tech hygiene" to detox periodically from digital stimulation. We can use technology intentionally to deepen existing relationships rather than as a substitute for connecting . . . choosing voice and video over text whenever possible, for example. Technology isn't inherently good or bad; it's a tool. The question is: Does your use of technology expand or contract your capacity for genuine human connection?

BEYOND LONELINESS: FINDING OUR WAY BACK TO CONNECTION

These insights from anthropology, psychology, and neuroscience underscore a fundamental truth: We are not meant to go it alone. We are wired for connection, and our well-being depends on it. The erosion of genuine connection in modern society has created a void, a dissonance that is reflected in the rising tide of loneliness.

THE CONNECTED VS. ISOLATED BRAIN

This is not just metaphorical: Loneliness literally changes your brain. Cognition, decision-making, and emotional regulation are impaired in the socially isolated brain. But the good news? Connection can reverse these changes, creating new neural pathways and restoring optimal brain function.

My own journey through this darkness took an unexpected turn when my father, sensing my descent into isolation after a particularly difficult period, rallied his men's group to support me. This group of men, who had gone through a men's training called the ManKind Project back in the eighties, offered to fund a weekend training for me. It was an invitation to step into a space of vulnerability and connection, something I had long avoided.

That weekend was a turning point. Surrounded by a circle of men committed to their own growth and to supporting each other, I found the courage to confront my own pain and begin the process of healing. My father's presence there, as the only father among the volunteers, was a powerful testament to his unwavering love and support. He didn't try to fix me or offer easy answers. He simply offered his presence, his willingness to stand by me as I navigated the turbulent waters of my inner world.

This experience showed me that healing and transformation are possible, even from the depths of loneliness and despair. It ignited within me a deep appreciation for the power of authentic connection and the importance of being an offering to others. It was a living example of how resonant relationships can provide the safety, support, and understanding we need to heal, grow, and find our way back to ourselves. It also planted a seed for what would eventually grow into a lifelong mission of helping others create resonant lives.

FROM THE RESEARCH: THE SCIENCE OF SOCIAL HEALING

Recent studies reveal the remarkable power of connection to restore health:

- A 2019 Harvard study found that strong social connections improve immune function as effectively as regular exercise.
- Research from Emory University shows that resilience after trauma increases by up to 40 percent when survivors have access to a supportive community.
- An eighty-year longitudinal study concluded that relationship quality was the strongest predictor of both happiness and longevity—more powerful than genetics, wealth, or social status
- Neuroimaging reveals that empathic listening activates the same neural circuits as physical healing, suggesting that being truly heard creates actual brain repair.

These findings explain why my experience with my father's men's group wasn't just emotionally supportive; it may have literally rewired my traumatized nervous system, creating new pathways for trust and connection.

Resonance Session

THE POWER OF SUPPORT

Artist Spotlight: Bill Withers, "Lean on Me"

If you can, before continuing, play this song and notice how its simple melody and straightforward message create an immediate sense of connection.

Bill Withers grew up in the coal-mining town of Slab Fork, West Virginia, where community wasn't just a concept—it was survival. In this small town, people relied on each other through hardship and struggle, creating bonds of mutual support that transcended individual differences.

Years after leaving his hometown, Withers found himself in Los Angeles, a sprawling city where that natural sense of community was often missing. Reflecting on the contrast between his upbringing and his new urban environment, he composed "Lean on Me" in 1972 as a reminder of the simple, essential truth he'd learned in Slab Fork: We all need somebody to lean on.

In a 2015 interview, Withers explained: "It's a rural song that translates probably across cultures, because people do need each other. That's all." The song's enduring power comes from this universality—the recognition that vulnerability and interdependence aren't weaknesses but the very foundation of human strength.

With its gospel-influenced piano progression and straightforward lyrics, "Lean on Me" became Withers's only number one hit on both the Billboard Hot 100 and R&B charts. More important, it has transcended its time to become an anthem of support and solidarity, performed at presidential inaugurations, benefit concerts, and countless moments when communities come together in times of challenge.

The song's message—that we all have times of strength and times of need—offers a powerful antidote to the isolation of modern life and the false ideal of complete self-sufficiency.

Resonance Question: Think about times when you've leaned on others and times when you've been the support for someone else. How did these experiences of mutual support create a sense of connection? What makes it difficult to ask for or offer support in our current culture?

Resonance Session

ISOLATION IN THE DIGITAL AGE

Artist Spotlight: Radiohead, "How to Disappear Completely"
If you can, before reading further, listen to this haunting meditation on disconnection.

In the late 1990s, as technology was beginning to reshape human connection, Thom Yorke of Radiohead found himself overwhelmed by fame and increasing dissociation. During a particularly difficult tour, Michael Stipe of R.E.M. offered him this advice for coping with overwhelming situations: "I'm not here, this isn't happening."

This mantra became the central refrain of "How to Disappear Completely," a song that captures the paradoxical experience of feeling unreal in an increasingly connected yet isolated world. Released on Radiohead's groundbreaking 2000 album *Kid A*, the song pairs Yorke's ethereal vocals with orchestral strings to create a soundscape of beautiful alienation.

The lyrics "I'm not here / This isn't happening" express a universal experience in our hyperconnected age—the sense of detachment that comes from living through screens, the feeling of watching your own life from a distance rather than fully inhabiting it.

Resonance Question: When have you caught yourself "disappearing" in plain sight—present physically but absent emotionally? What brings you back to full presence in your own life and with those around you?

THE VALUE OF INTENTIONAL CONNECTION

The research clearly demonstrates the profound impact of connection on our physical and mental well-being, but the benefits are not just a consequence of having relationships; they depend on the quality of those relationships. The value comes from creating moments of genuine connection, moments where we feel seen, heard, and valued. And sometimes, the simplest traditions can be the most effective in fostering this sense of connection.

YOUR CONNECTION QUOTIENT (CQ): A SELF-ASSESSMENT

Rate yourself from 1 (rarely) to 5 (consistently) on each dimension:

1. **Presence**
   - I give my full attention to others during interactions.
   - I notice when I'm distracted and can bring myself back to presence.
   - I'm aware of both verbal and nonverbal signals from others.
2. **Authenticity**
   - I show my true self rather than a curated image.
   - I share my genuine thoughts and feelings appropriately.
   - I'm willing to be vulnerable about my challenges.
3. **Curiosity**
   - I ask questions that invite meaningful sharing.
   - I'm genuinely interested in others' perspectives.
   - I listen to understand rather than to respond.
4. **Empathy**
   - I can sense others' emotional states.
   - I validate others' experiences without judgment.
   - I can be with others in difficult emotions without needing to fix them.
5. **Consistency**
   - I follow through on commitments to others.
   - I maintain connections even when busy.
   - I invest time in nurturing important relationships.

Scoring:

- 60–75: High CQ (Strong foundation for resonant relationships)
- 45–59: Moderate CQ (Good capacity with room for growth)
- 30–44: Developing CQ (Specific areas need attention)
- Below 30: Opportunity CQ (Significant room for transformation)

Your score isn't a judgment but a starting point. The practices in this book will naturally increase your CQ over time.

Take, for example, the Swedish practice of *fika*. On the surface, fika appears to be just a coffee break, but it is much more; it's a cultural institution, a cherished ritual that emphasizes the importance of slowing down, connecting with others, and savoring the present moment.

Typically observed twice a day, once in the morning and once in the afternoon, fika involves taking a break from work or other activities to enjoy coffee, pastries, and conversation with colleagues, friends, or family. But there's more going on than just the refreshments. The significance comes from the intention behind the act. Fika is a dedicated time to pause, to step away from the demands of the day, and to connect with others on a human level.

In Sweden, fika is considered essential for building strong social bonds, both in the workplace and in personal life. It's a time to catch up, to share stories, to offer support, and to simply enjoy each other's company. It's a recognition that human connection is not a luxury but a necessity, and that taking the time to nurture our relationships is just as important as any other task or responsibility.

RESONANCE IN ACTION: A PLACE AT THE TABLE

Location: Durham, North Carolina

Founder: Maggie Kane

Mission: Transforming community isolation through intentional gathering spaces and inclusive meal experiences.

In 2018, Maggie Kane witnessed a profound disconnect in her neighborhood: Families were eating alone behind closed doors, neighbors rarely gathered, and the simple act of sharing a meal had become a rarity rather than a foundation of community life.

Her solution was beautifully elegant: A Place at the Table, which creates sacred gathering spaces where food becomes the bridge to deeper human connection. The initiative includes:

Community Kitchens. Shared cooking spaces in neighborhoods where residents prepare meals together, learning from each other's traditions and stories

Table Hosts. Trained volunteers who open their homes monthly for inclusive dinners, welcoming neighbors, newcomers, and anyone seeking connection

Story Suppers. Regular gatherings where sharing a meal accompanies the sharing of personal narratives, creating deeper understanding across cultural and generational lines

Empty Chair Commitment. A practice where participants always set one extra place, symbolically welcoming the stranger and staying open to unexpected connection

The transformation has been profound. Communities implementing A Place at the Table report:

- Measurable increases in neighborhood social cohesion and trust
- Reduced anxiety and depression among regular participants
- Stronger support networks during personal and community crises
- Breaking down of cultural barriers through food and storytelling
- Renewed sense of belonging among isolated residents

Kane's work demonstrates how the ancient practice of breaking bread together can heal the fragmentation of modern life, one conversation at a time.

Resonance Question: What would it mean to create "a place at the table" in your own life? How might you use the simple act of sharing food to deepen connection with those around you?

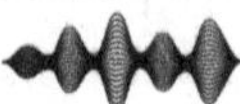

BRIDGE NOTE: CULTURAL PRACTICES OF CONNECTION

Many cultures have developed intentional practices that foster connection:

- **Japanese Tea Ceremony (*Chado*):** A ritualized practice emphasizing presence, respect, and harmony
- **Indigenous Talking Circles:** A tradition where participants speak and listen from the heart, often using a talking piece
- **Greek Symposium:** Originally a drinking party that combined conviviality with intellectual discourse
- **West African Griot Traditions:** Storytelling gatherings that preserve history and strengthen community bonds

These practices vary widely but share common elements: They create dedicated time and space for connection, they often involve sharing food or drink, they establish rituals that signal a shift from ordinary activities, and they emphasize quality of attention over quantity of time.

Resonance Question: What might we learn from these traditions about creating more meaningful connection in our own lives? How might you adapt one of these practices to fit your own context?

Resonance Instrument

THE CONNECTION INVENTORY

Purpose: To assess your current relationship landscape and identify opportunities for deeper resonance

Time Required: 30–45 minutes initially, with 15-minute quarterly updates

Materials: Your Resonance Journal; colored pens or highlighters (optional)

Practice:

1. **Map Your Current Connections.** List all the significant relationships in your life across these categories:
    - **Inner Circle:** Those you turn to in crisis (typically 3–5 people)
    - **Close Connections:** Regular, meaningful contact (typically 10–15 people)
    - **Community:** Important but less frequent contact (typically 30–50 people)
    - **Peripheral:** Occasional meaningful interactions (the rest of your social world)
2. **Assess Resonance Quality.** Rate each relationship in your inner circle and close connections, using a scale of 1 (minimum) to 10 (maximum).
    - How seen and understood do you feel in this relationship? (Scale 1–10)
    - How authentic can you be? (Scale 1–10)

- How energized do you feel after spending time with this person? (Scale 1–10)
- Which of the Seven Pillars of Resonance are present or missing?

3. **Identify Connection Deserts and Oases.**
    - Which areas of your life (e.g., work, community, family) are **connection deserts**, offering little meaningful interaction?
    - Which areas are **connection oases**, where you consistently experience resonance?
4. **Create a Connection Priority Plan.**
    - Select ONE relationship in which you want to create more resonance.
    - Identify which pillar, if strengthened, would have the most impact.
    - Design a small, daily practice to strengthen this pillar in this relationship.

Success Metrics: You'll know this practice is working when:

- You have greater clarity about where authentic connection exists in your life;
- You make more intentional choices about where to invest your relational energy;
- You see measurable improvement in the quality of your priority relationship.

Variations:

- **Visual Mapping:** Create a visual "connection ecosystem" using concentric circles to represent the relationships in your life. Place your inner circle in the center, then the close connections outside that, and so on.

- **Digital Tracking:** Use your preferred app to log meaningful interactions.
- **Conversation Version:** Complete this exercise with a partner or small group.

Resonance Instrument

THE FIKA BREAK

Purpose: To create intentional moments of connection throughout your day

Time Required: 15–30 minutes per break

Materials: A favorite beverage, a simple snack (optional), and the willingness to be present

Practice:

1. **Schedule the Break:** Choose a specific time each day (or several times a week) for your "fika break." This could be a coffee break with a colleague, a phone call with a friend, or a shared meal with your family.
2. **Create the Space:** Make it a ritual. Put away your phones, turn off screens, and create a distraction-free zone where you can truly connect.
3. **Prepare Something Simple:** The focus isn't on elaborate preparation but on the act of sharing. A simple coffee, tea, or snack is sufficient.

4. **Be Fully Present:** During your fika break, practice being fully present with the person or people you're with. Listen actively, engage in meaningful conversation, and savor both the refreshment and the company.
5. **Make It a Habit:** The key is consistency. The more you practice fika, the more natural it will become and the stronger your connections will grow.

Success Metrics: You'll know this practice is working when:

- Conversations during fika breaks become progressively deeper and more authentic;
- You find yourself looking forward to these moments as highlights of your day;
- Others begin to protect and prioritize these times as well.

Common Obstacles:

- "We're too busy." Remember that connection enhances productivity; these breaks make the rest of your time more effective.
- "Conversations feel awkward." Start with simple prompts: "What's energizing you lately?" or "What are you looking forward to?"
- "People keep checking phones." Establish a gentle norm at the beginning: "Let's enjoy being fully present for the next twenty minutes."

Variations:

- **Solo Fika:** Even alone, you can practice a mindful break, perhaps journaling or simply being present with your thoughts.
- **Virtual Fika:** Schedule a video call with distant friends or family specifically for sharing a coffee and conversation.

- **Walking Fika:** Combine the connection of fika with the benefits of nature by taking a walk with a friend.

Real-World Application: In work environments, advocate for regular fika breaks as a team-building practice. Many organizations find that these short breaks actually increase productivity by improving morale, communication, and creativity.

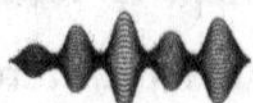

BRIDGE NOTE: LONELINESS ACROSS THE LIFESPAN

Loneliness manifests differently at various life stages, requiring different approaches.

Childhood (ages 5–12)

How It Shows Up: Difficulty making friends, withdrawal from play, physical complaints

Critical Needs: Guided social skills development, structured opportunities for peer connection

Adolescence (ages 13–19)

How It Shows Up: Social media obsession, risk-taking behavior, identity confusion

Critical Needs: Authentic mentorship, belonging to positive peer groups, space for identity exploration

Young Adulthood (ages 20–35)

How It Shows Up: Career-focused isolation, comparison with peers, moving away from support networks

Critical Needs: New community formation, meaningful group activities, work-life integration

Midlife (ages 36–65)

How It Shows Up: Busy isolation, caregiver burnout, friendship attrition

Critical Needs: Intentional friendship maintenance, vulnerability with age peers, cross-generational connection

Older Adulthood (age 65+)

How It Shows Up: Loss of purpose, reduced mobility, loss of peers

Critical Needs: Continued contribution opportunities, accessible community, technology bridges to family

Understanding these patterns helps us recognize and address loneliness appropriately, whether in ourselves or others at different life stages.

FROM CRISIS TO OPPORTUNITY

As we confront the loneliness epidemic, it's easy to focus on the problem—the statistics, the health implications, the societal costs. But perhaps we should also see this moment as an opportunity, a call to reexamine how we live and connect with one another. The very depth of the crisis suggests the depth of our hunger for authentic connection, for relationships that resonate with our core values and needs.

As we discussed in "The Upward Spiral of Connection" section of chapter 1, the journey from isolation to connection isn't linear but spiral—each positive experience of connection creates the conditions for deeper connection to emerge. It begins with safety, which allows for vulnerability, which enables recognition, which builds trust, which creates resonance, which expands safety even further, continuing the upward spiral.

This spiral works in both directions. When safety is broken, we move inward toward self-protection and disconnection. But a single moment of intentional connection can reverse the direction, starting an upward spiral of increasing resonance.

In the chapters ahead, we'll explore the Seven Pillars of Resonant Relationships, beginning with the foundation, the first pillar: Being Generous of Time and Energy/Being an Offering. You'll discover how the simple shift from "What can I get?" to "What can I give?" transforms not just your relationships but your entire experience of life.

The journey from isolation to connection begins with a single step—a deliberate choice to move toward others rather than away, to offer yourself authentically rather than hiding behind walls of protection. As we continue, you'll gain practical tools to make this shift in your daily interactions, creating ripples of connection that extend far beyond your immediate circle.

For now, if you haven't already, I encourage you to complete the Connection Inventory and begin your Resonance Journal with the exercises we've discussed. These practices will increase your awareness of your current relationship landscape and help you identify opportunities for intentional growth. Remember, awareness precedes change—the simple act of noticing your patterns of connection and disconnection creates the possibility for transformation.

The antidote to loneliness isn't just more people; it's more resonance. Let's continue our exploration of how to create it.

POWER PLAYLIST

As we conclude our exploration of the loneliness epidemic, I invite you to begin building your Resonant Relationships Power Playlist. Music offers a unique pathway to understanding and transformation, bypassing our analytical defenses to speak directly to our emotional core. Below are some suggestions to get you started.

The Soundtrack of Disconnection and Connection

- **"Mad World" by Gary Jules.** Listen for: The haunting echo of disconnection in our digital age.

- **"Lean on Me" by Bill Withers.** Listen for: How mutual support becomes life's most natural rhythm.
- **"The Night We Met" by Lord Huron.** Listen for: Nostalgia that awakens a longing for real connection.

Listening Practice:

Find a quiet space free from distractions. Choose one song each day this week. Before listening, take three deep breaths to center yourself. Play the song with your full attention, perhaps with eyes closed. Notice:

- Where in your body you feel the music's emotional impact
- Which lyrics resonate most deeply with your own experience
- How the melody and rhythm themselves (beyond the words) express connection or disconnection

After listening, take five minutes to reflect in your Resonance Journal on how the song illuminates your own journey from isolation to connection.

Creating Your Personal Additions

Which songs have been companions during your own moments of loneliness? Which have reminded you of your capacity for connection? Add at least two or three personal selections to this playlist that reflect your unique journey. Consider sharing these with someone close to you, explaining why each song matters.

Music has been called "the shorthand of emotion" because it can express and evoke feelings that words alone cannot capture. As we continue our exploration of resonant relationships, these songs will serve as both mirrors and maps—reflecting our current experiences while pointing the way toward deeper connection. In the coming chapters you will be presented with more songs that illuminate the themes presented here. Some songs will resonate, some won't. The practice is to listen for the deeper notes within and make the playlist and experience your own.

YOUR RESONANCE MOMENT

Take a moment to complete these thoughts in your journal:

The most important insight I'm taking from this chapter is:

One specific action I commit to taking this week is:

I will know this action is working when I notice:

CHAPTER 3

Become an Offering: The Generosity Principle

Close your eyes and breathe deeply. Recall a moment when someone was unexpectedly generous to you—not with money or gifts, but with their presence, their attention, their understanding. Perhaps it was a friend who truly listened during a difficult time, a stranger who offered help without being asked, or a mentor who believed in you when you couldn't believe in yourself.

Notice what happens in your body as you remember this moment. Feel the warmth that spreads through your chest. Notice how your shoulders relax, how your breath deepens. This physiological response isn't coincidental—it's your body's recognition of a fundamental truth: We are wired to resonate with genuine giving.

Now, shift your focus to a moment when you gave freely to another—when you became an offering without expectation of return. Feel the expansive sensation, the quiet joy that accompanies true generosity. This is the vibrational signature of what we're exploring in this chapter, the first pillar of resonant relationships.

FROM CONSUMPTION TO CONTRIBUTION

In the previous chapters, we explored the loneliness epidemic devastating our modern world and the profound human need for meaningful connection. We discovered that despite our technological interconnectedness, many of us suffer from a starvation of authentic relationship—a hunger for something real in a world of superficial interaction.

This chapter introduces the first pillar of resonant relationships: **Be Generous of Time and Energy.** Like the hands of a musician that draw sound from an instrument, our generosity creates the initial vibration from which all resonance flows.

But this isn't about random acts of kindness or transactional giving. It's about a radical shift in orientation—from "What can I get?" to "What can I give?" This shift represents nothing less than a revolution in how we approach our relationships and, ultimately, our lives.

The journey from consumption to contribution unfolds through several distinct stages:

Taking. At this first stage, we operate from a scarcity mindset, the belief that resources are limited and we must secure our share before others take it. Relationships are primarily transactional, focused on what we can extract.

Exchanging. Here we evolve to a "tit-for-tat" approach, a fairness mindset of carefully tracking what we give and receive to ensure balance. While more evolved than mere taking, this mindset still restricts the flow of generosity.

Giving. At this stage, we begin to offer without explicit expectation of return, with a generosity mindset, recognizing that giving creates value beyond the immediate exchange. We still maintain some separation between ourselves and our gifts.

Offering. Now we move beyond giving things to offering our presence—our full attention, empathy, and authentic being. With a presence mindset, we become more interested in the quality of our giving than its quantity.

Becoming (embodied generosity): In this most evolved stage, one of embodied generosity, our very presence becomes a gift. Generosity isn't something we do but who we are, and giving flows naturally without effort or thought.

Take a moment to place yourself on this map. Where do you feel you are right now in your journey? What would it take to move one step forward?

THE ALCHEMY OF OFFERING

In 1992, as the world witnessed the fall of the Berlin Wall and unprecedented global change, Leonard Cohen released "Anthem," a meditation on imperfection and offering. The song emerged from Cohen's own period of personal darkness—he had lost most of his savings and was rebuilding his life from scratch at age fifty-eight.

What makes "Anthem" extraordinary is its embrace of brokenness as the very source of light. The chorus reminds us that "There is a crack in everything, that's how the light gets in." This profound insight mirrors the Japanese art of ***kintsugi***, where broken pottery is repaired with gold, honoring the breaks as part of the object's history rather than something to disguise.

Cohen spent a decade perfecting this song, working through eighty verses before distilling it to its essence. The song's enduring message is that perfection is not a prerequisite for offering ourselves to the world. In fact, it is often through our wounds and imperfections that we have the most to give.

How might embracing your own "cracks" allow more light to flow through you to others? What parts of yourself have you been hiding that, if offered generously, might become your greatest gift?

THE CALL TO BE AN OFFERING

The concept of "being an offering" stands in stark contrast to the dominant cultural narrative that prioritizes acquisition, achievement, and self-advancement. To be an offering means approaching life and relationships with the primary question "What can I contribute?" rather than "What can I gain?"

This principle calls us to recognize that the most meaningful connections are built on a foundation of generosity—of time, energy, and spirit. Being an offering means showing up fully in our relationships, not just physically, but emotionally and mentally as well. It means being present, being attuned, and being willing to give of ourselves in ways that nourish and support those around us.

The poet David Whyte captures this beautifully when he writes: "The antidote to exhaustion is not necessarily rest; the antidote to exhaustion is wholeheartedness." When we give partially, guardedly, or begrudgingly, we deplete ourselves. But when we give wholeheartedly—when we become an offering—we often discover an unexpected source of energy and vitality.

The science behind this paradoxical energy gain is fascinating. When we give generously, our brains respond with a cascade of beneficial neurochemical reactions. The act of giving activates the mesolimbic pathway—the brain's reward system—releasing dopamine and creating what scientists call a "helper's high." The ventral striatum, part of this reward circuit, shows increased activity during acts of generosity, similar to when we receive rewards ourselves.

Generosity also triggers the release of oxytocin, which increases our sense of trust and connection with others. This creates a positive feedback loop: Giving leads to oxytocin release, which leads to more trust, which in turn leads to more giving.

Perhaps most remarkably, acts of generosity decrease activity in the amygdala, the brain's fear center. This reduces the production of stress hormones like cortisol. Regular giving is associated with lower blood pressure and reduced inflammation—physiological benefits that explain why volunteers consistently report better health outcomes than non-volunteers.

These neurological responses suggest that we're literally wired to benefit from generosity—that giving is not just morally virtuous but biologically advantageous. We're designed to thrive when we contribute to others' well-being.

GENEROSITY IN CRISIS: OUR NATURAL STATE REVEALED

There are moments in life when the principle of generosity moves from aspirational to essential—times of collective crisis when becoming an offering isn't just about personal transformation but about collective survival and resilience.

Throughout human history, we've witnessed how disasters, hardships, and challenges often reveal our deepest capacity for connection. From the aftermath of natural disasters to periods of social upheaval, stories of extraordinary generosity emerge alongside the suffering.

Rebecca Solnit, in her remarkable book *A Paradise Built in Hell*, documents how disasters often produce what she calls "disaster communities"—temporary utopias of mutual aid and cooperation. Studying events from the 1906 San Francisco earthquake to Hurricane Katrina, she found that contrary to popular myths about panic and selfishness, most people respond to crisis with remarkable altruism and resourcefulness.

What makes crisis generosity particularly powerful is that it often transcends the boundaries that typically divide us. Political differences, social status, and other distinctions fade in importance when survival and recovery demand our shared humanity. In these moments, we discover our innate capacity for what sociologists call "emergent altruism"—spontaneous, selfless behavior that arises without external incentives or organization.

The COVID-19 pandemic offered countless examples of this phenomenon—from healthcare workers risking their lives to neighborhood mutual aid networks ensuring vulnerable community members received food and medicine. These weren't just isolated acts of kindness but demonstrations of our collective capacity to become an offering when circumstances demand it.

The generosity shown in crisis reveals something profound about human nature: Beneath our cultivated individualism lies a deeper instinct for connection and mutual care. We are, at our core, wired to help each other through difficulty. The challenge isn't creating this capacity but removing the barriers that prevent its expression in ordinary times.

When have you witnessed or participated in extraordinary generosity during a crisis? What might everyday life look like if we maintained that level of mutual care and offering outside of emergencies?

THE FLOWER BLESSING: SMALL OFFERINGS, PROFOUND IMPACT

The transformative power of becoming an offering often manifests in unexpected moments of spontaneous generosity. Let me share a personal story that illustrates this principle in action.

When my father was diagnosed with dementia, I was overwhelmed with fear and grief—particularly at the prospect of him eventually needing care in a memory facility. Rather than avoiding this fear, I decided to face it directly through an act of giving.

One morning, I purchased dozens of fresh flowers and drove to a local memory care center. With no appointment or connection to the facility, I simply arrived with my arms full of blooms and asked to visit with residents. The staff, though initially surprised, welcomed this unexpected offering.

For the next two hours, I moved from room to room, presenting each resident with a flower and the gift of my full attention. I listened to their stories, held their hands, and witnessed their humanity. Some were confused, others clear minded but physically frail, and all hungry for genuine connection.

What happened next surprised me. The act of giving—of becoming an offering to these strangers—shifted something profound within me. My fear began to dissolve, replaced by a sense of peace and even wonder. In giving presence to these elders, I received an unexpected gift: the realization that connection transcends cognitive decline, that our capacity for resonance remains even when memory fades.

This experience, which I came to call "the Flower Blessing," taught me something essential about generosity: When we give from a place of authenticity, we often receive exactly what we need—not because we sought it, but because it is the natural consequence of genuine offering.

CULTIVATING AWARENESS: THE GENEROSITY CHRONICLE

To cultivate awareness of giving and receiving in your daily life, consider creating a generosity chronicle. This simple practice requires just five or ten minutes daily but can profoundly shift your relationship to giving and receiving.

Begin each day by writing a single sentence in your Resonance Journal (or keep a separate generosity journal, if you prefer) about how you intend to be an offering today. Be specific rather than general. Not "I'll be more generous," but "I'll give my colleague my full attention when they share their project concerns."

At the end of each day, reflect on three questions:

- How did I show up as an offering today? (Celebrate specific moments of generosity.)
- What made it easy or difficult to give? (Notice patterns of resistance or flow.)
- What unexpected gifts did I receive when I wasn't seeking them? (Develop awareness of the reciprocal nature of generosity.)

At the end of each week, review your daily entries and identify:

- One insight about your giving patterns
- One area where you'd like to expand your capacity for generosity
- One relationship where you could experiment with deeper offering

Use your generosity chronicle to identify relationships or situations where you tend to contract rather than expand. These are precisely the areas where conscious offering can create the most transformation—both for others and yourself.

You'll know this practice is working when you begin noticing opportunities for offering that previously went unrecognized; when your definition of generosity expands beyond material giving to include presence, attention, and emotional support; and when you experience less depletion and more energy when giving authentically.

THE SCIENCE OF CONNECTION THROUGH GIVING

The imperative to give, to be an offering, is not just a poetic notion or spiritual ideal. It is increasingly supported by rigorous scientific research across multiple disciplines.

Evolutionary biology suggests that our capacity for generosity evolved as a survival advantage. In hunter-gatherer societies, those who shared resources and supported group members were more likely to receive support when they needed it. This reciprocal altruism became encoded in our DNA, explaining why generosity feels natural when we remove the barriers of fear and scarcity thinking.

Longitudinal research on happiness and well-being consistently identifies giving behavior as a key predictor of life satisfaction. The Harvard Study of Adult Development, one of the longest-running studies on human happiness, has followed participants for over eighty years. Its director, Robert Waldinger, summarizes the findings simply: "Good relationships keep us happier and healthier. Period." And what creates good relationships? The study points to reciprocity, support, and generosity as critical factors.

Social psychology experiments have demonstrated that spending money on others produces more happiness than spending it on ourselves. In a landmark study by Elizabeth Dunn and colleagues, participants who were given money to spend on others reported greater happiness than those instructed to spend the same amount on themselves—regardless of the amount.

Public health research reveals that regular volunteering is associated with lower mortality rates, reduced depression, and better self-reported health. A meta-analysis of forty studies found volunteers had a 20 percent reduced mortality risk compared to non-volunteers, and this benefit remained even when controlling for factors like physical health, socioeconomic status, and social support.

This growing body of evidence suggests that generosity is not just morally virtuous but biologically adaptive. We are, quite literally, designed to thrive when we give.

THE RHYTHM OF RECIPROCITY: LESSONS FROM JAZZ

In 1959, Miles Davis gathered six musicians in a New York studio with minimal instructions and skeletal compositions. The result was *Kind of Blue*, widely regarded as one of the greatest albums ever recorded. What makes this recording so extraordinary is not just the individual brilliance of the players but the way they create space for each other—the way they listen, respond, and build upon each other's offerings.

Davis revolutionized jazz with this album by moving from the complex chord progressions of bebop to a simpler approach, creating more space for intuitive musical conversation. The musicians—Davis, John Coltrane, Cannonball Adderley, Bill Evans, Paul Chambers, and Jimmy Cobb—demonstrate the essence of resonant relationships through their playing.

Listen to the album yourself, and hear how each soloist becomes an offering to the group, neither dominating nor disappearing, but contributing their unique voice while remaining attuned to the whole. Notice how they leave space, how they build upon each other's ideas, how they create something together that none could create alone.

This is musical generosity in action—not diminishing oneself but offering one's gifts in service to something larger. It's the perfect sonic illustration of what happens in resonant relationships when each person brings their authentic self as an offering to the connection.

Think about your own "ensemble" of relationships. Where are you playing too loudly, taking up too much space? Where are you holding back, not offering your unique "sound"? How might you create more balance in your relational "music"?

THE BIOLOGY OF BELONGING

Our need for connection, and the transformative power of generosity in creating it, is rooted in our biology. We are wired to belong, to bond, to create meaningful connections with others. This isn't just a psychological preference; it's a physiological imperative.

The vagus nerve—the longest cranial nerve in the body—plays a crucial role in our capacity for connection and generosity. This nerve connects the brain to the heart, lungs, and digestive tract. Higher "vagal tone" (activity in this nerve) is associated with greater empathy, better emotion regulation, and stronger social bonds. Researchers like Stephen Porges and Dacher Keltner have found that acts of generosity and compassion activate and strengthen the vagus nerve, creating an upward spiral: giving leads to vagal activation, which increases our capacity for connection, which leads to more giving.

Practices that stimulate the vagus nerve—deep breathing, singing, meditation, cold exposure—can actually enhance our biological capacity for generosity and connection. This physiological understanding gives new meaning to ancient wisdom traditions, which have long taught that generosity opens the heart.

This intersection of neuroscience and relational wisdom reveals that being an offering isn't just a nice idea. It's aligned with our deepest biological design.

BEYOND THE TRANSACTION: TRUE GENEROSITY

In exploring generosity as the foundation of resonant relationships, it's important to distinguish authentic giving from its counterfeits. True generosity differs from transactional giving in several critical ways:

True generosity is intrinsically motivated. It emerges from an internal desire to contribute rather than external pressure or expectation. When we give because we "should" or to gain approval, the giving depletes us. When we give from authentic desire, it energizes us.

True generosity has no strings attached. It comes without expectation of return or reciprocity. This doesn't mean we don't receive—ironically, no-strings giving often returns to us multiplied—but return isn't the motivation.

True generosity honors both giver and receiver. It respects the dignity of both parties rather than creating dependency or power imbalance. It recognizes the gift of being allowed to give, honoring the receiver for creating the opportunity for generosity.

True generosity aligns with personal values. It expresses what matters most to us rather than conforming to external norms of "charitable behavior." When our giving aligns with our deepest values, it becomes an authentic expression of who we are.

Psychologist Adam Grant categorizes people as "givers," "takers," or "matchers" in his research on workplace dynamics. His findings reveal that givers fall into two categories: successful givers and burned-out givers. The difference? Successful givers practice what Grant calls "otherish" giving—they maintain awareness of their own needs while giving generously to others. They give in areas where they have strength and energy, and they aren't afraid to receive when needed.

This research affirms what wisdom traditions have long taught: Sustainable generosity requires self-awareness and appropriate boundaries. Being an offering doesn't mean depleting yourself—it means giving from your authentic center in ways that energize rather than exhaust you.

OVERCOMING OBSTACLES TO GENEROSITY

Even when we understand the value of becoming an offering, we may encounter internal or external obstacles. Here are common barriers and strategies to overcome them:

Fear of exploitation. When the belief that "If I give freely, others will take advantage of my generosity" produces concern about being taken advantage of, consider these resolution strategies:

- Practice "otherish" giving—generosity with appropriate boundaries that protect your own needs.
- Start with low-risk forms of giving to build confidence.
- Notice when your fear is based on past wounds rather than present reality.
- Develop discernment about which relationships merit deeper investment.

Depletion and burnout. If the belief that "I must keep giving even when it costs me too much" leads to exhaustion, decreased joy, or resentment about giving, try these approaches:

- Practice the counterintuitive discipline of receiving.
- Schedule regular renewal practices that replenish your giving capacity.
- Learn to recognize early warning signs of depletion.
- Give from your strengths and passions rather than your areas of struggle.

Unhealthy motivations. If believing "My worth depends on what I can provide for others" means that you're giving to be liked, to control outcomes, or to avoid rejection, consider these strategies:

- Practice giving anonymously to disentangle ego from generosity.
- Explore the difference between healthy and unhealthy motivations.
- Develop practices that affirm your inherent worth apart from what you do for others.
- Seek support to heal underlying wounds that drive compulsive giving.

Scarcity thinking. When the belief that "There isn't enough to go around; I must protect what I have," triggers withholding, anxiety about having "enough," or a competitive mindset, try these approaches:

- Challenge scarcity assumptions with evidence of abundance.
- Practice giving in small ways that build your "abundance muscle."
- Surround yourself with models of generous living.
- Create "enough" metrics for different areas of your life.

Remember, these obstacles aren't signs of failure but normal aspects of the journey toward embodied generosity. Each challenge offers an opportunity to deepen your understanding and practice of authentic offering.

THE GENEROSITY AUDIT: REBALANCING YOUR GIVING

To assess and rebalance your giving patterns for greater sustainability and impact, set aside sixty minutes initially (with quarterly thirty-minute updates) for a generosity audit. This practice helps you identify where your giving is aligned with your values and energizing, and where it might be depleting or misaligned. You can record your audit in your Resonance Journal or keep a separate record.

Begin by documenting your current giving habits in these categories:

- **Time and Attention:** Who receives your focused presence? How often?
- **Emotional Labor:** Whose feelings do you help process or manage?
- **Practical Support:** What tangible assistance do you provide and to whom?
- **Knowledge/Skills:** With whom do you share your expertise?
- **Financial Resources:** Where does your money go as conscious giving?

For each answer, rate these four dimensions from 1–10:

- **Alignment:** How aligned is this with your values and purpose?
- **Energy:** Does this giving energize (+) or deplete (-) you?
- **Impact:** How meaningful is the difference this makes?
- **Reciprocity:** Is there appropriate give-and-take over time?

As patterns emerge, look for:

- **Depletion Zones:** Areas where you give beyond sustainable limits
- **Resentment Indicators:** Giving that comes with strings or expectations
- **Impact Opportunities:** High-alignment, high-energy giving to amplify
- **Boundary Needs:** Areas requiring clearer limits

Based on these insights, create a rebalancing plan that includes:

- One giving pattern to mindfully reduce or transform
- One offering to amplify or develop further
- One new form of giving to explore that aligns with your values
- One way to become more comfortable receiving from others

Remember that reducing unsustainable giving isn't selfish—it creates space for more impactful, energizing generosity. The goal isn't to give less overall but to give more authentically and effectively.

THE ART OF RECEIVING: THE FORGOTTEN HALF OF GENEROSITY

A complete understanding of generosity must include its essential counterpart: the art of receiving. Many of us find it easier to give than to receive, yet without receptivity, the cycle of generosity remains incomplete. Gracious receiving is itself a form of giving—it offers others the gift of contributing, of mattering, of making a difference.

The poet and philosopher Rabindranath Tagore writes: "Everything comes to us that belongs to us if we create the capacity to receive it."

This reluctance to receive stems from various sources: pride, self-sufficiency, unworthiness beliefs, fear of obligation, or past experiences of manipulation through giving. Whatever its origins, this blockage disrupts the natural flow of generosity that sustains healthy relationships and communities.

Indigenous cultures often demonstrate a more balanced understanding of this flow. Many Native American traditions include elaborate gift-giving ceremonies like the potlatch of the Pacific Northwest, where social bonds are strengthened through cycles of generous giving and gracious receiving. In these traditions, both giving and receiving are seen as honorable acts that contribute to community resilience.

THE MORNING GRATITUDE PRACTICE

To cultivate generosity through meaningful expressions of appreciation, try this simple daily practice that requires just five to ten minutes:

Each morning, select one to three people to whom you'd like to express gratitude. These can be close friends, family members, colleagues, or even acquaintances who have positively impacted your life.

Craft a brief, specific message of appreciation:

- Be specific about what you appreciate (e.g., "I was thinking about our conversation last week, and I really valued your insight about . . .).
- Connect to a quality you admire in them (e.g., "Your thoughtfulness reminds me to slow down and consider others").
- Express how they've impacted you (e.g., "Your support gave me courage to try something new").

Choose the most appropriate medium for your message—a handwritten note for deeper impact, a text message for immediacy, a voice message for personal connection, or an email for more detailed appreciation.

Send without expectation, making it clear that no response is needed: "No need to reply—I just wanted you to know you made a difference."

After sending your messages, take a moment to notice how it feels to express gratitude. Does your emotional state shift? How does this practice affect your perspective on your relationships? Record these feelings in your Resonance Journal.

This practice isn't just about feeling good; it's about strengthening your "generosity muscles" and creating a foundation for the day centered on abundance rather than scarcity. Research shows that people who regularly express gratitude report stronger relationships, better health outcomes, and greater resilience in the face of challenges.

THE ABUNDANCE MINDSET: BREAKING THE SCARCITY TRAP

A fundamental shift that underlies generous living is moving from a scarcity mindset to an abundance mindset. With scarcity thinking, we believe there isn't enough to go around—not enough love, recognition, opportunity, or resources. This belief creates a contracted state where giving feels threatening to our security.

An abundance mindset recognizes that many of the most important things in life—love, creativity, knowledge, connection—are not diminished when shared but actually multiply. When I share knowledge with you, I don't have less knowledge—we both have more. When I offer love, my capacity for love expands rather than depletes.

This shift is particularly important in how we approach relationships. A scarcity mindset in relationships manifests as possessiveness, jealousy, and competitiveness. We view others' relationships as threats to our own, fearing that if our friend connects with someone new, it diminishes our connection.

An abundance mindset in relationships embraces the reality that meaningful connections can multiply without diminishing each other. We celebrate when people we care about form new bonds, recognizing that a wider web of connection strengthens rather than weakens our own place in the relationship ecosystem.

Network science offers fascinating insights into the dynamics of relationship abundance. Sociologist Mark Granovetter discovered that some of our most valuable opportunities come through "weak ties"—acquaintances rather than close friends. These connections create bridges between social clusters, allowing ideas and opportunities to flow more widely. The implication: An abundant approach to relationships (maintaining a diverse network) creates more possibilities than a scarcity approach (investing only in a few close ties).

Similarly, the "six degrees of separation" phenomenon demonstrates the highly connected nature of human social networks. When we connect people we know with each other, we exponentially increase the overall connectivity of the network. Each introduction we make strengthens the collective web of relationships.

Computational models show that generosity tends to cluster and spread through networks. When we act generously, we influence not just the recipient but also observers who are more likely to pass on similar generosity. This creates "contagious generosity" that amplifies our individual contributions.

These scientific insights validate the abundance mindset: Our generous connections create ripple effects far beyond what we can directly observe.

THE DISCIPLINE OF OFFERING: BEYOND FEELING GENEROUS

Being an offering isn't merely a matter of feeling generous. It's a discipline—a commitment to show up fully regardless of emotional fluctuations. Just as a musician practices scales even when uninspired, we can practice generosity even when we don't particularly feel like giving.

The concept of "emotional labor"—work that involves managing feelings and expressions to fulfill the emotional requirements of a job—has gained recognition in professional contexts. But emotional labor is also essential in personal relationships. Being fully present, listening deeply, celebrating others' successes, and offering comfort during struggles all require emotional work.

The key is developing sustainable practices rather than depleting ourselves through unsustainable giving. This means:

Recognizing our own needs and limitations. Sustainable generosity acknowledges that we have finite energy and resources. Setting appropriate boundaries isn't selfish—it's the foundation of long-term giving capacity.

Cultivating renewal practices. Just as a well needs to be refilled, our capacity for giving requires regular replenishment through self-care, solitude, and receiving support from others.

Aligning giving with purpose and values. When our generosity expresses our deepest values, it energizes rather than depletes us. This is why clarifying our purpose is essential for sustainable offering.

Practicing presence. The discipline of being fully present—bringing our whole attention to interactions rather than being mentally elsewhere—is perhaps the most valuable offering we can make.

THE OFFERING MEDITATION

To cultivate the inner state of generosity that precedes external giving, try this ten- to fifteen-minute daily meditation practice:

Begin by sitting in a comfortable position with your spine tall and dignified. Place your hands palms up on your thighs or knees as a physical representation of openness and offering.

Start with one to two minutes of simple breath awareness, noticing the natural flow of breath in and out of your body.

For the next three or four minutes, focus on receiving. Imagine yourself receiving what you need—love, support, understanding, strength. With each inhale, visualize these qualities filling your being. Notice any resistance to receiving, and gently release it. Allow yourself to be filled, recognizing that you must receive in order to give.

Then, for three or four minutes, shift your awareness to giving from your fullness. With each exhale, imagine offering your presence, care, and unique gifts to others. Begin with those close to you, then expand to acquaintances, then to all beings. Notice the sensation of generous offering in your body.

For the final three or four minutes, rest in the balanced flow of receiving and giving. Notice the expansive feeling of participating in this natural cycle. Set an intention to carry this awareness into your day.

After the meditation, you might briefly consider what you noticed about your capacity to receive, what you noticed about your capacity to give, and one specific way you intend to be an offering today.

This meditation cultivates the inner state from which authentic giving flows. Practice it before challenging interactions or when you notice yourself contracting into scarcity thinking. It serves as a reset button, helping you return to your natural generosity.

THE RIPPLE EFFECT: HOW SMALL OFFERINGS CREATE WAVES OF CHANGE

The impact of generosity extends far beyond the immediate exchange between giver and receiver. Like a stone dropped in a pond, each act of giving creates ripples that extend outward in ways we may never fully witness.

Researchers Nicholas Christakis and James Fowler have documented this "contagious" quality of human behavior. Their studies suggest that our actions influence not just those directly connected to us but also their connections, and their connections' connections—extending out to three degrees of separation. When you act generously, you potentially influence thousands of people through this ripple effect.

This understanding transforms how we view small acts of offering. The smile you offer a stranger, the encouraging word to a colleague, the attentive listening you give a friend—these aren't isolated moments but potential catalysts for wider transformation.

Anthropologist Margaret Mead famously said, "Never doubt that a small group of thoughtful, committed citizens can change the world; indeed, it's the only thing that ever has." Her insight speaks to the exponential power of generosity when it becomes a shared practice. What begins as individual acts of offering can coalesce into movements, organizations, and cultural shifts that transform communities and societies.

A single act of generosity creates ripples of impact.

First ripple immediately affects both the giver (increased well-being, neural reward activation) and the direct recipient.

Second ripple transforms existing relationships and influences the recipient's behavior toward others.

Third ripple spreads through extended networks and communities as others are inspired to similar acts.

Fourth ripple creates long-term cultural and systemic changes that may continue for generations.

The most remarkable aspect of this ripple effect is that much of a generous act's impact remains unseen by the original giver. This "invisible legacy" of generosity suggests that the full value of our offerings can never be fully measured in the moment.

Think about a time when someone's generous act toward you inspired you to be generous toward others. How far might those ripples have traveled beyond your awareness? How might your own acts of generosity be creating ripples you cannot see?

THE GIVING MOVEMENT: PLAYING FOR CHANGE

In 2005, a small team of filmmakers and musicians set out with a mobile recording studio and a dream: to connect the world through music. The Playing For Change project began by recording street musicians around the globe performing the same songs, then mixing these recordings into unified performances that transcend geography, language, and culture.

Their breakthrough moment came with a rendition of "Stand By Me" that featured dozens of musicians from New Orleans to Santa Monica, from the Himalayan mountains to the streets of Barcelona—none of whom ever met. The video went viral, touching millions of viewers with its visualization of harmony across difference.

What began as a creative project evolved into a movement. The Playing For Change Foundation now builds music schools in underserved communities worldwide, creating educational opportunities for children who might otherwise have none. More than two thousand children receive free music education through these programs, and many have gone on to become teachers themselves, creating a self-sustaining cycle of giving.

This initiative exemplifies the ripple effect of generosity. By offering their talents and voices, individual musicians created something far greater than any could accomplish alone. The project reminds us that when we become an offering—when we contribute our authentic gifts without concern for recognition or reward—we participate in a global symphony of connection.

What unique "instrument" do you play in the symphony of life? What gift or quality can you offer that creates harmony in your relationships and communities? How might sharing that gift create ripples beyond what you can immediately see?

THE PARADOXICAL MATHEMATICS OF GIVING

Traditional mathematics teaches us that when we give something away, we have less. If I have five apples and give you two, I'm left with three. But the mathematics of generosity operates by different principles:

The multiplication principle. Some resources—like knowledge, love, and creativity—multiply when shared. When I teach you something, we both know it. When I offer love, my capacity for love expands.

The inverse relationship. Often, the less we have materially, the more willing we are to share. Studies show that lower-income individuals often give a higher percentage of their income to charity than the wealthy. Those who have experienced hardship frequently demonstrate greater empathy and generosity.

The compounding effect. Small acts of generosity, repeated over time, create exponential rather than linear growth in relationship quality and community strength. Like compound interest, the returns accelerate over time.

The zero-sum fallacy. Many operate from the assumption that human relationships are a zero-sum game—that someone else's gain must come at our expense. Network theory demonstrates that the opposite is true: Well-connected networks create value for all participants.

These paradoxical principles suggest that the conventional wisdom of scarcity—"Look out for number one" and "Get yours before someone else does"—isn't just morally questionable but mathematically flawed. The most effective strategy for individual and collective flourishing is generous collaboration rather than protective competition.

Generosity in Digital Spaces

In our increasingly digital world, the principle of generosity takes on new dimensions and challenges. How do we become an offering in spaces where physical presence is impossible and attention is fragmented?

Digital generosity requires intentional practice but can create powerful resonance when done authentically:

Digital presence. Just as physical presence is a gift, digital presence—your full, undivided attention during video calls or thoughtful engagement in written exchanges—is increasingly valuable in a distracted world.

Amplification. One of the unique forms of digital generosity is in amplifying others' contributions—sharing their work, highlighting their insights, and connecting them with opportunities or resources.

Knowledge sharing. The digital realm offers unprecedented opportunities to share expertise, resources, and information that might benefit others, transforming private knowledge into public good.

Constructive engagement. In online spaces often characterized by conflict and criticism, offering thoughtful, nuanced contributions and assuming good intentions can be revolutionary acts of generosity.

Digital boundaries. Paradoxically, an important aspect of sustainable digital generosity is setting boundaries around your online availability and attention. This models a healthy relationship with technology for others while preserving your capacity to give meaningfully.

The key distinction in digital generosity is between passive consumption and active contribution. Many of us spend hours scrolling through content created by others without ever adding our own voice or value. The invitation of this chapter applies equally to digital relationships: Shift from "What can I get from this platform?" to "What can I offer this community?"

How might you transform one of your digital spaces from a consumption experience to a contribution opportunity? What unique value could you offer that aligns with your authentic gifts?

THE WISDOM OF GIFT ECONOMIES

Writer Lewis Hyde distinguishes between market economies (based on exchange) and gift economies (based on circulation). In gift economies, the value of a gift increases as it moves from person to person, because each transaction strengthens community bonds. This ancient wisdom offers a powerful alternative to transactional thinking. When we become an offering, we participate in this circular flow of giving that has sustained human communities throughout history.

This concept isn't limited to one culture or tradition. Across the globe, we find powerful examples of gift-based connection:

Potlatch (Pacific Northwest Indigenous Peoples). A ceremonial feast where chiefs display their wealth and status through elaborate gift giving, establishing reciprocal relationships between communities.

Ubuntu (Southern Africa). A philosophy captured in the Zulu phrase "*Umuntu ngumuntu ngabantu*," meaning "a person is a person through other persons." It emphasizes generosity and responsibility to the collective.

Dana (Buddhist tradition). The practice of cultivating generosity through giving without attachment to recognition or reward, considered essential for spiritual development.

Kula ring (Trobriand Islands). An elaborate exchange system where ceremonial items circulate among island communities, creating bonds that supersede potential conflicts.

Meitheal (Ireland). A traditional practice of neighbors coming together to help with harvests or other labor-intensive projects, creating community resilience through reciprocal assistance.

What unites these diverse traditions is recognition that generosity creates something more valuable than material wealth: It weaves the social fabric that allows communities to thrive. In each case, the act of giving isn't just about transferring resources—it's about creating and strengthening bonds of mutual care and responsibility.

How might incorporating elements of gift economies into your own relationships create more resonance? Where do you already participate in circles of giving that operate outside market exchanges?

LIVING FROM GENEROSITY: THE PRACTICE OF DAILY OFFERING

As we prepare to move into the next chapter, it's important to recognize that becoming an offering isn't an ideal to achieve but a practice to embody daily. It's about making the shift from "What can I get?" to "What can I give?" in countless small moments throughout our days.

This shift doesn't require grand gestures or dramatic sacrifices. It begins with simple practices:

The practice of presence—offering your undivided attention when someone speaks to you, putting away your phone during conversations, listening to understand rather than to respond.

The practice of appreciation—actively looking for what you can genuinely acknowledge in others, expressing specific gratitude rather than generic thanks.

The practice of service—finding small ways to make others' lives easier or more pleasant without being asked, from holding doors to taking on tasks that no one wants to do.

The practice of invitation—creating spaces where others feel welcome, included, and valued for who they truly are.

These practices may seem small, but their cumulative effect is transformative. As the Zen proverb reminds us, "Before enlightenment, chop wood, carry water. After enlightenment, chop wood, carry water." The profound awakening to generosity happens not in rare moments of insight but in the ordinary actions of daily life.

LOOKING AHEAD: FROM GIVING TO LISTENING

We've explored how generosity creates the foundation for resonant relationships. But giving alone is not enough. To create truly resonant connections, we must also develop the capacity to listen deeply—to attune ourselves to others with curiosity and presence.

In the next chapter, we'll explore the second pillar of resonant relationships: **Listen Deeply and Be Curious (the Ear).** We'll discover how the quality of our attention can either constrict or expand the possibilities for connection, and we'll learn practical techniques for developing the art of deep listening.

The journey from giving to listening is natural. When we approach relationships from a generosity mindset, we create the safety and openness that make deep listening possible. And when we listen with full presence, we discover new ways to offer ourselves authentically to others.

As you move forward, consider this: What if the most valuable gift you have to offer is not your advice, your solutions, or even your support, but the quality of your attention? What if the practice of truly hearing another person is itself a profound act of generosity?

In our next chapter we'll explore how generosity expresses itself in various rituals and customs as a way of seeking inspiration for our own generosity rituals. And in the following chapter we'll discover how deep listening creates the resonance that transforms relationships from transactional to transcendent. But first, take time to integrate what you've learned about generosity. Begin practicing the art of becoming an offering in your daily interactions. Notice what shifts when you approach each encounter with the question "What can I give?" rather than "What can I get?"

The journey of resonance has begun. You've taken the first step—recognizing that connection starts with generosity. Now, carry this awareness forward as we continue to explore the principles and practices that create truly resonant relationships.

CHALLENGE: THE SEVEN-DAY OFFERING

For the next seven days, commit to becoming a conscious offering in your relationships through this structured experiment:

Day 1: The Gift of Presence

Choose three interactions today where you'll offer your complete, undivided attention. Put away all devices, maintain eye contact, and listen not just to words but to the emotions behind them.

Day 2: The Gift of Appreciation

Identify five people to whom you'll express specific, genuine appreciation. Focus not just on what they do but on who they are—qualities you value in them.

Day 3: The Gift of Service

Look for three opportunities to make someone's life easier without being asked and without drawing attention to your assistance.

Day 4: The Gift of Invitation

Create space for someone who might feel excluded or unheard. This could be as simple as asking a quiet colleague for their opinion or inviting someone new to join your lunch table.

Day 5: The Gift of Vulnerability

Share something authentic about yourself—a challenge, a hope, a fear—with someone you trust. Offering our true selves is perhaps the most valuable gift we can give.

Day 6: The Gift of Boundaries

Practice saying no to something that would deplete you, recognizing that sustainable generosity requires honest boundaries. This, too, is a gift—to yourself and ultimately to others.

Day 7: The Gift of Integration

Reflect on your experiences over the week. Which forms of offering felt most natural? Which were challenging? How did others respond? What did you learn about yourself and your relationships?

Journal Prompts

At the end of each day, spend five minutes reflecting in your Resonance Journal:

- What surprised me about being an offering today?
- Where did I feel resistance to giving, and what might that tell me?
- How did my offering affect my own state and energy?
- What did I notice about others' responses to my offering?

This seven-day experiment isn't about perfection but about awareness. By intentionally practicing different forms of giving, you'll begin to discover your unique "generosity signature"—the ways of offering that feel most authentic and energizing for you.

POWER PLAYLIST

BECOMING AN OFFERING

As you continue your journey of becoming an offering, these songs illuminate the transformative power of authentic generosity. Music offers a unique pathway to understanding how giving and receiving create the foundation of resonant relationships. In the chapters ahead, we will use listening to integrate the principles discussed and unleash our own creativity.

- **"Anthem" by Leonard Cohen.** Listen for: How acknowledging our brokenness becomes our greatest offering, the cracks where light gets in.
- **"Give Yourself Away" by Glen Hansard.** Listen for: The raw passion that emerges when we surrender completely to generosity rather than holding back.
- **"So What" by Miles Davis.** Listen for: How musicians create space for each other—true listening as the ultimate gift we can offer.

Listening Practice: Choose one song to focus on. Before listening, reflect on a recent moment when you either gave or received generously. Play the song with full attention, noticing how the music itself demonstrates generosity, how artists offer their vulnerability, how instruments support rather than compete, how silence creates space for expression. After listening, spend five minutes in your Resonance Journal exploring: What would change in my relationships if I approached them as opportunities to give rather than to get?

Creating Your Personal Additions: Add songs that remind you of moments when you felt most generous or most grateful for someone's generosity toward you. Consider sharing one of these with someone who has been an offering in your life, explaining why the song captures what their generosity meant to you.

Remember that generosity is contagious. These songs can serve as powerful reminders of your capacity to be an offering, especially in moments when scarcity thinking tempts you to contract rather than expand.

RESONANCE REFLECTION: THE ECHO OF YOUR GIFTS

As we close this chapter, take a moment for this final reflection:

Imagine that every offering you've ever made—every act of kindness, every moment of presence, every genuine expression of care—has created a ripple that continues to move outward. These ripples cross and intersect, creating complex patterns of influence far beyond what you can see.

Now imagine that you could hear these ripples as sound—as music. What would the symphony of your generosity sound like? Which notes would resonate most strongly? Which harmonies would emerge from the relationships you've nurtured?

This isn't just a poetic image. It's a reminder that we're each creating music through our interactions—through what we choose to give and how we choose to show up. The quality of that music—whether it's discordant or harmonious, whether it lifts others or brings them down—is determined by countless small choices we make each day.

The invitation of this chapter is to become more conscious of the music you're creating, to recognize your power to add beauty and harmony to the world through the simple yet profound act of becoming an offering.

What note will you contribute today?

CHAPTER 4

Ancient Roots and Modern Rituals: The Heart Rhythm of Connection

In chapter 3, we established generosity as the cornerstone of resonant relationships—the willingness to be an offering of time, energy, and authentic presence. This foundational pillar creates the conditions for genuine connection to flourish and sets the stage for deeper, more meaningful relationships.

Now, we turn our attention to how this generosity takes form in the world, manifesting through intentional practices and rituals that have sustained human connection across cultures and throughout history. The art of creating resonant relationships isn't a modern innovation but ancient wisdom reawakened for our disconnected age.

THE MODERN PARADOX OF DISCONNECTION

Look around you. We live in the most technologically connected era in human history. With a few taps on a screen, we can video chat with someone on the other side of the world or send a message to thousands of "friends" simultaneously. Yet paradoxically, rates of loneliness, isolation, and disconnection have reached epidemic proportions.

More Americans report feeling lonely than ever before—a staggering 61 percent in recent surveys. The US surgeon general has declared loneliness a public health crisis, with research showing that chronic isolation carries the same mortality risk as smoking fifteen cigarettes a day. Young people, despite growing up in a hyperconnected digital world, report the highest levels of loneliness across all generations.

How did we arrive at this paradox of connection without connection?

I found myself pondering this question as I sat cross-legged on a woven mat in a small village outside Kandy, Sri Lanka. Before me, a traditional healer named Ananda prepared a ritual space with meticulous care—arranging flowers, lighting oil lamps, and setting out small bowls of herbs and spices. I had traveled there to learn about traditional healing practices, but what I discovered would transform my understanding of human connection itself.

"Modern medicine treats the body as a machine with broken parts," he told me in carefully measured English. "But the body is an instrument that plays in harmony with others. When that harmony is broken, illness follows."

I watched as he welcomed a young woman suffering from what we might call depression. Instead of isolating her for treatment, Ananda gathered her family and several village elders. He facilitated a ceremony involving shared singing, storytelling, and symbolic actions that acknowledged her pain while weaving her back into the fabric of community.

This experience taught me something profound: What we often label as personal pain—anxiety, depression, listlessness—the healer recognized as symptoms of disconnection from our natural rhythm, from community, from something larger than ourselves. And his remedies weren't pharmaceutical but relational, not isolation but immersion in shared ritual.

What struck me most was how the healer described the heart rhythm and its role in human connection. He explained that when people gather in authentic community, their hearts begin to synchronize—not just metaphorically, but literally. Modern science confirms this phenomenon: Researchers have documented how heart rhythms can synchronize between people during moments of deep connection, a biological resonance that mirrors the emotional one.

"The heart speaks to heart," Ananda told me. "This is not poetry; this is medicine."

This wisdom isn't unique to Sri Lanka. Across cultures and throughout history, humans have developed practices that foster this heart-level synchrony, that create the conditions for genuine connection to flourish. In this chapter, we'll explore how ancient wisdom about connection can transform your relationships today.

What my time with the Sri Lankan healer taught me is that connection isn't just a pleasant addition to our lives—it's essential medicine for our well-being.

THE MEDICINE OF RITUAL

From my time with the healer in Sri Lanka, I learned that effective healing rituals share certain fundamental elements, regardless of their cultural origin:

Creating Sacred Space: Rituals establish a boundary between ordinary time and sacred time, between mundane space and space dedicated to connection. The intentional preparation of a physical setting signals to participants that something special is happening.

Engaging the Senses: Effective rituals involve multiple senses—sound, smell, taste, touch, and sight—creating a full-bodied experience that bypasses our analytical mind.

Shared Rhythm: Whether through music, movement, breath, or speech, rituals often create a shared rhythm that allows participants' heart rates and breathing to synchronize. This physiological synchrony creates the conditions for emotional resonance.

Community Witnessing: The presence of others who witness and participate amplifies the power of ritual, creating a container of mutual support.

Symbolic Actions: Meaningful gestures and objects serve as bridges between the visible and invisible worlds, between what we can articulate and what we can only feel.

These elements aren't mere cultural decorations—they're sophisticated psychological and neurological tools that facilitate connection. Modern research increasingly validates what traditional cultures have long known: These practices change our physiology, affecting everything from heart rate variability to immune function to neurochemistry.

When we engage in connection rituals, we aren't just following pleasant social customs; we're accessing powerful medicine for our disconnected hearts.

A GLOBAL SYMPHONY OF CONNECTION PRACTICES

As I returned from Sri Lanka, I discovered that many cultures have developed unique traditions that prioritize connection, each offering its own variation on the elements Ananda had taught me. These practices, often rooted in a deep understanding of human needs and the natural world, offer valuable lessons for us today as we seek to build more resonant relationships.

The Swedish Art of Fika

As we discussed in chapter 2, in Sweden, fika is more than just a coffee break; it is a dedicated moment to pause, connect, and be present with others. Typically involving coffee and something sweet like a cinnamon bun (***kanelbullar***), the focus isn't on the refreshments but on the conversation and companionship they facilitate.

Hygge: Creating Warmth in Connection

Similar to fika, *hygge* (pronounced "hoo-gah") from Denmark and Norway embodies a feeling of cozy contentment through enjoying life's simple pleasures. It's about creating a warm atmosphere, often involving candles, soft blankets, and comforting food. While hygge can be enjoyed alone, it's particularly powerful as a shared experience.

During the darkest winter months when sunlight is scarce, Danes create literal and figurative warmth through hygge gatherings. These aren't elaborate dinner parties but intentional spaces for authentic connection. The emphasis is on creating a sanctuary from the outside world where people can be fully present with each other.

Ubuntu: I Am Because We Are

Perhaps no cultural concept captures the essence of human interconnectedness more powerfully than *Ubuntu* from Southern Africa. This Nguni Bantu term, often translated as "I am because we are," encapsulates a philosophy that recognizes our fundamental interdependence.

Archbishop Desmond Tutu explained Ubuntu this way: "A person with Ubuntu is open and available to others, affirming of others, does not feel threatened that others are able and good, for he or she has a proper self-assurance that comes from knowing that he or she belongs in a greater whole."

During my time in post-apartheid South Africa, I witnessed how Ubuntu principles were applied in community rebuilding efforts. What impressed me most was how even the most marginalized community members were given space to speak and be heard—a living demonstration of the belief that everyone's well-being matters to the collective good.

Moai: Lifelong Circles of Support

On the Japanese island of Okinawa, home to some of the world's longest-lived people, there exists a social structure that might explain their remarkable longevity: the *moai*.

A moai is a group of five to seven people who commit to supporting each other for life. Formed often in childhood, these groups meet regularly to share meals, experiences, and resources. They celebrate each other's joys and shoulder each other's burdens, creating a safety net of social connection that lasts decades.

Shinrin-Yoku: Finding Connection in Nature

The Japanese practice of *shinrin-yoku* or "forest bathing" represents a different kind of connection—one that recognizes our need to maintain a relationship not just with other humans but with the natural world.

Developed in the 1980s as a response to increasing urbanization and technological saturation, shinrin-yoku involves immersing oneself mindfully in nature. It's not hiking or exercising but simply being present in the forest, engaging all senses, and allowing nature to enter through our eyes, ears, nose, mouth, hands, and feet.

Ho'oponopono: The Practice of Reconciliation

How we handle conflict and repair harm in relationships may be the ultimate test of our commitment to connection. The ancient Hawaiian practice of *ho'oponopono* offers a powerful framework for this essential work.

Traditionally used within families to restore harmony, ho'oponopono means "to make right" or "to correct." It involves a structured process of acknowledgment, responsibility, forgiveness, and gratitude, guided by four key phrases:

- "I'm sorry" (taking responsibility)
- "Please forgive me" (requesting reconciliation)
- "Thank you" (expressing gratitude)
- "I love you" (reaffirming connection)

These simple phrases, when spoken with genuine intent, can break through resentment and defensiveness, creating a path back to connection even after serious breaches of trust.

CREATING YOUR OWN CONNECTION RITUALS

After my return from Sri Lanka, I found myself continually drawing parallels between Ananda's healing ceremonies and the diverse connection practices I encountered in my research and travels. Despite their cultural differences, these traditions all embody what Ananda called "the medicine of togetherness." They teach us that resonance is not a passive state but an active practice, something we can cultivate through intentional rituals, shared experiences, and a commitment to being present with one another.

As Ananda taught me, it's not enough to intellectually understand these principles—we must embody them through regular practice. Just as he prescribed specific rhythmic movements and communal activities as medicine for disconnection, we, too, can create intentional practices that restore our natural rhythms of connection.

Rituals, in essence, are intentional, repeated actions that carry symbolic meaning and connect us to something larger than ourselves. They can be simple everyday practices, like sharing a meal or a morning cup of coffee, or more elaborate ceremonies that mark important life transitions. What they all have in common is their ability to create a sense of shared identity, to reinforce values, and to provide a framework for meaningful interaction. They are, in a sense, the rhythm section of our relationships, providing a steady beat that anchors us in connection.

"In your modern world," Ananda once told me, "you have many machines but few rituals. You have lost the technology of the heart." When I asked him to explain, he smiled and said, "Ritual is the technology of the heart. It is how we have always synchronized our spirits and restored our natural rhythms."

In my work with individuals and organizations, I've found that those who create and maintain simple connection rituals are significantly more resilient in the face of life's challenges. They have built-in systems for support, celebration, and creating meaning that sustain them through difficult times and enhance their experience of good times.

THE RHYTHM INTEGRATION MAP

Now that we've explored these diverse traditions and practices, how do we integrate them into our modern lives? How do we translate these ancient technologies of connection into a practical approach for today?

The Rhythm Integration Map on the next page offers a framework for incorporating these practices into your weekly life, creating a rhythm of connection that sustains your relationships and nourishes your well-being.

Daily Practices	Weekly Rituals	Monthly Ceremonies	Seasonal Celebrations
Morning gratitude practice	Shared meal	Nature immersion	Community gathering
Digital sunset	Creative collaboration	Resonance circle	Seasonal transition ritual
Heart-centered check-in	Dedicated listening space	Service project	Personal reflection retreat

This framework isn't meant to be prescriptive but adaptive. The specific practices you choose should reflect your cultural background, personal preferences, and current life circumstances. What matters is establishing a consistent rhythm that creates containers for connection in your life.

Remember what Ananda taught: It's the regularity of practice, not its complexity, that establishes new patterns. A simple daily practice sustained over time will create more profound shifts than occasional elaborate ceremonies.

THE POWER OF THE SHARED TABLE

Among all the practices we've explored, one stands out for its accessibility, power, and universality: the shared meal. This practice transcends cultural boundaries and has been at the heart of human connection since our earliest beginnings.

During my final week in Sri Lanka, Ananda invited me to his home for a traditional meal. I expected a simple dinner, but what I experienced was a profound ritual of connection. Before we ate, he carefully prepared the space, lighting oil lamps and arranging fresh flowers. Family members arrived, each bringing a dish prepared with intention. Before the meal began, we sat in silence for several moments, acknowledging the hands that had grown and prepared the food. Throughout the meal, stories were shared—some joyful, some poignant—but all received with equal attention and respect.

"The meal is medicine," Ananda told me that night. "Not just the plants and spices, but the way we come together to share it. In your country, you eat quickly, often alone, sometimes in your cars. This is not nourishment. True nourishment happens when food and presence are shared."

Think of the shared table as the heart of the home, the central gathering place where families and friends come together to connect, share stories, and break bread. It's a space where we can slow down, put aside distractions, and be fully present with one another. It's a place where we can practice the art of deep listening, offer our time and attention as a gift, and create a sense of belonging.

Ananda emphasized the power of shared meals as medicine for disconnection. "When we eat together," he would say, "we share more than food—we share life force."

Drawing Inspiration from Shabbat

One powerful example of the shared meal as a resonant ritual can be found in the Jewish tradition of *Shabbat*. Every week, from Friday evening to Saturday evening, Jewish families around the world gather to observe Shabbat, a day of rest and spiritual rejuvenation. Central to this observance is the Shabbat dinner, a time for family and friends to come together, share a meal, and connect with each other and with their traditions.

My friend Leah invited me to experience her family's Shabbat dinner after hearing about my work on resonant relationships. "Shabbat has sustained the Jewish people through centuries of hardship," she told me. "It's a practice of collective resilience."

The evening began with the lighting of candles, which Leah explained creates a boundary between ordinary time and sacred time. "This simple act tells our nervous systems that we can put down our burdens and just be present," she said. Blessings were recited over wine and challah (a special braided bread), and then we shared a leisurely meal filled with conversation, laughter, and occasional silence. What struck me most was how the ritual elements created a container that made deep connection feel natural and effortless.

More than just a meal, the Shabbat dinner is a carefully orchestrated ritual filled with symbolic meaning. It begins with the lighting of candles, symbolizing the creation of a sacred space, separate from the worries and demands of the week. Blessings are recited over wine and challah, expressing gratitude for the gifts of life. The meal itself is often a festive affair, with special dishes prepared and enjoyed together.

But perhaps the most important element of the Shabbat dinner is the conversation. It's a time for families to share their experiences from the week, to discuss meaningful topics, and to simply enjoy each other's company. It's a time for deep listening, for storytelling, and for strengthening the bonds that tie the family together. The structure of the Shabbat dinner—the set time, the specific rituals, the emphasis on presence and connection—creates a container for resonance to flourish.

THE SCIENCE OF BREAKING BREAD

The benefits of shared meals, whether as elaborate as a Shabbat dinner or as simple as a weeknight supper, are increasingly supported by research:

- **Family Meals and Child Development:** Studies have consistently shown that children who regularly eat meals with their families tend to have better academic outcomes, lower rates of substance abuse, and improved mental health. The shared meal provides a consistent opportunity for communication, connection, and the transmission of values.
- **Strengthening Relationships:** Research on adult relationships also highlights the importance of shared meals. Couples who regularly eat dinner together report higher levels of relationship satisfaction and intimacy. The shared meal provides a dedicated time for conversation, connection, and emotional support.
- **Reducing Stress and Promoting Well-Being:** The act of sharing a meal with loved ones can be a powerful stress reliever. It provides a sense of comfort, security, and belonging, all of which contribute to overall well-being. Studies have shown that eating together can lower levels of cortisol, a stress hormone.
- **Building Community:** Beyond the family, shared meals can be a

powerful tool for building community. Potlucks, community dinners, and other shared meal events create opportunities for people to connect with their neighbors, build relationships, and foster a sense of belonging.

The shared table, then, is more than just a place to eat; it's a crucible for connection, a space where we can practice the principles of resonance and unlock The More in our relationships. It's a place where we can offer our presence, our attention, and our authentic selves to those we care about, creating a ripple effect of positive energy that extends far beyond the meal itself.

As Ananda would often say, "The medicine is in the gathering." The transformative power of the shared meal isn't in any single element but in the synergy created when all elements work together: the sacred space, the sensory experience, the shared rhythm, the community witnessing, and the symbolic actions. Together, these create what he called a "healing field" where our natural capacity for connection can flourish.

PRACTICAL CONNECTION INSTRUMENTS

Here are some tools for developing the kind of connection that happens in a community gathering.

Resonance Instrument

THE SHARED TABLE

This instrument transforms a simple meal into a powerful ritual for connection. Like a well-rehearsed ensemble, it brings together different elements—food, conversation, presence—to create a harmonious and nourishing experience.

How to Play It:

1. **Choose a time.** Designate a specific time for a shared meal—it could be dinner, lunch, or even breakfast. Aim for at least once a week but more often if possible. Consistency is key to creating a rhythm that people can count on.
2. **Invite your circle.** Invite the people you want to connect with—family, friends, colleagues, or even new acquaintances. Consider who might benefit from being included, especially those who might otherwise eat alone.
3. **Create a sacred space.** Set the table with intention. This doesn't have to be fancy; it simply means creating a welcoming and inviting atmosphere. You might light candles or open the shades to allow natural light. Put on some soft music, or perhaps arrange a simple centerpiece. The key is to create a space that feels special and conducive to connection.
4. **Prepare food together (optional).** If possible, involve your guests in the preparation of the meal. Cooking together can be a fun and collaborative activity that strengthens bonds. Even simple tasks like washing vegetables or setting the table can create a sense of shared purpose.
5. **Disconnect to connect.** Before you begin eating, put away your phones, turn off the TV, and commit to being fully present with each other. Consider creating a "phone stack" in the center of the table or designating a basket where devices are placed during the meal.
6. **Start with a moment of gratitude.** Before everyone begins eating, take a moment to express gratitude for the food, the company, and the opportunity to connect. This could be a formal blessing or a simple round of "What I'm grateful for today . . ." Ananda emphasized that gratitude practices physically change our heart rhythm, creating what he called a "coherent

heart state" that is optimal for connection. Research from the HeartMath Institute confirms this physiological effect, showing that gratitude practices increase heart rate variability and improve nervous system regulation.

7. **Engage in meaningful conversation.** Use this time to connect on a deeper level. Share stories, ask open-ended questions, and practice active listening. Here are some conversation starters:
   - What was the most meaningful moment of your week?
   - What's something you're looking forward to?
   - What's been challenging you lately?
   - What's something you're curious about or learning?
   - What's a memory that this meal reminds you of?
8. **End with a closing ritual.** Just as you began with intention, end with intention. This could be a final expression of gratitude, a toast, or simply acknowledging the time shared. The closing ritual signals a transition back to ordinary time and carries the connection energy forward.

Variations:

- **Potluck Style:** Have each person bring a dish that has meaning to them and invite them to share the story behind it.
- **Theme Meals:** Create meals around a theme—a country's cuisine, a seasonal celebration, or dishes from family heritage.
- **Story Meals:** Designate each meal as a time to share specific types of stories—childhood memories, professional challenges, travel adventures.
- **Question Bowl:** Place conversation-starting questions in a bowl and take turns drawing and answering them.

Start small and build consistency. A single weekly shared meal with intention is more powerful than occasional elaborate gatherings.

Pay attention to which elements create the most resonance for your particular group and adapt accordingly. Remember that the goal isn't perfection but presence.

Resonance Instrument

THE TECH-FREE ZONE

This instrument creates physical and temporal spaces free from digital distraction, allowing natural rhythms of connection to emerge. Like clearing static from a radio signal, removing technology creates clarity for the subtle frequencies of human relationship to be heard.

How to Play It:

1. **Define your boundaries.** Decide on specific times and spaces that will be technology-free. This could be a physical space (the dining room, bedroom, or a particular corner of your home), a time period (the first hour after waking, evenings after 8 PM), or during a particular activity like meals or family game nights.
2. **Communicate expectations.** Clearly explain the purpose of the tech-free zone to everyone involved. Frame it positively—not as a restriction but as a gift of presence and connection.
3. **Create a "parking lot" for devices.** Designate a specific place where devices are stored during tech-free times. This might be a basket, drawer, or shelf located at the edge of your tech-free zone.
4. **Fill the space with alternatives.** Nature abhors a vacuum, and so does human attention. Stock your tech-free zone with books,

games, art supplies, musical instruments, or other non-digital activities that encourage interaction and creativity.

5. **Start small and build.** Begin with short periods—perhaps thirty minutes—and gradually extend as the practice becomes more comfortable. This allows your nervous system time to adjust to the absence of digital stimulation.
6. **Notice what emerges.** Pay attention to how conversation, connection, and general awareness shift in the absence of technology. What do you notice about yourself and others when screens aren't competing for attention?
7. **Reset when needed.** If the boundary gets broken (and it will), simply notice, reset, and begin again without judgment. Consistency over time matters more than perfection in the moment.

Variations:

- **Digital Sabbath:** Spend a full twenty-four-hour period (typically weekly) without technology.
- **Nature Tech Detox:** Combine tech-free time with outdoor experiences.
- **Progressive Expansion:** Start with just phones, then include all screens, then all electronic devices.
- **Silent Tech Break:** Combine tech-free time with periods of intentional silence.

This instrument directly counters one of the primary barriers to connection in modern life: divided attention. Research consistently shows that even the presence of a phone (even face down) measurably reduces the depth of conversation and empathy between people. By creating intentional spaces free from digital distraction, we allow our natural capacity for resonance to emerge.

Resonance Instrument

PERSONAL RITUAL DESIGN

This instrument empowers you to create your own connection rituals tailored to your specific relationships and needs. Like a composer creating a new piece of music, you'll draw on traditional elements while adding your unique voice to create practices that foster resonance in your life.

How to Play It:

1. **Identify a relationship or relationship domain** that would benefit from a more intentional connection practice. This could be your romantic partnership, your family, a friendship or group of friends, your work team, your community.
2. **Define your intention.** What specific quality of connection do you want to cultivate? Is it deeper understanding, more playfulness, increased support, or something else? Be as specific as possible.
3. **Consider the elements of effective ritual** that we discussed earlier in this chapter, and how you might incorporate them:
    - Creating a sacred space (How will you distinguish this time/place from ordinary life?)
    - Engaging the senses (What sensory elements will you include?)
    - Establishing shared rhythm (How will you create synchrony?)
    - Witnessing community (Who will participate, and how?)
    - Symbolic actions (What meaningful gestures will represent your intention?)
4. **Start with a simple design** that you can consistently implement.

A ritual that happens regularly with fewer elements is more powerful than an elaborate one that rarely occurs.

5. **Test and refine.** After implementing your ritual a few times, reflect on what's working and what could be adjusted. Invite feedback from other participants.
6. **Document and evolve.** Write down your ritual design so it can be replicated. Allow it to evolve over time as you discover what creates the most resonance.

Examples:

- **Morning Connection Ritual:** A couple takes five minutes each morning to sit knee to knee, make eye contact, and share one hope for the day and one concern, followed by a brief touch (hand on heart, forehead touch, or hug).
- **Friendship Check-in:** Friends commit to a monthly video call where each person shares their "rose" (a celebration), "thorn" (a challenge), and "bud" (something they're looking forward to), followed by supportive witnessing without giving advice.
- **Team Alignment Practice:** A work team begins each week with a circle where each person shares their key focus for the week and one way others could support them, with a brief moment of silence between speakers.
- **Family Gratitude Jar:** Family members write moments of gratitude on slips of paper throughout the week, placing them in a special jar; then they read them aloud during a weekly meal.

When designing your ritual, remember Ananda's wisdom: "The power is not in complexity but in consistency." Simple practices done regularly create more transformation than elaborate ceremonies done occasionally. Start small, be consistent, and allow your ritual to evolve naturally.

CREATING YOUR RESONANCE RHYTHM

Throughout this chapter, we've explored traditional practices from around the world that foster genuine connection. Now, the invitation is to create your own resonance rhythm—a pattern of intentional practices that support the quality of connection you desire in your life.

This isn't about perfectly replicating ancient rituals or adopting practices that feel foreign to your cultural background. It's about extracting the wisdom embedded in these traditions and applying it in ways that make sense for your unique circumstances and relationships.

Your resonance rhythm might include:

Daily Practices: Small, consistent actions that create moments of connection throughout your day; a morning check-in with your partner or family, a midday fika, an evening ritual of sharing highlights and challenges.

Weekly Rituals: More substantial practices that create deeper connection. A device-free dinner with family or friends, a nature walk with a loved one, an online gathering with distant connections.

Monthly Ceremonies: More elaborate experiences that foster community and deeper bonds. A potluck meal with neighbors, a service project with friends, a creativity circle with like-minded people.

Seasonal Celebrations: Marking natural transitions with intentional gathering. Solstice or equinox observances, harvest or planting celebrations, year-end reflection and setting intentions for the new year.

The specific practices you choose don't matter; what does is their alignment with the principles we've explored: creating sacred space, engaging the senses, establishing shared rhythm, enabling community witnessing, and incorporating meaningful symbolic actions.

Ananda's guidance applies here: "The most powerful rituals are not the most elaborate but the most consistent." A simple practice done daily will create more connection than an elaborate ceremony done once a year. Start where you are, with what feels accessible and sustainable, then build from there.

THE TECHNOLOGY OF TOGETHERNESS

As we conclude this chapter on ancient roots and modern rituals, it's worth returning to Ananda's powerful phrase: "Ritual is the technology of the heart." This reframing helps us see the practices we've explored not as quaint cultural artifacts but as sophisticated tools for creating the connection our hearts and minds require to thrive.

In our rush toward digital innovation, we've often neglected these time-tested technologies of togetherness. The result is a society with unprecedented tools for communication but diminishing capacity for communion—for the heart-to-heart resonance that gives our lives meaning and sustains us through challenges.

Yet there is hope in the growing recognition of this imbalance. From the corporate boardrooms of Silicon Valley to suburban living rooms, people are rediscovering the power of intentional connection practices. Companies are implementing device-free meetings, families are creating tech-free dinner zones, and communities are reviving traditional gathering practices.

This isn't regression but integration—bringing forward the wisdom of our ancestors while navigating the complexities of modern life. It's about reclaiming our attention from the forces that would fragment it and redirecting it toward what matters most: our presence with each other.

As you move forward from this chapter, I invite you to become not just a consumer of connection but a creator of it. Design your own rituals, establish your rhythms of togetherness, and become a steward of spaces where hearts can speak to hearts.

In his book *To Bless the Space Between Us*, poet and philosopher John O'Donohue describes a blessing as an act that evokes a "privileged intimacy." This is what intentional connection practices offer—a blessed intimacy, a privileged space where we remember our belonging to each other and to something larger than ourselves.

The disconnection epidemic of our time isn't inevitable; it's a call to remember and revive the technologies of togetherness that have sustained human communities through millennia. By integrating these practices into our modern lives, we create islands of resonance in a sea of distraction—spaces where The More can emerge and flourish.

CHALLENGE: THE THREE-RITUALS EXPERIMENT

For the next month, commit to implementing three connection rituals in your life:

A daily micro ritual (2–5 minutes). Design a brief daily practice that creates a moment of intentional connection. This might be:

- A morning check-in with your partner or family
- A gratitude text to someone different each day
- A tech-free tea break where you simply observe your surroundings
- A moment of silence before meals to establish presence

A weekly mini ritual (15–30 minutes). Create a weekly practice that allows for deeper connection. This could be:

- A device-free family meal
- A friend check-in with a specific sharing format
- A nature walk, alone or with others
- A creative practice that connects you with your inner experience

A monthly macro ritual (1–3 hours). Establish a monthly gathering or practice that creates community and deeper bonds:

- A potluck dinner with friends or neighbors
- A service project that contributes to your community
- A reflection circle where people can share current challenges and celebrations
- A seasonal celebration connected to the natural world

Throughout this experiment, record in your Resonance Journal:

- What elements of your rituals create the strongest sense of connection?
- What resistances or obstacles emerge, and how might you address them?
- What subtle shifts do you notice in the quality of your relationships?

- How does the rhythm of these practices affect your overall sense of well-being?

This challenge isn't about perfection but exploration. Allow your rituals to evolve based on what you discover works best for your particular relationships and circumstances.

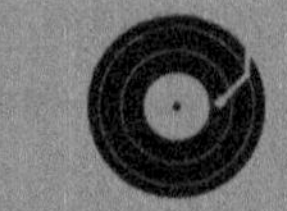

POWER PLAYLIST

RITUAL AND THE MORE

Across cultures and throughout history, music has been the heartbeat of human ritual—from celebrations to ceremonies, from work songs to worship. These songs demonstrate how shared rhythms create the foundation for meaningful connection and community bonds.

- **"Lean on Me" by Bill Withers.** Listen for: The call-and-response structure that transforms individual need into collective strength—notice how the rhythm itself creates community.
- **"Circle of Life" by Elton John.** Listen for: How African-influenced arrangements connect us to ancestral wisdom and the timeless cycles that bind all generations.
- **"We Are Family" by Sister Sledge.** Listen for: The disco beat that makes chosen community feel like celebration—how rhythm creates belonging beyond blood relations.

Listening Practice: This week, pay attention to the rhythms in your daily life. Choose one song and listen while moving—whether swaying, clapping, or walking. Notice how your body naturally wants to synchronize with the music. After listening, reflect in your Resonance Journal: What rituals or rhythms in my life create the strongest sense of connection? How might I be more intentional about creating shared rhythmic experiences with others?

Creating Your Personal Additions: Add songs that connect you to your cultural heritage or that have been part of meaningful rituals in your life—wedding songs, holiday music, or tunes that always bring your family or community together. Consider how these songs serve as bridges across time and difference.

Music is humanity's oldest technology for creating unity across diversity. These songs remind us that beneath our surface differences, we all respond to rhythm, melody, and the profound human need to move and celebrate together.

RESONANCE REFLECTION: THE RHYTHM OF YOUR LIFE

As we close this chapter, take a moment for this final reflection:

Think about the natural rhythms that currently exist in your life—the patterns of connection and disconnection, gathering and solitude, giving and receiving. These rhythms may be intentional or unconscious, supportive or depleting.

Now imagine your ideal rhythm of connection. Not a fantasy that ignores real-world constraints but an authentic, sustainable pattern that would nourish your relationships and well-being.

What elements of this ideal rhythm already exist in your life? What small shifts would create the greatest positive impact? Who might be allies in creating more intentional connection practices?

The invitation of this chapter is to move from passive participation in cultural patterns to active creation of resonant rhythms. As the conductor of your life's symphony, you have the power to establish tempos, create movements, and invite others into harmonious rituals and collaboration.

What beat will you set? What melody will you play? What harmonies will you invite? The rhythm of resonance awaits your creative touch.

PART 2

Finding Your Authentic Note

Before you can create resonance with others, you must first discover the music within yourself.

WHERE YOU ARE NOW

You've recognized resonance, understood connection, practiced generosity. Now comes the crucial turning point: discovering your authentic voice.

THE CHALLENGE AHEAD

Many of us live out of alignment with our true selves. We perform roles written by others, play notes composed for different instruments, and wonder why our relationships feel hollow. This disconnection from self creates a dissonance that echoes through all our connections.

THE BIGGER TRUTH

You cannot create resonant relationships if you're playing someone else's song. The journey to connection begins with self-connection. The work in this section is the fulcrum upon which all your future relationships will balance—because you cannot share what you haven't yet discovered within yourself.

YOUR INVITATION

As we prepare to explore the inner landscape of authenticity and integrity in the chapters ahead, I invite you to approach this section with particular openness. The journey inward can be both the most challenging and the most rewarding part of creating resonant relationships.

When we turn our attention to our own authentic voice, we often encounter resistance—the accumulated expectations, beliefs, and protective patterns that have kept us safe but small. This resistance is normal. It's the sound of your system recognizing that change is coming.

Throughout the next two chapters, remember that finding your authentic note isn't about perfection—it's about alignment. It's about removing the layers of expectation, conditioning, and fear that have muffled your true voice, allowing your unique song to emerge.

Are you ready to find your authentic note?

CHAPTER 5

Finding Your True Song

The privilege of a lifetime is to become who you truly are.

JOSEPH CAMPBELL

Don't ask yourself what the world needs. Ask yourself what makes you come alive, and go do that, because what the world needs is people who have come alive.

HOWARD THURMAN

To be nobody-but-yourself—in a world which is doing its best, night and day, to make you everybody else—means to fight the hardest battle which any human being can fight; and never stop fighting.

E. E. CUMMINGS

Imagine standing at the edge of a vast canyon.

You call out, but instead of hearing your own voice echo back, you hear someone else's words—words that sound nothing like you. This is the dissonance many of us live with every day: speaking in voices that aren't our own, playing melodies composed by others, living lives orchestrated by external expectations rather than internal truth.

Have you ever heard a voice that stopped you in your tracks? A voice so authentic, so powerful that it seemed to bypass your ears and strike directly at your heart? That's what happens when someone finds their true song.

But what is your song?

We've explored the profound value of connection and learned how to be an offering in our relationships. But creating resonant relationships doesn't just happen by chance. It requires a willingness to turn inward, to understand our own inner music before we can truly harmonize with others. It requires us to become aware of our own needs, values, and desires—to find our authentic note.

This chapter is about finding our true song, the authentic expression of who we are. It's about recognizing that alignment is the inner thermostat that regulates our energy levels and attracts the right people into our lives.

THE CACOPHONY OF INAUTHENTICITY

Imagine a symphony orchestra where every musician is playing a different tune, out of sync and out of harmony. The result would be a cacophony, a jarring dissonance that grates on the ears. Yet, this is how many of us live our lives: disconnected from our inner music, playing a tune that doesn't resonate with our true selves.

Are you playing your authentic melody or someone else's arrangement?

We conform to societal expectations, chase after external validation, and suppress our authentic voices, creating a dissonance within that leaves us feeling unfulfilled and disconnected. But what if you could discover your own unique melody, the song that only you can sing? What if you could learn to play your inner instrument in perfect harmony with your values, passions, and purpose?

ARETHA'S JOURNEY TO AUTHENTIC EXPRESSION

She grew up singing in her father's church, her voice soaring through the rafters, filled with the raw emotion and power of gospel music. But when she stepped into the world of professional recording, she found herself being molded into something she wasn't. They dressed her in elegant gowns, smoothed out her edges, and handed her jazz standards to sing. She had a beautiful voice, no doubt, and she achieved a degree of success. But something was missing. The music felt hollow, forced. It didn't resonate with her soul. It wasn't her song.

Year after year, she chased a sound that wasn't hers, trying to fit into a mold that didn't quite fit. She was singing, but she wasn't singing *her* song. The dissonance between her true self and the image she projected was growing.

Then, a change in direction. A new record label. A producer who saw beyond the surface, who recognized the fire that burned within her. He encouraged her to return to her roots, to embrace the music that had shaped her, to sing with the raw, unbridled passion she'd learned in her father's church.

And so, she did. She stepped up to the microphone, not as a polished jazz singer but as a woman who had something to say. She sang about respect—respect for herself, respect for her community, respect for all women. She sang about love, loss, and the struggles of everyday life. She sang with a power and conviction that shook the foundations of the music industry. And when she sang, the world listened.

That woman was Aretha Franklin, the "Queen of Soul." It was her willingness to embrace her authentic voice, to sing her true song, that made her a legend. She didn't try to fit into a preexisting mold; she created her own. She listened to her inner music, honed her craft, and shared her unique song with the world, forging deep connections with fans who saw themselves reflected in her music.

What would happen if you sang your song with the same conviction as Aretha?

Aretha's story is a powerful reminder that true resonance begins with self-discovery. It's about finding your authentic note amid the noise of the world and having the courage to play it, loud and clear.

THE FIRST STEPS: DEEP LISTENING AND SELF-DISCOVERY

Aretha's journey highlights the essential first steps on the path to resonant relationships: learning to listen deeply to the whispers of our own hearts and embracing the unique combination of experiences, talents, and passions that make us who we are. This is where we discover our true song, the authentic melody that wants to be expressed through us.

It requires turning inward, paying attention to our thoughts, feelings, values, and desires. It's about becoming curious about what makes us tick, what brings us joy, and what creates dissonance within us.

Reflection: When was the last time you felt completely aligned with yourself—when your outer actions matched your inner values? What were you doing? Who were you with? How did it feel? Take a moment to write this memory in your Resonance Journal.

THE AUTHENTIC VOICE JOURNEY

Finding your true song isn't a linear process but a journey with distinct phases that often spiral and repeat throughout our lives. Understanding where you are in this journey can help you navigate the process with greater awareness and intention:

1. **Dissonance:** Recognizing when your outer expression doesn't match your inner truth
2. **Deep Listening:** Tuning in to your values, desires, and authentic voice
3. **Experimentation:** Trying new ways of expressing your authentic self
4. **Integration:** Embedding authentic expression into your relationships and life
5. **Evolution:** Growing and adapting while maintaining authenticity

Throughout this chapter, we'll explore practices for each phase of this journey, helping you find and express your true song.

CULTURAL WISDOM: SONGS OF IDENTITY AROUND THE WORLD

This journey of self-discovery, of finding our authentic note, is not a new concept. Cultures around the world have long understood the importance of connecting with one's inner essence and expressing it outwardly.

The Sami Joik

The Sami people, an indigenous group from northern Scandinavia, have a unique musical tradition called the "joik." A joik is more than just a song; it is a person, a place, or a thing. It's not a song *about* something; it *is* that something, expressed through sound. Every Sami person has their own joik. Places have joiks too—a mountain, a river, a forest can all have their own distinct song. If your life were a joik—not a song about you, but the very essence of you expressed as sound—what would it sound like?

Australian Aboriginal Songlines

For Aboriginal Australians, songlines are ancient pathways across the land that are recorded and maintained through songs, stories, and ceremonies. These songs contain practical knowledge about the landscape as well as spiritual knowledge about one's place within it. Like musical maps, they help individuals and communities navigate not just physical terrain but also their spiritual and cultural identity. If you were to trace your own songline across the landscape of your life, where would it lead?

Japanese Ikigai

The Japanese concept of *ikigai*—often translated as "a reason for being"—offers another lens for understanding authenticity. Ikigai emerges at the intersection of four elements: what you love, what you're good at, what the world needs, and what you can be paid for. What is your ikigai, the purpose that aligns your passions, talents, and the world's needs?

West African Griot Traditions

In many West African societies, griots serve as historians, storytellers, and musicians who preserve and share the authentic stories of their communities. Through their songs and tales, griots maintain cultural identity across generations. This tradition reminds us that authenticity isn't just about individual expression but can also involve carrying forward and honoring the authentic stories and values of our communities. What authentic stories do you carry that need to be expressed?

THE RESONANCE PRINCIPLES OF AUTHENTICITY

This chapter delves into two interconnected pillars of resonant relationships, both essential for finding your authentic note and creating alignment in your life.

Pillar #2: Listen Deeply and Be Curious (the Ear)

This pillar emphasizes the importance of listening not only to others but also to ourselves. It involves turning inward and paying attention to our own thoughts, feelings, values, and desires. It's about becoming curious about what makes us tick, what brings us joy, and what creates dissonance within us.

In the context of finding your true song, it means listening deeply to your inner voice, the subtle cues that reveal your passions, strengths, and values. It also means recognizing that alignment is the inner thermostat that regulates our energy levels and attracts the right people into our lives.

Pillar #5: Find Uncommon Common Ground (the Strings)

This pillar builds upon the first, suggesting that true connection begins with finding the uncommon common ground within ourselves. It's about recognizing and embracing the unique combination of experiences, talents, and passions that make us who we are.

Once we understand our own inner landscape, we can then seek out and create resonant connections with others based on shared values and authentic self-expression. It all starts with aligning with our own truth. By understanding and embracing our unique blend of talents and experiences, we can then use that self-knowledge to find common ground with others, creating relationships that are both authentic and mutually beneficial.

The Neuroscience and Psychology of Authenticity

The journey of self-discovery is not just a feel-good concept; it's backed by robust scientific research. Studies in neuroscience, psychology, and relationship science reveal why authenticity matters not just for personal well-being but for creating meaningful connections.

Authenticity and Relationship Outcomes

Relationship science confirms what we intuitively sense: Authenticity creates stronger bonds. Research has found that authenticity in close relationships is positively associated with relationship satisfaction, intimacy, and commitment. When we feel safe to be ourselves in a relationship, we are more likely to experience deeper levels of connection and fulfillment.

Furthermore, studies have demonstrated that authenticity in romantic relationships is linked to greater relationship stability and lower levels of conflict. When partners feel they can be open and honest with each other, they are better equipped to navigate disagreements and challenges constructively.

Personal Well-Being and Authenticity

The benefits of authenticity extend beyond our relationships. Research has found that individuals who report higher levels of authenticity also experience greater life satisfaction, more positive emotions, and higher self-esteem. They are more likely to feel a sense of purpose and meaning in their lives.

Recent studies using a combination of self-reporting and physiological measures have demonstrated that people who regularly express their authentic selves show lower levels of cortisol (a stress hormone) and higher heart rate variability (an indicator of emotional regulation). This suggests that authenticity may have direct physical health benefits.

This alignment with our authentic selves is not just about personal fulfillment. It's also about unlocking "The More"—that exponential potential that emerges when we connect with others from a place of truth and genuine self-expression. When we are authentic, we tap into a wellspring of inner power, a resonance that attracts the right people and repels the wrong ones.

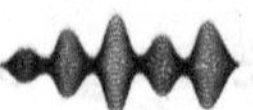

BRIDGE NOTE: AUTHENTICITY IN PROFESSIONAL RELATIONSHIPS

Therapist-Client Authenticity: Research in the realm of psychotherapy highlights the critical role of authenticity in fostering successful therapeutic relationships. Studies have found that therapist authenticity, characterized by genuineness and congruence, is a significant predictor of positive therapy outcomes. This suggests that even in professional settings, authenticity fosters trust and facilitates growth.

Authenticity and Reduced Stress: Research on cognitive dissonance—the mental discomfort that arises when our actions are inconsistent with our beliefs—demonstrates the negative impact of inauthenticity. When we suppress our true selves or try to conform to external pressures, we create inner dissonance that can lead to stress, anxiety, and even physical health problems. Studies have found that individuals who are more authentic in their daily lives report lower levels of stress and greater psychological well-being. This highlights the importance of aligning our actions with our values, not just in our close relationships but in all areas of our lives.

Authenticity as a Skill: Importantly, authenticity is not a fixed trait but a skill that can be developed. Research shows that individuals can increase their authenticity through self-reflection, mindfulness practices, and therapy. This means that even if we struggle with being authentic, we can learn to cultivate this quality over time.

THE MAGNETIC POWER OF AUTHENTICITY: BATTERIES AND BLACK HOLES

Think of it this way: Every relationship in your life either charges you up or drains you. When we are surrounded by people who resonate with our authentic self, who appreciate our unique song and encourage us to play it fully, we thrive. These are the "batteries" in our lives—the relationships that energize us, inspire us, and amplify our impact. They are the people who see us for who we truly are and support us in becoming the best version of ourselves.

Conversely, when we are in relationships that are out of alignment with our values, where we feel pressured to conform or hide our true selves, we experience a drain on our energy. These are the "black holes," the relationships that deplete us, leaving us feeling exhausted, unfulfilled, and disconnected from our inner music. They are the people or situations that dim our light and prevent us from sharing our unique gifts with the world.

Take a moment right now to identify one "battery" and one "black hole" in your life. What makes the "battery" relationship so energizing? What makes the "black hole" relationship so draining? Write these insights in your Resonance Journal.

Your Inner Thermostat

Just as a thermostat regulates the temperature of a room, you have an inner thermostat that regulates the energy in your life. This inner thermostat is calibrated to your level of self-worth and your beliefs about what you deserve. When you surround yourself with batteries—people who uplift and energize you—your inner thermostat rises. You begin to expect and attract more positive, supportive relationships.

Conversely, when you tolerate black holes—relationships that drain you and leave you feeling depleted—your inner thermostat gets set lower. You may start to believe that you don't deserve fulfilling connections, and you may unconsciously sabotage relationships that could potentially nourish you.

What is your inner thermostat currently set to? What temperature would you like it to be?

NAVIGATING RESISTANCE: WHEN FINDING YOUR SONG FEELS RISKY

While the benefits of authenticity are clear, the path to finding and expressing your true song isn't always easy. Most of us encounter resistance—both internal and external—when we begin to align with our authentic selves.

Common Forms of Resistance

Fear of Rejection: Perhaps the most common barrier to authenticity is the fear that others won't accept our true selves. The human need for belonging is so fundamental that we often suppress our authentic expression to fit in.

Imposter Syndrome: The nagging feeling that you're not "qualified" to express your authentic voice can be paralyzing. You might hear an inner critic asking: "Who are you to speak your truth? Who would listen anyway?"

Practical Constraints: Real-world obligations and relationships may seem incompatible with authentic expression. You might worry: "If I'm truly myself, will I still be able to support my family? Will I lose important relationships?"

Identity Entrenchment: Sometimes we've played a role for so long that it feels like our identity. The thought of letting go—even of a false self—can feel like a kind of death.

Cultural and Social Conditioning: Many of us have been taught from childhood to suppress certain aspects of ourselves to conform to cultural, religious, or social expectations.

Strategies for Moving Through Resistance

Start Small: You don't need to overhaul your entire life overnight. Begin by expressing your authentic self in low-risk situations or with trusted individuals.

Name the Fear: Simply identifying and acknowledging your specific fears can reduce their power. Write them down in your Resonance Journal.

Create a Safety Net: Before making major changes, ensure you have emotional support from people who value your authentic self.

Reframe "Failure": If someone rejects your authentic expression, it doesn't mean you've failed—it means you've gained clarity about whether they're a "battery" or "black hole" for you.

Find Models of Courage: Seek out stories of people who have navigated similar resistance to find and express their authentic voices.

THE POWER OF SILENCE

In his book *Silence: The Power of Quiet in a World Full of Noise*, Buddhist monk and peace activist Thich Nhat Hanh wrote, "Silence is essential. We need silence, just as much as we need air, just as much as plants need light. If our minds are crowded with words and thoughts, there is no space for us."

In a world filled with noise, silence can be a powerful tool for self-discovery. It's in the quiet moments that we can truly hear our inner music, connect with our intuition, and discern the authentic notes of our being. Make space for silence in your day, even if it's just for a few minutes. Turn off the distractions, close your eyes, and listen to the wisdom that resides within.

AUTHENTICITY IN THE DIGITAL AGE

Finding and expressing your authentic self brings about unique challenges in the digital age. Social media platforms encourage us to create carefully curated versions of ourselves, often disconnected from our actual lived experience. The constant exposure to others' highlight reels can make our own authentic journey seem inadequate by comparison.

Yet digital spaces can also be laboratories for authentic expression when approached mindfully:

Digital Experimentation: Online communities centered around specific interests can provide safe spaces to explore aspects of your authentic self before bringing them into your everyday life.

Intentional Curation: Rather than mindlessly consuming content that reinforces inauthenticity, curate your digital environment to include voices that encourage authentic expression.

Digital Boundaries: Establish clear boundaries around your digital presence. Ask yourself: "Am I sharing this from a place of authenticity or from a need for validation?"

Authentic Connection: Use digital tools to deepen real-world connections rather than as substitutes for them. Technology can amplify authenticity when it brings together people with shared values and interests.

FINDING YOUR TRUE SONG: A PROGRESSIVE PATH

Now that we understand the importance of authenticity, let's explore how to embark on this journey of self-discovery. The following progressive path will guide you through this process, helping you uncover the unique melody that resides within you and setting the stage for creating a life of greater authenticity and resonance.

Days 1–3: Awakening Awareness

Daily Silence Practice: Begin with just five minutes of complete silence each day. No music, no podcasts, no talking. Just sit with yourself and notice what arises. If thoughts come, acknowledge them without judgment and return to silence.

Dissonance Check-Ins: Three times each day, take thirty seconds to notice how you're feeling. Are you energized or drained? Connected or disconnected? In alignment or out of alignment? Make a quick note in your journal or on your phone.

Evening Reflection: Before bed, ask yourself: "When did I feel most alive today? When did I feel most drained?" Write down one sentence for each.

Week 1: Mapping Dissonance

In your Resonance Journal, dedicate a section to creating a "Dissonance Diary." For one week (including your Awakening Awareness days), make a daily entry noting any instances where you experienced inner dissonance. This could manifest as feelings of anxiety, frustration, self-doubt, or a sense of being out of alignment with your values. For each entry, briefly describe the situation that triggered the dissonance and the motions and physical sensations you experienced. Reflect on the underlying cause of the dissonance. What belief, value, or expectation was challenged? If this dissonance were a musical note, what kind of sound would it be (e.g., jarring, out of tune, too loud, too soft)? At the end of the week, review your entries. Look for patterns and recurring themes.

Be honest with yourself and practice self-compassion throughout this process. Connect your observations to your core values.

Week 2: Inner Exploration

Find a quiet space where you can relax and reflect without distractions. Reflect on the following questions, writing down your answers in your Resonance Journal. Take your time with each question, allowing your thoughts and feelings to flow freely onto the page.

Values: What principles guide your life? What truly matters to you? (For instance, honesty, compassion, creativity, courage, justice?)

Strengths and Talents: What are you naturally good at? What unique gifts do you bring to the world? (For example, communication skills, problem-solving, empathy, leadership?)

Passions: What activities make you feel most alive and engaged? What ignites your soul? (Music, art, writing, social justice, technology?)

Limiting Beliefs: What negative thoughts about yourself hold you back? How can you challenge these beliefs? (For instance, "I'm not good enough," "I'm too old to change.")

Connect to The More: How can your unique combination of values, strengths, and passions contribute to something larger than yourself?

Be completely honest—there are no right or wrong answers. Dig deep, stay open to unexpected insights, and trust your intuition.

Week 3: Values Clarification Collage

With this practice you'll use visual imagery to help you connect with your core values.

1. **Gather Materials:** Collect magazines, newspapers, printed images, scissors, glue, and a large sheet of paper or poster board.
2. **Reflect on Your Values:** Before beginning, take a few moments to reflect on the values most important to you.
3. **Create the Collage:** Look through your materials and select images, words, phrases, and colors that resonate with your core values. Don't overthink it—trust your intuition and choose what speaks to you. Cut out these elements and arrange them in a meaningful way. Glue them down to create your collage.
4. **Reflect and Connect:** When your collage is complete, take time to reflect on it. What do you notice about your choices? How do they relate to your values? What insights does the collage offer about your authentic self? Write your reflections in your Resonance Journal.

Throughout this exercise, let your intuition guide your choices rather than overthinking. Embrace creativity—there's no "right way" to create your collage. Use symbols and abstract images to represent complex values. Display your finished collage where you'll see it daily as a reminder.

Monthlong Challenge: The Authentic Voice

Building on everything you've discovered about your authentic self, commit to one small act of authentic expression each day for thirty days. These can be as simple as:

- Speaking up in a meeting when you would normally stay silent;
- Wearing something that feels true to you rather than what's expected;
- Having a difficult but honest conversation you've been avoiding;
- Pursuing a passion project for fifteen minutes daily;
- Setting a boundary with someone who drains your energy;
- Expressing gratitude to someone who energizes you.

Record your experiences in your Resonance Journal, noting:

- What was the authentic expression?
- How did it feel before, during, and after?
- What, if any, resistance did you encounter?
- What impact did it have on your relationships?

As the month progresses, you'll likely find that authentic expression becomes easier and that the positive feedback loop between authenticity and resonant relationships grows stronger.

THE ONGOING SYMPHONY OF SELF-DISCOVERY

Discovering your inner music is not a one-time event; it's an ongoing process of exploration, refinement, and growth. It's about learning to listen deeply to yourself, to honor your values, to embrace your strengths, and to challenge your limiting beliefs. As you become more attuned to your authentic self, you'll find it easier to connect with others on a deeper level, to find the uncommon common ground that forms the basis of resonant relationships.

You'll also become more adept at recognizing and attracting the batteries in your life, those who support and uplift you, and setting boundaries with the black holes that drain your energy.

But self-discovery is only the first step. In the next chapter, we'll explore how to create harmony in our relationships by embracing the foundational principle of integrity, learning to align our actions with our values, and building trust through consistent honesty and ethical behavior. Just as a skilled musician must master their instrument before they can create beautiful music with others, so, too, must we cultivate inner harmony before we can create truly resonant connections with those around us.

And it all begins with a commitment to living in alignment with our deepest truth, allowing our actions to be a true reflection of the music within. Remember the canyon from the beginning of this chapter? Imagine standing there again, calling out, and hearing your own authentic voice echo back—powerful, clear, unmistakably you. This is the beginning of resonance. This is the journey to your true song.

Final Reflection: What one step will you take today to begin finding your true song? Write your commitment in your Resonance Journal and take that step. Your authentic melody is waiting to be discovered, and the world is waiting to hear it.

POWER PLAYLIST

AUTHENTICITY AND SELF-DISCOVERY

The journey toward authentic self-expression requires both courage and compassion—for ourselves and others. These songs celebrate the transformative power of honoring your true voice, even when the world pressures you to conform.

- **"Respect" by Aretha Franklin.** Listen for: How demanding recognition becomes an act of authentic self-advocacy—the power of knowing your worth and insisting that others acknowledge it.
- **"This Is Me" by Keala Settle.** Listen for: The explosive moment when shame transforms into defiant self-acceptance—notice how vulnerability becomes unstoppable strength.
- **"I Am What I Am" by La Cage aux Folles.** Listen for: The theatrical boldness of complete self-acceptance—how owning every part of yourself becomes an act of liberation.

Listening Practice: This week, choose one song and listen while looking at yourself in a mirror. Notice what emotions arise—discomfort, joy, resistance, or acceptance. Pay attention to the physical sensations of hearing your authentic self celebrated in music. After listening, reflect in your Resonance Journal: What parts of myself do I hide to gain acceptance? What would change in my relationships if I showed up completely as I am?

Creating Your Personal Additions: Add songs that make you feel most like yourself—whether they celebrate your heritage, your struggles, your joy, or your uniqueness. Consider sharing one of these with someone close to you, explaining what authentic self-expression means to you.

Authenticity is not a destination but a practice—the daily choice to honor your true voice even when it's easier to blend in. These songs remind us that our genuine selves are not just acceptable but essential contributions to the world's symphony.

CHAPTER 6

The Resonant Truth: Amplifying Your Signal

What if the most powerful force in your relationships isn't what you say or do but the alignment between them?

Imagine trying to tune in to your favorite radio station, but all you hear is static. You turn the dial, searching for that clear, strong signal, but the noise keeps interfering. This is what it's like when we try to build relationships without integrity. Our actions, our words, our very being, become a jumble of conflicting signals, creating a "noise" that prevents genuine connection.

We've embarked on a journey of self-discovery, learning to listen to our inner music and find our true song. In chapter 5, you identified your core values—the fundamental notes that compose your authentic self. Now we move to the crucial next step: amplifying that signal by aligning your inner truth with your outer actions.

This chapter is about tuning out the noise and broadcasting your authentic signal with crystal clarity. It is about integrity—the bridge between knowing your values and living them.

ONE-MINUTE PRACTICE: SIGNAL STRENGTH

Take a deep breath and ask yourself: *What's one area of my life where my actions and my values are perfectly aligned?* Feel the sense of congruence, the absence of static. This is your authentic signal at its strongest. We'll be working to extend this alignment to all areas of your life.

Resonance Session

THE COURAGE OF CONVICTION

In the late 1960s, Marvin Gaye found himself at a crossroads. His record label, Motown, was known for its polished, radio-friendly sound—a sound that had brought him immense success. Yet, he felt a growing unease, a dissonance between the music he was making and the social and political turmoil unfolding around him.

The Vietnam War was raging, civil rights protests were erupting across the country, and he felt a deep responsibility to use his platform to speak truth to power. He began writing songs that reflected his concerns—songs about war, poverty, injustice, and the environment. His label was resistant, fearing that such controversial themes would alienate his audience and damage his commercial success. They urged him to stick to the formula.

But Gaye couldn't ignore the call of his conscience. The noise of external pressure was strong, but the signal of his inner truth was stronger. He knew he had to be true to himself, to his values, even if it meant risking everything. He poured his heart and soul into a new project, a powerful statement of his beliefs, a musical testament to his unwavering commitment to social justice.

What's Going On, released in 1971, was unlike anything he had done before. It was a concept album, a cohesive work of art that tackled themes of war, poverty, environmental destruction, and the urgent need for peace and understanding. It was a risky move, a bold departure from the Motown sound that had made him famous.

Berry Gordy, Motown's founder, was initially resistant, reportedly telling Gaye: "This is the worst thing I've ever heard in my life." But Gaye stood firm.

The album became iconic. It was a critical and commercial success, defying the label's expectations and solidifying Gaye's status as a visionary artist. It resonated deeply with a generation yearning for authenticity and social change.

Reflection: Think about a time when you've felt pressure to compromise your values for success, acceptance, or convenience. How did you respond? If you stood firm in your integrity, what gave you the courage to do so? If you compromised, how did that affect your sense of self and your relationships?

WHEN THE SIGNAL BREAKS DOWN

Jack was rising quickly in his company. His innovative thinking and problem-solving skills made him a favorite for promotion. There was just one problem: His boss routinely took credit for his ideas and expected him to inflate numbers on quarterly reports to make the department look better.

At first, Jack justified his silence. *It's just office politics,* he told himself. *Everyone does it.* But as months passed, he couldn't ignore the growing knot in his stomach during meetings, the difficulty sleeping, the increasing irritability with his family. Most troubling was how he started to see himself—as someone who could be bought, whose values had a price tag.

His relationships suffered. Friends noticed he'd become guarded, less present. His wife sensed he was holding something back. Trust began to erode, not because they knew what was happening at work but because they could feel the dissonance in his presence. His authentic signal had become distorted with static.

The turning point came when his daughter asked innocently at dinner, "Dad, what did you do at work today that made you proud?" The question hit him like a thunderbolt. He couldn't remember the last time he'd felt proud at work.

The next day, Jack had an honest conversation with his boss. It wasn't easy, but setting that boundary—refusing to compromise his integrity any longer—lifted an immense weight. Some things at work became more difficult, but his relationships at home immediately improved. Friends commented that "the real Jack is back."

Sometimes the clearest demonstration of integrity's importance is seeing what happens when it breaks down.

One-Minute Practice: Integrity Scan

Close your eyes and scan your body right now. Where do you feel tension or discomfort? This physical sensation might be pointing to an area where your actions and values are misaligned. Simply noting this without judgment is the first step toward realignment.

PILLAR #3: BE AT INTEGRITY IN WORD AND ACTION

Being at integrity means living in a state of wholeness, where your inner values and your outer actions are aligned. It's about being honest with yourself and with others, keeping your promises, and acting ethically, even when it's difficult.

When you live with integrity, you create a sense of inner harmony that radiates outward, attracting relationships that are built on a foundation of trust and mutual respect. You become like a tuning fork, emitting a clear and consistent tone that others can rely on.

THE TUNING FORK OF INTEGRITY

The tuning fork is a perfect metaphor for integrity. When struck, a tuning fork produces a pure, unwavering tone—a single note of perfect clarity. It doesn't produce multiple frequencies or conflicting sounds—just one clear, consistent signal.

Similarly, people with integrity send a clear signal to the world. Their words match their actions. Their private behavior aligns with their public personas. Their promises are kept. There's no static or interference in their relationships because people know exactly what to expect.

Just as musicians use a tuning fork to ensure their instruments are playing the correct notes, we can use our values to check whether our actions are in alignment with our authentic selves. When there's dissonance between our values and actions, we can make adjustments until we achieve harmony.

And like a tuning fork that helps an entire orchestra find the same pitch, our integrity creates a standard that influences those around us, encouraging others to heighten their own alignment and authenticity.

One-Minute Practice: The Tuning Moment

Think of a decision you need to make today. Hold that decision up against your core values like a musician would hold a note against a tuning fork. Does it resonate clearly or create dissonance? Let this quick check guide your choice.

SIGNAL VS. NOISE: THE ESSENCE OF INTEGRITY

Think of integrity as the clarity of your "signal" in the world. When your actions, words, and values are aligned, you broadcast a strong, clear signal—a message of authenticity, trustworthiness, and genuine connection. This signal attracts resonant relationships, drawing to you people who appreciate and value who you truly are.

But when there's a disconnect between your inner values and your outer actions, you create "noise." This noise can take many forms:

- **Inconsistent Behavior:** Saying one thing and doing another
- **Broken Promises:** Failing to follow through on commitments
- **Dishonesty:** Lying, withholding information, or manipulating others
- **Lack of Transparency:** Hiding your true thoughts and feelings
- **Compromising Your Values:** Acting in ways that go against your core beliefs

This "noise" interferes with your ability to connect authentically with others. It creates dissonance, eroding trust and making it difficult to build strong, lasting relationships. People may sense that something is "off," even if they can't put their finger on it. Your signal becomes weak, distorted, and unreliable.

THE SCIENCE OF TRUST AND INTEGRITY

The importance of integrity in building and maintaining resonant relationships is not just a matter of philosophical musing; it's backed by a wealth of scientific research. Studies from various fields, including psychology, sociology, and even neuroscience, converge on a fundamental truth: Trust, born out of consistent integrity, is the bedrock of healthy and enduring connections.

Trust and Longevity

One of the most compelling arguments for integrity in relationships comes from studies on relationship longevity. Research consistently demonstrates a direct link between integrity, trust, and the long-term success of relationships.

For instance, a longitudinal study by Jeffrey Larson and Thomas Holman found that trust was a key predictor of marital stability and satisfaction over time. Couples who perceived each other as honest, reliable, and consistent in their actions were more likely to report higher levels of trust and relationship satisfaction. This makes intuitive sense—when someone consistently demonstrates integrity, it creates a sense of security and predictability, fostering a deeper bond.

"The most fundamental skill in creating resonant relationships is the ability to create trust," explains Dr. Brené Brown, relationship researcher and author. "And you cannot have trust without reliability, which is essentially integrity over time."

Conversely, breaches of trust, whether through dishonesty, infidelity, or broken promises, can cause irreparable damage to a relationship. As researchers Dr. John Gottman and Dr. Robert Levenson discovered in their extensive work on marital stability, betrayals of trust are often cited as a primary reason for relationship dissolution. The erosion of trust creates a dissonance that can be difficult, if not impossible, to overcome.

Psychological Safety

Integrity also plays a crucial role in creating what researchers call "psychological safety" within relationships. Psychological safety, a concept popularized by Harvard Business School professor Amy Edmondson, refers to a shared belief that it's safe to take interpersonal risks, to express vulnerabilities, and to be authentic without fear of negative consequences.

Edmondson's research, originally focused on team performance, has clear implications for personal relationships. When we perceive our partners, friends, or family members as acting with integrity, it creates an environment where we feel safe to be ourselves, to share our true thoughts and feelings, and to be vulnerable. This openness, in turn, fosters deeper intimacy and strengthens the bonds of connection.

In a psychologically safe relationship, we can make mistakes, express doubts, and even disagree without fearing judgment or rejection. This is because integrity has built a foundation of trust that can withstand the inevitable challenges of human interaction.

Resonance Session

INTEGRITY IN ACTION

In 1963, Nina Simone was at a pivotal point in her career. Already acclaimed for her unique blend of jazz, classical, and blues, she was building a reputation in the entertainment industry. Then came news that shattered her world: A church bombing in Birmingham, Alabama, killed four young Black girls, following closely after the assassination of civil rights leader Medgar Evers.

Simone's response was immediate and visceral. In under an hour, she wrote "Mississippi Goddam," a song that abandoned the coded language many Black artists used when addressing racism. Instead, she directly confronted segregation and violence with raw, unfiltered truth.

Many radio stations banned the song. Records were returned to her label broken in half. Her career suffered as venues and industry professionals distanced themselves from her increasingly political stance.

Yet Simone remained unwavering. When asked why she would jeopardize her success, she famously responded: "An artist's duty is to reflect the times." She continued to use her platform to speak truth, recording songs like "To Be Young, Gifted and Black" and performing at civil rights rallies.

Her integrity—this alignment between her values and her art—came at considerable personal cost. She faced financial hardship, industry blacklisting, and tremendous stress. But decades later, history vindicates her choice. Nina Simone is remembered not just as a brilliant musician but as a voice of moral courage whose art helped change the world.

As her daughter Lisa Simone Kelly later reflected: "My mother was one of the artists who used her voice to speak truth in a time when truth was dangerous. That's integrity."

Reflection: Where in your life might you be choosing comfort over truth? What might it look like to align your actions more fully with your deepest values, even when there's a cost?

Authenticity and Well-Being

A growing body of research demonstrates a strong connection between authenticity, integrity, and overall well-being. When we live in alignment with our values—a core component of integrity—we experience a greater sense of purpose, meaning, and life satisfaction.

Kennon M. Sheldon from the University of Missouri found that individuals who scored high on measures of authenticity also reported higher levels of self-esteem, positive emotions, and overall life satisfaction. This suggests that being true to ourselves is not just good for our relationships, but also for our individual well-being.

Integrity, then, can be seen as a bridge between authenticity and well-being, creating a positive feedback loop where being true to ourselves allows us to build more fulfilling relationships, which in turn further enhances our sense of self.

The Neuroscience of Trust

Even our brains are wired to respond to integrity. Studies have shown that oxytocin is released during acts of trust and generosity, and that it plays a crucial role in social bonding.

In one study, researchers found that participants who received a dose of oxytocin were more likely to trust strangers in a financial exchange game. This suggests that integrity, by fostering trust, can actually trigger neurochemical responses that strengthen our connections with others.

When we consistently act with integrity, we create a biological environment that promotes bonding and strengthens the neural pathways associated with trust and connection.

ONE-MINUTE PRACTICE: INTEGRITY AFFIRMATION

Place your hand over your heart and say aloud: "My integrity is nonnegotiable. I choose alignment between my values and actions." Feel the resonance of these words in your body. You're literally strengthening neural pathways associated with integrity each time you affirm this commitment.

THE DISSONANCE WITHIN

Inner dissonance arises when our actions are out of alignment with our values. It's the uncomfortable feeling when we betray our own sense of what is right—when the signal of our true self is disrupted by the noise of external pressures or internal conflicts.

This feeling has a scientific name: **cognitive dissonance**. First identified by psychologist Leon Festinger in 1957, cognitive dissonance is the mental discomfort that occurs when we hold contradictory beliefs or when our actions contradict our values.

This discomfort isn't just psychological—it can manifest physically as:

- Increased heart rate
- Elevated stress hormones
- Disrupted sleep patterns
- Compromised immune function
- Digestive disturbances

Our bodies literally react to the discord between our values and actions.

Pay attention to this inner dissonance. It's a signal that something needs to change. What adjustments can you make to create greater harmony within yourself? What "noise" do you need to tune out to hear your authentic voice more clearly?

Just as a musician might wince at an out-of-tune string, your discomfort is a valuable feedback mechanism—not something to ignore but something to address by realigning your actions with your values.

YOUR FUTURE SELF: A VISUALIZATION

Close your eyes and imagine yourself one year from today, living with complete integrity in all areas of your life. See yourself making decisions, both large and small, that align perfectly with your core values. Notice how you carry yourself—the confidence in your posture, the clarity in your eyes, the ease in your smile.

Picture your relationships—how they've transformed as people have come to trust your word completely. See how conflicts resolve more quickly because people know you speak your truth. Imagine the quality of people now drawn into your life—others with a similar commitment to authenticity and integrity.

Feel the inner peace that comes from this alignment—the absence of cognitive dissonance, the energy freed up now that you're not maintaining inconsistencies. This is who you're becoming as you commit to integrity as a daily practice.

Take a deep breath and know that this version of you isn't just possible—it's already emerging through each choice you make to align your actions with your values.

THE SOCIAL DIMENSION OF INTEGRITY

Integrity isn't just about personal alignment—it has profound social implications. When we act with integrity, we don't just benefit ourselves; we contribute to a culture of trust and authenticity that enhances all our relationships. By embodying our values consistently, we create safe spaces for others to do the same.

This ripple effect extends beyond our immediate circle. As social beings, we're constantly influencing and being influenced by those around us. When we demonstrate integrity, we implicitly invite others to raise their own standards, creating an upward spiral of authentic connection and trust.

But living with integrity doesn't mean isolation in your values. It requires engaging with the world while maintaining your authentic core. It's about finding the balance between standing firm in your values and remaining open to connection with others.

TUNING YOUR INNER INSTRUMENT

Just as a musician regularly tunes their instrument, we must also regularly "tune" our inner selves. This means taking time for self-reflection, examining our values, and ensuring that our actions are in alignment with our deepest beliefs. It's an ongoing process of refinement, a commitment to living with integrity and authenticity.

Consider implementing these tuning practices:

Daily check-in. Take five minutes each evening to reflect on moments when your actions aligned with your values and moments when they didn't. This simple practice builds self-awareness.

Weekly alignment. Choose one value each week to focus on embodying more fully. Notice opportunities to express this value in your daily interactions.

Monthly recalibration. Schedule time each month for deeper reflection. Ask yourself: "Am I moving toward greater integrity or away from it?"

Situational tuning. Before important decisions or conversations, pause to connect with your core values. Ask: "What would integrity look like in this moment?"

Remember, this isn't about perfection. Even the finest instruments require regular tuning. The goal is progress—becoming increasingly resonant over time.

By consistently aligning your actions with your values, you tune your social instrument, expanding your range and creating a more vibrant and resonant life. You'll be surprised at the connections you make and the opportunities that arise when you make a conscious effort to engage with the world around you from a place of integrity.

PRACTICAL TOOLS FOR LIVING WITH INTEGRITY

Now that we've explored the importance of integrity and its impact on our relationships, let's turn to practical tools that can help you live with greater alignment between your values and actions. These exercises are designed to be integrated into your daily life, helping you strengthen your integrity muscle over time.

Resonance Instrument

THE INTEGRITY AUDIT

Purpose: To assess the alignment between your values and actions, identifying areas for greater integrity

Time Required: 45-60 minutes initially, then regular check-ins

Material: Your Resonance Journal

Practice:

1. **Values Identification:** Begin by reviewing the values you identified in chapter 5. List your five to seven core values (e.g., honesty, compassion, courage) at the top of a fresh journal page.
2. **Values in Action—for Each Value:**
   - Write two or three specific ways this value currently shows up in your life.
   - Rate yourself on a scale of 1–10: How consistently do your actions align with this value?
   - Identify one situation where you fully embodied this value despite challenges.

3. **Integrity Gaps:**
    - For each value, identify any areas where your actions don't fully align.
    - Reflect on why these gaps exist (fear, convenience, external pressure, etc.).
    - Note any patterns across different values.
4. **Word and Deed Assessment:** Answer honestly.
    - Do I keep the promises I make to others? To myself?
    - Do I speak truth even when it's uncomfortable?
    - Do my public and private behaviors align?
    - How do I handle mistakes—do I take responsibility?
    - Do I treat others consistently with my values?
5. **Choice Point Analysis:**
    - Recall a recent difficult choice you faced.
    - Which values were at stake in this situation?
    - Did your choice align with these values? Why or why not?
    - What would acting with greater integrity have looked like?
6. **Integrity Growth Plan:**
    - Select one value where you want to strengthen your integrity.
    - Identify specific situations where this value is challenged.
    - Create three concrete action steps to align your behavior more fully with this value.
    - Determine how you'll measure success.

Resonance Instrument

THE SOCIAL STRETCH

Purpose: To practice integrity in increasingly diverse social contexts, building confidence in authentic connection

Time Required: Twenty-one days, with daily practice

Material: Your Resonance Journal

Practice: This twenty-one-day challenge helps you gradually expand your comfort zone for authentic connection while maintaining integrity. Each phase builds on the previous one.

Phase 1: Tuning Up (Days 1–7)

1. **Focus:** Start with familiar daily interactions.
2. **Goal:** Engage authentically with three people each day.
3. **Key Practice:** Be fully present and genuine in brief exchanges.

Phase 2: Expanding Your Range (Days 8–14)

1. **Focus:** Connect with people you know less well.
2. **Goal**: Initiate five authentic conversations daily.
3. **Key Practice:** Share something genuine while honoring your values.

Phase 3: Hitting the High Notes (Days 15–21)

1. **Focus:** Navigate more challenging social situations with integrity.
2. **Goal:** Create five to seven meaningful exchanges daily.

3. **Key Practice:** Stay true to your values even when socially difficult.

Daily Protocol:

1. **Morning Intention:** Identify your focus value for the day.
2. **Mindful Interactions:** Before each social exchange, briefly connect with your intention.
3. **Evening Reflection:** In your journal, record:
    - Who did you connect with authentically?
    - How did it feel to express your values?
    - What challenges did you face?
    - What did you learn about yourself?

Research from the University of British Columbia shows that even brief positive social interactions with strangers can significantly boost happiness and well-being. These "micro-moments of connection," as psychologist Barbara Fredrickson calls them, create cumulative effects on our neurochemistry, releasing oxytocin and reducing cortisol levels. This explains why the seemingly small interactions in the Social Stretch can have such profound impacts on your overall capacity for resonant relationships. Each interaction is literally rewiring your nervous system for greater connection.

Your Seven-Day Integrity Implementation Plan

To help you immediately apply the principles in this chapter, here's a simple seven-day plan:

Day 1: Awareness

- Complete the Integrity Audit.
- Identify your top integrity challenge area.
- Set a specific intention for how you'll approach this area differently.

Day 2: Truth Speaking

- Practice radical honesty in at least three conversations.
- Notice your impulse to be a people pleaser or withhold truth.
- Journal about what you observed.

Day 3: Promise Keeping

- Make only promises you're 100 percent committed to keeping.
- Follow through on a previous commitment you've been postponing.
- Acknowledge any promises you can't keep and communicate openly about them.

Day 4: Value Alignment

- Review your core values from chapter 5.
- Make three decisions explicitly guided by these values.
- Decline one thing that doesn't align with your values.

Day 5: Boundary Setting

- Identify one relationship where you need stronger boundaries.
- Clearly communicate a boundary that honors your values.
- Note how it feels to honor yourself in this way.

Day 6: Integrity Recovery

- Identify one relationship where trust has been damaged.
- Take a concrete step toward repair through honest communication.
- Practice self-forgiveness for past lapses in integrity.

Day 7: Integration

- Review your journal entries from the week.
- Note patterns, progress, and challenges.
- Set specific integrity intentions for the coming month.

Progress Markers: You'll know you're making progress when:

- You feel increased inner peace and reduced anxiety.
- You notice a greater willingness to speak uncomfortable truths.
- Others begin to trust your word more completely.
- You stop making excuses for misalignments.
- You feel more drawn to others who demonstrate integrity.
- You begin to value integrity over approval or convenience.

MOVING FORWARD: THE BRIDGE TO PART 3

In part 1, we explored the fundamental value of connection in our lives. In part 2, we've discovered our authentic voice and learned how to amplify it through integrity. Now we stand at the threshold of part 3, where we'll apply these principles to our closest relationships.

The authentic voice you discovered in chapter 5, now amplified through the integrity practices in this chapter, will become your guide as you learn to strike the right chord in family relationships, intimate partnerships, and friendships. The alignment you're creating now between your inner and outer self will serve as the foundation for all the connection practices to come.

Like Marvin Gaye and Nina Simone, you may find that your greatest impact comes not from compromising your values for acceptance but from having the courage to express them authentically. Your integrity becomes a clear, unwavering signal that cuts through the noise of superficial connection, creating the conditions for true resonance to flourish.

FINAL REFLECTION

As we conclude this chapter, take a moment to consider: What one step will you take today to strengthen your integrity? How might greater alignment between your values and actions transform your relationships? Write your commitment in your Resonance Journal and take that step. Your journey toward resonant relationships continues with each choice to live with integrity.

POWER PLAYLIST

INTEGRITY AND AUTHENTIC COURAGE

When authenticity meets injustice, integrity demands we speak truth to power. These songs demonstrate the courage required to align your actions with your deepest values, even when the cost is high. This is where self-discovery becomes service to something greater.

- **"What's Going On" by Marvin Gaye.** Listen for: How urgent love can sound like protest—notice the conversational tenderness that makes social justice feel like intimate care.
- **"Mississippi Goddam" by Nina Simone.** Listen for: Righteous anger transformed into focused power—how personal pain becomes collective healing when channeled through courage.
- **"Brave" by Sara Bareilles.** Theme: Courage to speak authentic truth.

Listening Practice: This week, sit with discomfort. Choose one song and listen while thinking about a situation where you know what's right but haven't acted on it. Notice where you feel tension in your body—this is integrity calling. After listening, write in your Resonance Journal: What truth am I avoiding? What would it cost me to speak it? What would it cost others if I remain silent?

Creating Your Personal Additions: Add songs that have given you courage during difficult moments or that connect you to causes larger than yourself. Consider how these songs bridge personal authenticity (from chapter 5) with moral courage that serves others.

Integrity is authenticity under pressure—the willingness to let your inner truth create outer change, even when it's uncomfortable. These songs remind us that our individual courage to stand in truth creates the foundation for relationships and communities built on genuine rather than convenient connection.

CHAPTER 7

Dealing with Dissonance, Bringing Your Authentic Self into Harmonious Connection

THE THRESHOLD MOMENT

You stand at a critical juncture.

You've discovered the value of connection and developed your individual resonance—finding your authentic voice and cultivating integrity. You've tuned your instrument in the privacy of your own space. But instruments aren't meant to be played alone forever.

Think of a violinist who has mastered technique in isolation. The true test comes when they join an ensemble. Will they maintain their distinctive sound while harmonizing with others? Or will they either dominate the group or fade into timid silence?

This is your threshold moment: bringing your authentic self into meaningful contact with others, navigating the inevitable dissonance that arises when unique individuals connect. The moment of truth in any journey is not when you discover who you are but when you bring that self into contact with other people.

THE BRIDGE IN MUSIC AND LIFE

In musical composition, the bridge serves a profound purpose. It creates tension and anticipation, providing contrast before the song returns to the familiar chorus with renewed meaning. Think of how the bridge in Leonard Cohen's "Hallelujah" shifts both melody and perspective, creating a moment of revelation before returning to the triumphant chorus.

Your personal journey follows this same pattern. You've developed your melody (your authentic voice) and established your rhythm (your integrity). Now comes the bridge—that crucial passage where tension increases as you bring your authentic self into contact with others, creating the necessary dissonance that precedes a more powerful harmony.

WHY THIS BRIDGE MATTERS

Most relationship journeys fail precisely at this juncture. We learn to find our voice, only to lose it again in the presence of others. Or we maintain our authenticity but struggle to create true harmony with different personalities, perspectives, and needs.

The bridge between self-discovery and relationship resonance is rarely addressed, yet it's the most crucial passage in personal transformation.

THE PARADOX OF AUTHENTIC CONNECTION

Here lies one of life's great paradoxes: Our most authentic self emerges not in isolation but in relationships. Just as a musical note reveals its full character when it resonates with others, your authentic voice finds its fullest expression when it enters into meaningful dialogue with different perspectives.

This is supported by social psychologist Susan Fiske's research on the "stereotype content model," which demonstrates that warmth and competence are the two primary dimensions by which we evaluate others. Individuals who project both qualities—authenticity (competence in being oneself) and connection (warmth toward others)—create what Fiske calls a "golden quadrant" of social perception.

In other words, the science confirms what great spiritual traditions have long taught: We become most fully ourselves in relationship with others.

RESEARCH INSIGHT: THE SCIENCE OF SOCIAL EXPANSION

Recent neuroscience research reveals why this bridge is so challenging. Brain imaging studies conducted at UCLA show that social rejection activates the same neural pathways as physical pain. This explains why many people retreat from authentic expression in social contexts—the risk feels literally painful.

Yet the research also reveals something extraordinary. As psychologist Matthew Lieberman documented in his landmark studies, these same neural pathways become less reactive with practice. The brain actually rewires itself through repeated social interaction, reducing sensitivity to rejection while enhancing capacity for connection.

THE THREE FORMS OF DISSONANCE

As you bring your authentic self into deeper relationship with others, you'll encounter three forms of dissonance:

1. **External dissonance.** When your authentic expression meets resistance from others who are accustomed to your old patterns. They may say: "You've changed," or "This isn't like you." This dissonance tests your commitment to your true self.
2. **Internal dissonance.** The voice inside that questions: "Am I being too much?" or "Am I worthy of being heard?" This dissonance reveals where you still doubt your own authentic value.
3. **Relational dissonance.** The natural friction that occurs when authentic selves interact. Like instruments tuning together, this productive dissonance is not to be avoided but navigated skillfully.

DISSONANCE AS A SIGNAL AND CATALYST FOR GROWTH

Dissonance in relationships, like dissonance in music, creates tension. But it's how we respond to that tension that determines whether it leads to breakdown or breakthrough. We can view dissonance as:

A signal. A sign that something is out of alignment—a miscommunication, an unmet need, a clash of values. It's an invitation to pay attention, to listen more deeply, and to seek understanding.

A catalyst for growth. An opportunity to learn, to adapt, and to strengthen the relationship. By navigating dissonance constructively, we can deepen our empathy, improve our communication skills, and create more resilient bonds.

THE CELLIST'S JOURNEY: A RESONANCE STORY

Consider the story of Yo-Yo Ma, perhaps the world's most celebrated cellist. As a child prodigy, he mastered the technical aspects of his instrument in isolation, practicing for hours daily. His 1983 recording of Bach's Cello Suites showcased flawless technique, but also what Ma himself later described as a youthful "I know everything" approach.

What followed was a deliberate journey outward. He began collaborating with musicians from radically different traditions, from Appalachian folk to Mongolian throat singing. Each collaboration required vulnerability, curiosity, and the willingness to release control.

The result wasn't a diminishment of his distinctive voice, but its amplification. Today, Ma is known not just for his technical brilliance but for his profound capacity to create resonance that transcends cultural boundaries.

Your journey follows this same trajectory—from mastery of self to meaningful connection with others.

Resonance Session

FINDING HARMONY IN TENSION

Artist Spotlight: Fleetwood Mac

When Fleetwood Mac began recording their album *Rumours* in 1976, the band wasn't just making music, they were navigating an emotional minefield. The romantic relationships within the group were disintegrating: Christine and John McVie were divorcing after eight years of marriage, Stevie Nicks and Lindsey Buckingham's long-term relationship was ending bitterly, and Mick Fleetwood was experiencing the pain of discovering his wife's affair.

The studio sessions were fraught with tension. There were tears, arguments, and moments when it seemed the album—and the band—might not survive.

Yet remarkably, Fleetwood Mac channeled this profound dissonance directly into their music. Songs like "Go Your Own Way," "Dreams," and "The Chain" emerged from their personal pain.

Christine McVie later reflected: "I think it was kind of therapeutic, because we were in the studio about ten hours a day, working on these deeply personal songs about each other, playing and singing them together, with the people we were writing about right there in the room. It was emotional, but it became almost cathartic."

The result? An album that sold over forty million copies and is widely considered one of the greatest records ever made. Rather than destroying their music, the band's willingness to work through their interpersonal dissonance created something of lasting value.

Reflection: Consider a relationship where dissonance exists. What creative or constructive outcome might be possible if you channeled that energy? How might the tension, if approached with honesty and vulnerability, lead to something valuable neither of you could create alone?

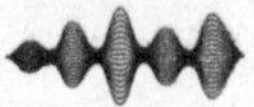

BRIDGE NOTE: THE BEAUTY OF IMPERFECTION

There is a crack in everything. That's how the light gets in.

LEONARD COHEN

In Japanese aesthetics, there exists a concept called *wabi-sabi*—the beauty of imperfection, impermanence, and incompleteness. Japanese craftsmen sometimes repair broken pottery with gold, creating ***kintsugi*** (golden joinery), highlighting rather than hiding the cracks. The repaired piece becomes more valuable and more beautiful because of its history, not in spite of it.

This philosophy offers a powerful metaphor for relationships. When we embrace the inevitable cracks—the misunderstandings, disagreements, and failures—and repair them with care and attention, we don't just restore the relationship to its former state. We create something stronger, more resilient, and often more beautiful than before.

The light that Leonard Cohen speaks of—wisdom, growth, compassion—enters precisely because of these cracks, not despite them. When we approach relationship dissonance with this mindset, we transform what could be perceived as flaws into unique opportunities for deeper connection.

TRANSFORMING DISSONANCE INTO HARMONY

The secret to crossing this bridge successfully lies not in avoiding dissonance but in transforming it into rich, complex harmony. This requires three capacities.

Courage: The willingness to express your authentic self even when it creates temporary discomfort.

Curiosity: The ability to remain open to others' authentic expression without defensive reaction.

Creativity: The skill to find the unexpected harmony that emerges when authentic voices interact.

THE TWO DIMENSIONS OF CONFLICT RESOLUTION

When navigating dissonance, we need to consider two equally important dimensions:

Task dimension. Addressing the practical issue at hand.

- What problem needs to be solved?
- What decision needs to be made?
- What compromise might work for both parties?

Relationship dimension. Maintaining and strengthening the connection.

- How do we preserve trust during disagreements?
- How can we ensure both people feel heard and respected?
- How do we reaffirm our commitment to each other despite differences?

Too often, we focus exclusively on the task dimension, trying to "win" the argument or solve the problem without attending to the relationship impact. But research shows that successful conflict resolution addresses both dimensions simultaneously.

Resonance Instrument

THE BREAKTHROUGH CONVERSATION

Purpose: To transform conflict into deeper understanding and connection

Time Required: 30–60 minutes

Materials: A private, comfortable space; your full presence

Preparation:

1. **Self-check.** Before initiating, assess your emotional state. Are you calm enough to listen? Can you approach this with curiosity rather than judgment?

2. **Timing.** Choose a moment when neither of you is hungry, tired, or rushed. Ask: "I'd like to talk about something important. Is this a good time, or would another time work better?"
3. **Setting.** Find a neutral space free from distractions. Turn off devices or set them to "Do not disturb."

Practice:

1. **Set a shared intention.** Begin by stating your desire for mutual understanding.
    - "I care about our relationship and want us both to feel heard and understood."
    - "I'm hoping we can find a way forward that works for both of us."
    - "My goal isn't to convince you I'm right but to understand each other better."
2. **Share your experience using "I" statements.**
    - "I feel ______ when ______ because ______."
    - "My experience is ______."
    - "One thing that's important to me is ______."
    - Avoid generalizations like "You always" or "You never."
3. **Listen deeply.** When the other person speaks,
    - Maintain eye contact and open body language;
    - Resist the urge to plan your response;
    - Notice their emotions as well as their words;
    - Wait until they've finished before responding.
4. **Reflect back.** Confirm your understanding.
    - "What I hear you saying is . . ."
    - "It sounds like you feel . . ."
    - "Am I understanding correctly that . . . ?"
    - Ask: "Is there anything else you want me to understand?"

5. **Find underlying needs.** Look beneath positions to discover needs.
    - "What makes this important to you?"
    - "What are you concerned might happen if . . . ?"
    - "What would an ideal outcome look like for you?"
6. **Seek common ground.** Identify shared values or goals.
    - "It seems we both value . . ."
    - "We both want . . ."
    - "We agree that . . ."
7. **Co-create solutions.** Brainstorm possibilities that address both sets of needs.
    - "What if we tried . . . ?"
    - "Would it work if . . . ?"
    - "How might we . . . "
8. **Agree on next steps.** Establish clear action items.
    - Who will do what by when?
    - When will you check in on progress?
    - How will you handle future conflicts on this issue?
9. **Express appreciation.** End by acknowledging the process.
    - "Thank you for being willing to have this conversation."
    - "I appreciate your openness/honesty/patience."
    - "This helps me understand you better."

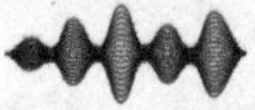

BRIDGE REFLECTION: CROSSING THE BRIDGE

Before continuing to part 3, take a moment for this powerful visualization:

Imagine yourself standing at the beginning of a bridge. Behind you lies the land of self-discovery—the terrain you've explored in parts 1 and 2. Ahead lies the landscape of resonant relationships that awaits in part 3.

The bridge itself represents this threshold moment—bringing your authentic self into meaningful contact with others.

As you visualize taking steps across this bridge, notice:

- What emotions arise?
- What do you carry with you from your journey so far?
- Who awaits you on the other side?
- What becomes possible when you bring your authentic self into full, resonant relationship with others? Write your reflections in your Resonance Journal.

The journey ahead isn't about perfection—it's about progression. Each interaction becomes a practice opportunity, each relationship a unique composition in your life's symphony.

The bridge has been built. The path is clear.

Are you ready to cross it?

POWER PLAYLIST

CROSSING THE BRIDGE TO AUTHENTIC CONNECTION

This is the threshold moment—where individual courage meets collective healing. Having discovered your authentic self and found your moral courage, you now face the sacred work of building bridges with others. These songs illuminate how personal transformation becomes relational transformation.

- **"Hallelujah" by Leonard Cohen.** Listen for: Brokenness becoming the very foundation of beauty—notice how vulnerability transforms into sacred connection.
- **"The Chain" by Fleetwood Mac.** Listen for: The musical tension that mirrors relationship complexity—how discord can strengthen rather than break the bonds between us.
- **"Here Comes the Sun" by The Beatles.** Listen for: Hope emerging after the longest winter—the gentle promise that authentic connection is possible after isolation.

Listening Practice: This week, think of a relationship that needs bridge-building. Choose one song and listen while holding both the difficulty and the possibility of that connection. Notice what emotions arise—fear, hope, resistance, longing. After listening, reflect in your Resonance Journal: What bridge am I avoiding building? What would it take to extend my authentic self toward someone who seems different or difficult?

Creating Your Personal Additions: Add songs that have helped you through relationship challenges or that remind you of successful reconciliations. Consider how these songs capture the alchemy of transforming tension into deeper understanding.

The bridge between self and community requires both the courage you've cultivated and the willingness to extend that courage toward others. These songs remind us that authentic connection often emerges not despite our struggles, but because we're willing to meet each other in the midst of them.

PART 3

Striking the Right Chord

The best and most beautiful things in the world cannot be seen or even touched, but just felt in the heart.

HELEN KELLER, QUOTING HER TEACHER ANNE SULLIVAN

THE INTIMATE SYMPHONY

You've laid the foundation. You've found your authentic voice. Now comes the true challenge—bringing these principles into your most intimate circles, where both the stakes and potential rewards are highest.

In the realm of your closest relationships—family, partnership, friendship—resonance isn't just a nice idea; it's the difference between a life of rich connection and one of persistent loneliness. These relationships are the crucible where your ability to create genuine resonance will be tested, refined, and ultimately mastered.

Think of this section as your intimate symphony—where the music becomes personal, vulnerable, and transformative. The notes you strike here will echo throughout your life.

THE COURAGE TO TRANSFORM

In the chapters ahead, you'll learn to transform inherited family patterns into intentional bonds of genuine connection, move beyond romance-focused relationships to resonance-centered partnerships that endure, and create friendships that evolve from circumstantial to purposeful connections.

This isn't about perfection. It's about presence, the deep skill of showing up fully in your most important relationships—even when it's difficult, even when old patterns threaten to pull you back into dissonance.

Each relationship carries within it the seed of profound transformation. When you approach family members, partners, and friends with the principles of resonance, you create a field of possibility—not just for yourself but for everyone in your circle.

THE PATH FORWARD

As you journey through these chapters, remember: This is where theory meets real life. The concepts we've explored become living practices with the people who matter most.

Some relationships will transform quickly; others may take time. Certain connections may reveal themselves as unable to hold resonance. This, too, is valuable information.

The path ahead requires both courage and compassion—for yourself and others. It invites you to see your closest relationships not merely as sources of comfort or obligation but as the sacred ground where resonance can flourish in its most meaningful form.

Let's begin.

CHAPTER 8

Family Ties: Resonance in Family Relationships

Call it a clan, call it a network, call it a tribe, call it a family: Whatever you call it, whoever you are, you need one.

JANE HOWARD

The family is one of nature's masterpieces.

GEORGE SANTAYANA

OPENING VIGNETTE: THE UNPLAYED NOTES

The Thanksgiving table gleamed with the reflected light of candles and the polish of silver. Steam rose from perfectly arranged dishes—recipes passed down through generations. To an observer, the scene appeared picture-perfect: a successful businessman father at the head of the table, his accomplished wife beside him, their three well-dressed children completing the tableau.

But beneath this harmonious exterior, currents of tension rippled. The eldest daughter's smile never quite reached her eyes. The middle son checked his watch every few minutes. The youngest child pushed food around her plate, speaking only when directly addressed. The mother maintained the conversation with practiced ease, while the father's knuckles whitened around his glass when certain topics arose.

They were playing their family song—a melody composed over decades—but several notes remained unplayed. Unspoken hurts, unresolved conflicts, and unexpressed love created dissonance beneath the surface harmony. Like musicians who had rehearsed their parts separately but never truly listened to each other, they performed their roles without creating true resonance.

In another home across town, a different family gathered. Their table wasn't as perfectly arranged, the food more potluck than gourmet. But their laughter was uninhibited, their conversations punctuated by playful disagreements and genuine curiosity. A grandmother taught her teenage grandson to play dominoes while his mother recorded the moment. Two siblings who had fought bitterly last month now collaborated on a dessert. When the youngest child knocked over a glass, the cleanup became a group effort rather than a source of tension.

This family wasn't perfect—they had their struggles and wounds too. But they had learned to play their instruments together, to listen for each other's melodies, to create space for solos and harmonies. They had discovered the art of family resonance.

Two families. Two symphonies. Which music would you rather create?

THE SYMPHONY OF ORIGIN

In the previous chapters, you developed self-knowledge, integrity, and tools for navigating dissonance. Now you'll apply these foundational skills to your most formative relationships—your family. The authenticity you've cultivated and the conflict resolution abilities you've gained will be especially valuable in this domain, where patterns run deep and emotional stakes are high.

We've learned that dissonance, those inevitable clashes and conflicts, can be opportunities for growth in any relationship. We've explored tools for turning breakdowns into breakthroughs, for transforming discordant notes into a richer harmony. Now, we turn to the first, and often most complex, orchestra of our lives: the family. It's here, amid the tangled melodies of shared history, ingrained patterns, and unconditional (yet often tested) love, that the principles of resonance can be both profoundly challenging and profoundly rewarding.

Imagine a family gathering. The room is filled with a mix of familiar sounds: laughter, conversation, the clinking of silverware, perhaps the background hum of music. But beneath the surface, a complex interplay of dynamics is at work. There are unspoken expectations, unresolved conflicts, ingrained patterns of communication that have been passed down through generations. There are moments of joy and connection—but also moments of tension and dissonance. The family, like a musical ensemble, is a collection of unique individuals, each with their own instrument to play, their own song to sing. And creating harmony within this ensemble requires intention, skill, and a willingness to navigate the inevitable clashes that arise.

BREAKTHROUGH QUESTIONS

- What is the unplayed melody in your family? What remains unsaid but needs to be expressed?
- What role do you typically play in your family orchestra? Is it a role you've chosen or one you've inherited?
- What would happen if you changed your part of the music, even slightly?

Resonance Session

THE FAMILY BAND

Artist Spotlight: The Jackson 5

They were a family band, quite literally. The patriarch, Joe Jackson, a charismatic but stern figure with ambitions for his children, led the group. His wife, Katherine, played supportive roles, and their nine children—particularly the five boys who formed the core performing group—each had their assigned instruments and roles. They toured the country from their humble beginnings in Gary, Indiana, performing soul music in clubs and theaters, their lives a whirlwind of rehearsals, travel, and family devotion.

Onstage, they were a picture of harmony. The infectious enthusiasm of young Michael Jackson leading songs like "ABC" and "I Want You Back" captivated audiences, creating the impression of a perfectly unified family.

But behind the scenes, the family dynamic was more complex. In his autobiography, *Moonwalk*, Michael Jackson revealed: "We were a show-business family, but we always remained a family first and show business second . . . We had our arguments and our areas of conflict, just like any family, but my mother and father kept it together."

The strict discipline imposed by their father, the pressure of early fame, and the normal rivalries between siblings created undercurrents of tension beneath the harmonious exterior. Later in life, siblings would express different memories and feelings about their shared experience—some remembering primarily the joy of creating music together, others focusing on the hardships and sacrifices.

Yet despite these challenges, the Jackson family persevered. As

Janet Jackson later reflected about her famous family: "We're just like any other family. We have our ups and downs, and we all have our issues . . . But at the end of the day, we're family, and that's what keeps us together."

Reflection: Consider your own family's "performance"—the public face versus private realities. How do the visible harmonies and hidden tensions in your family shape your relationships? What strengths have developed from navigating these complexities together?

DON'T LET YOUR LOVE DIE ON A NAPKIN: A PERSONAL JOURNEY OF GENERATIONAL HEALING

My relationship with my father was profoundly transformed when he showed up for me during my darkest hour. After moving across the country, my partner's betrayal left me shattered. My father didn't just offer sympathy—he guided me through the same men's work that had transformed him decades earlier. It was both an initiation and a confrontation with my deepest fears.

I can still feel the weight of his hand on my shoulder as we sat by the fire that first night. The crackling flames illuminated his face as he said, "This pain you're feeling—I've been there too. But this is where you get to decide what kind of man you'll become." His voice, steady and certain, anchored me when everything else felt unsteady.

My grandfather—my father's father—was the quintessential stoic military man. At six foot, four inches, always in a suit, he commanded respect as a captain in the US Air Force who shut down bases in Japan after World War II. He was stern, imposing, and a man of few words. Throughout his entire life, my grandfather never once told my father that he loved him. This absence became the source of deep, unresolved pain for my dad.

I remember the way my father's voice changed whenever he spoke about his own childhood—a slight tightening, a barely perceptible drop in volume, as if he were still that little boy longing for words of affirmation that never came. The pain echoed across decades, a dissonant note in his otherwise confident presence.

After completing his own transformational men's weekend, my father made a bold decision. He took his father to lunch at their favorite diner—the one with the red vinyl booths and the waitress who knew them by name. There, surrounded by the clinking of coffee cups and the murmur of conversations, he expressed how much he loved his father and what he meant to him—modeling the very behavior he had always longed to receive.

My grandfather sat silently, his weathered hands wrapped around his coffee mug, eyes fixed somewhere in the middle distance. He couldn't bring himself to say "I love you" in return. But his response spoke volumes: He gently folded the napkin from their lunch table—the one my father had unconsciously been drawing small circles on as he spoke—and tucked it into his inner suit pocket as a keepsake. He didn't have the emotional vocabulary to speak the words, but he showed up the best way he knew how.

"That napkin," my father told me years later, tears gathering at the corners of his eyes, "meant more to me than any words could have. It was his way of holding on to a moment he couldn't express but deeply felt."

This is why we must give without expectation of return. The generational pattern didn't continue between my father and me—he made absolutely certain I knew I was loved. He chose a career that allowed him to attend all my games, sitting in the same spot in the bleachers, his voice rising above all others when I made a good play. If I asked him to pick up a friend from the airport at 2 AM, he would be there without question, still in his pajama pants under his coat, a thermos of coffee in the cupholder, simply because it mattered to me. He showed up. The resonance between us was unquestionable.

When he was diagnosed with cancer and then dementia, our roles reversed, and I had the sacred privilege of showing up for him. During one late-night bedside vigil, while he slept, I noticed a folded, yellowed napkin in his wallet as I searched for his insurance card. It was from that lunch decades ago—carried every day as a talisman of unspoken love.

As Ram Dass wisely noted, "You think you're enlightened? Go spend a week with your family." Family dynamics quickly reveal our growth edges, exposing unprocessed emotions and testing our ability to remain centered in challenging situations. While our families often trigger us more than anyone else, they are also our greatest teachers. Within these dynamics—both challenging and joyful—lies the raw material for our most beautiful songs.

The question becomes: What is the song that wants to live through you? How have your family experiences—both the love and the triggers—informed the notes of that song? And most important, are you willing to sing it out loud?

Don't let your love die on a napkin. Express it. Share it. Let it resound in ways that heal not just your own heart but echo through generations to come.

PILLAR #6: CREATE EXPONENTIAL OPPORTUNITIES FOR CONNECTION (THE CONDUCTOR'S BATON)

This chapter focuses on Pillar #5: Create Exponential Opportunities for Connection, applying it specifically to the family context. The conductor's baton is our symbol for this pillar because, like a skilled conductor, we can learn to guide our family interactions with intentionality, bringing out the best in each member while creating a harmonious whole.

Within a family, this means intentionally creating moments of connection, both big and small, that strengthen bonds and foster a sense of belonging. It involves recognizing that family relationships, like any other relationship, require nurturing and effort. It's about moving beyond simply sharing a living space or a bloodline to creating a shared experience, a collective song that each member contributes to and draws strength from.

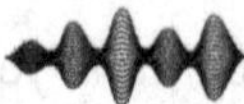

BRIDGE NOTE: THE FAMILY ORCHESTRA

Every family has its own unique sound—a distinctive blend of personalities, communication styles, traditions, and dynamics. Like an orchestra, each family member plays a different instrument:

- Some play **melody instruments** (taking center stage in family interactions);
- Others play **harmony instruments** (providing support and background structure);
- Some serve as **rhythm section** (maintaining traditions and routines);
- Others might be **improvisational soloists** (bringing spontaneity and creativity).

In music, no instrument is inherently more valuable than another—each contributes something essential to the whole. Similarly, in healthy families, each person's role is respected and valued for its unique contribution.

Just as orchestras need both structure (the written score) and flexibility (interpretation and expressiveness), families need both consistent patterns (traditions, values, boundaries) and adaptability (openness to change, growth, and individual expression).

What's your instrument in your family orchestra? How might recognizing and honoring the different "instruments" in your family create more harmony and appreciation for each person's contribution?

CREATING EXPONENTIAL OPPORTUNITIES WITHIN THE FAMILY

The word "exponential" might seem out of place when talking about family. We're not aiming for viral growth or massive scale. But the principle of exponential impact is deeply relevant. By creating intentional opportunities for connection, we create a ripple effect, strengthening not just individual relationships within the family but the family unit as a whole. One positive interaction can build momentum, leading to more positive interactions, creating a virtuous cycle of resonance.

Here are some ways to create these opportunities:

Family Rituals: Establishing regular family rituals, like a weekly family dinner, a monthly game night, or an annual vacation, creates shared experiences and strengthens bonds. These rituals provide a predictable rhythm to family life, creating a sense of stability and belonging. This builds on our earlier exploration of cultural rituals, like fika and moai, but applies them specifically to the family context.

Shared Activities: Engaging in activities that everyone enjoys, such as playing sports, making music, cooking together, working on a shared project, or exploring nature, fosters a sense of teamwork and camaraderie.

Open Communication: Creating a safe space for open and honest communication enables family members to feel comfortable expressing their thoughts and feelings without fear of judgment. This involves practicing active listening, empathy, and a willingness to understand different perspectives—skills we explored in chapter 7.

Celebrating Each Other: Recognizing and celebrating each other's accomplishments, both big and small, reinforces a sense of mutual support and appreciation. This could involve creating a family tradition of acknowledging birthdays, achievements, or milestones in a special way.

Navigating Conflict Constructively: Developing healthy communication patterns and conflict-resolution skills to address disagreements in a way that strengthens, rather than weakens, family bonds. The "Breakthrough Conversation" section from chapter 7 becomes especially valuable here.

Individuality Within Unity: Recognizing and supporting each individual's unique needs, talents, and aspirations while fostering a strong sense of family identity. This is about finding the balance between individual expression and collective harmony, allowing each family member to play their unique note while contributing to the overall symphony of the family.

Breakthrough Questions

- What moments of genuine connection stand out in your family history? What made those moments special?
- Which family member do you find it hardest to connect with and why? What would it take to create a bridge?
- What one ritual could you initiate that would create more opportunities for meaningful connection in your family?

Resonance Session

HEALING FAMILY WOUNDS

Artist Spotlight: Rosanne Cash

Focal Point: *The List* Album and Paternal Reconciliation

When country music legend Johnny Cash discovered that his eighteen-year-old daughter, Rosanne, had limited knowledge of country music history, he took action. He sat down and wrote a list of what he considered the one hundred essential country songs she needed to know—a musical education from father to daughter.

For years, Rosanne kept this handwritten list folded in her wallet as she forged her own path in music, often deliberately moving away from her father's style to establish her independent voice. Their relationship, while loving, was complicated by Johnny's long absences during her childhood, his struggles with addiction, and the inevitable challenges of growing up in the shadow of an icon.

In 2009, six years after her father's death and after establishing herself as an acclaimed artist in her own right, Rosanne Cash finally recorded *The List*—an album featuring twelve songs from her father's handwritten catalog.

In interviews about the project, she explained: "It was an act of love and honor and reconciliation . . . I had to grow up enough to realize how valuable this musical inheritance was, and to claim it on my own terms."

The project became much more than a tribute album. It represented a healing of old wounds, an acceptance of her musical heritage, and a reconciliation with her father's memory. The album went on to win a Grammy nomination and critical acclaim, but its greater significance was personal—a demonstration of how families can create opportunities for connection and healing across time, even after loss.

Reflection: What unresolved relationships in your family might benefit from a creative approach to reconciliation? Is there a family legacy—musical or otherwise—that you've resisted embracing but might now be ready to explore on your own terms?

THE SCIENCE OF FAMILY CONNECTION

The importance of creating these opportunities for connection within the family is not just anecdotal; it's supported by a robust body of research:

Family systems theory. A prominent approach in family therapy, family systems theory views the family as an interconnected unit where the actions of one member affect all others. This theory highlights that a family is not simply a collection of individuals but a dynamic system in which relationships and interactions create patterns that can be either resonant or dissonant. A change in one part of the system, such as introducing a new ritual or improving communication patterns, can have a ripple effect throughout the entire family.

Benefits of family rituals. Research has consistently shown that families that engage in regular rituals, such as shared meals, tend to have stronger bonds, better communication, and improved overall well-being. These rituals provide a sense of predictability and security, especially for children, and they create shared memories that strengthen family identity over time. For example, studies have found that families who eat dinner together regularly report higher levels of family satisfaction and lower rates of adolescent substance abuse and depression.

Impact of shared activities. Studies have demonstrated that participating in shared activities can enhance family cohesion and create positive memories that strengthen relationships over time. This is because shared activities provide opportunities for interaction, communication, and mutual enjoyment, fostering a sense of togetherness and belonging.

Communication and family satisfaction. Research on family communication patterns has identified specific behaviors that contribute to healthy family functioning. For example, studies have shown that families who communicate openly and honestly, who listen to each other with empathy, and who express affection regularly tend to report higher levels of satisfaction and well-being. This underscores the importance of creating a safe space for communication within the family, where each member feels heard, valued, and respected.

Resilience and family support. Research has also shown that strong family relationships can act as a buffer against stress and adversity, promoting resilience in the face of challenges. Families that provide emotional support, practical assistance, and a sense of belonging help their members cope with difficult life events and emerge stronger on the other side.

FAMILY RESONANCE ASSESSMENT

Rate each statement from 1 (rarely true) to 5 (consistently true) for your family:

Communication Harmony

- Family members express thoughts and feelings openly. ____
- We listen to understand rather than to respond. ____
- Conflicts are addressed rather than avoided. ____
- Different opinions are respected even when there's disagreement. ____
- We can be vulnerable with each other. ____

Emotional Attunement

- We recognize when someone is struggling without them having to say it. ____
- Joy is shared and celebrated collectively. ____
- Support is offered without having to be requested. ____
- Individual needs are acknowledged and honored. ____
- There's a sense of emotional safety within the family. ____

Structural Resonance

- We have meaningful family rituals we all value. ____
- Roles within the family are flexible rather than rigid. ____
- Time together is prioritized despite busy schedules. ____
- There's a balance between togetherness and individual space. ____
- Family rules and expectations adapt as needs change. ____

Resilience Rhythm

- We face challenges as a united front. ____
- Mistakes are treated as learning opportunities. ____
- We help each other through difficult times. ____
- The family can adapt to unexpected changes. ____
- We celebrate overcoming obstacles together. ____

Legacy Harmonies

- Positive family traditions are maintained and valued. ____
- Harmful patterns from previous generations are recognized. ____
- We actively create new, healthier patterns. ____
- Family history and stories are shared and preserved. ____
- There's a sense of creating something meaningful together. ____

Scoring:

- **100–125:** Strong resonance. Your family demonstrates exceptional harmony.
- **75–99:** Developing resonance. You have a solid foundation with room for deeper connection.
- **50–74:** Mixed resonance. There are some strengths alongside significant challenges.
- **25–49:** Struggling resonance. Major dissonance needs addressing.
- **Under 25:** Disconnected. This requires fundamental rebuilding of family connections.

Reflection: Look at your lowest-scoring categories. These represent your family's greatest opportunities for growth. Choose one category to focus on first and select a specific practice from this chapter to strengthen that area.

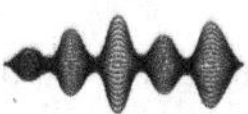

BRIDGE NOTE: BREAKING THE CYCLE

Family patterns, both positive and negative, can be passed down through generations like melodies in a song. We inherit not just genetic traits but also communication styles, emotional responses, and relationship dynamics.

Some of these inherited patterns create beautiful harmony—traditions of celebration, ways of showing love, values that guide decision-making. Others create dissonance—unhealthy conflict styles, emotional distance, or harmful behaviors.

Neuroscience shows that these patterns become encoded in our neural pathways through repeated exposure. But our brains remain plastic—capable of forming new connections and breaking old ones. This means we have the power to:

1. **Recognize** the patterns (becoming aware of the "music" we've inherited)
2. **Evaluate** which patterns serve us and which create dissonance
3. **Maintain** the harmonious traditions we value
4. **Transform** the discordant patterns into healthier alternatives

REAL-WORLD EXAMPLES OF BREAKING GENERATIONAL CYCLES

Consider the story shared earlier in this chapter—how my father broke the cycle of emotional distance that had characterized his relationship with his own father. By consciously choosing to express love openly to both his father and to me, he transformed a generational pattern of emotional restraint into one of emotional availability and affirmation.

Similarly, many people have found ways to transform other inherited patterns:

- A mother who grew up with harsh criticism learns to offer her children constructive feedback wrapped in encouragement.

- A father raised in a household where anger exploded into violence develops healthy ways to express and process his emotions.
- Parents who experienced financial insecurity create open conversations about money with their children rather than passing on anxiety and scarcity mindsets.

This process of conscious choice—deciding which family patterns to carry forward and which to leave behind—is one of the most powerful ways we can create positive change that extends beyond our own lives into future generations.

What cycles in your family are you committed to changing? What harmonies are you determined to preserve?

BEING A CONDUCTOR IN YOUR FAMILY

Just as a conductor guides an orchestra, bringing different instruments and sections together to create a harmonious whole, we can each take a leadership role in creating a more resonant family dynamic. This can involve:

Creating a Family Song: Establishing shared values, traditions, and rituals that create a sense of unity and belonging. This is like composing a unique melody that defines your family's identity.

Tuning In to Each Other's Needs: Paying attention to the emotional cues of family members and responding with empathy and understanding. It's akin to listening for the subtle nuances in each instrument's performance, ensuring that everyone is in tune.

Navigating Dissonance: Using healthy communication patterns and conflict-resolution skills to address disagreements constructively. This is comparable to resolving discordant notes in a musical piece, finding a way to create harmony even amid differences.

Amplifying Each Other's Strengths: Recognizing and celebrating the unique talents and contributions of each family member, creating space for everyone to shine. This is like highlighting the soloists in an orchestra, allowing their individual voices to be heard while still contributing to the overall harmony.

NAVIGATING DIFFICULT FAMILY CONVERSATIONS: A PRACTICE GUIDE

Below are frameworks for addressing common challenging family situations. These aren't scripts to be recited verbatim but rather structures to adapt to your own authentic voice and specific situations.

Addressing Hurtful Behavior

Framework: "When you [specific behavior], I felt [emotion] because [impact on you]. I value our relationship, and I'm wondering if we could talk about how we might [proposed solution]."

Example: "When you criticized my parenting approach in front of everyone at dinner, I felt undermined and embarrassed because raising my children well is important to me. I value your experience and wisdom, and I'm wondering if we could talk about how you might share your insights with me privately instead."

Setting Boundaries

Framework: "I care about you and want us to have a good relationship. For that to work well for me, I need [your boundary]. This would help me feel [desired outcome]. How might we work together to make this happen?"

Example: "I care about you and want us to have a good relationship. For that to work well for me, I need some advance notice before you come over to visit. This would help me feel respected and prepared to truly enjoy our time together. How might we work together to make this happen?"

Addressing Unequal Responsibilities

Framework: "I've noticed that [objective observation about current situation]. I'm feeling [emotion] about this because [reason]. I'd like to explore how we might [proposed solution]. What are your thoughts?"

Example: "I've noticed that I've been handling most of the household finances and decisions lately. I'm feeling overwhelmed about this because it's a lot to manage alone. I'd like to explore how we might share these responsibilities in a way that works for both of us. What are your thoughts?"

Discussing Sensitive Family History

Framework: "I've been thinking about [topic]. My understanding is [your perspective], but I realize I might not have the full picture. I'm asking because [your authentic reason]. Would you be open to sharing your perspective?"

Example: "I've been thinking about Grandpa's alcoholism and how it affected our family. My understanding is that it created a lot of tension between you and him when you were growing up, but I realize I might not have the full picture. I'm asking because I'm trying to understand our family patterns better. Would you be open to sharing your perspective?"

Key Principles

1. Focus on specific behaviors rather than character judgments.
2. Express your own feelings using "I" statements.
3. Explain the impact on you without accusation.
4. Propose solutions that could work for everyone.
5. Listen with genuine curiosity and openness to their perspective.
6. Look toward the future rather than dwelling on past grievances.

WHEN YOU'RE THE BLACK SHEEP: FINDING YOUR PLACE IN THE FAMILY MELODY

Being the family outlier—the one who thinks differently, chooses an unconventional path, or simply doesn't fit the family mold—presents unique challenges in creating resonance. If you identify as your family's "black sheep," consider the following strategies.

Recognize the Value of Your Different Note

Every orchestra needs instruments that provide contrast and tension within the larger composition. Your different perspective, approach, or choices may be exactly what your family system needs, even if that contribution isn't yet recognized. Your unique voice can expand the range and depth of your family's collective song.

Find Authentic Connection Points

You don't need to share every value or interest to connect meaningfully. Look for genuine areas of common ground, however small. Perhaps it's a shared sense of humor, appreciation for certain foods, or family stories everyone enjoys revisiting. Build connections around these authentic points of resonance rather than trying to force harmony where it doesn't exist.

Set Compassionate Boundaries

Being true to yourself while maintaining family connections often requires thoughtful boundaries. Learn to distinguish between moments when compromise serves connection and when it undermines your authenticity. Develop clear, kind limits around topics, behaviors, or situations that consistently create distress. Remember that boundaries aren't walls—they're guidelines that protect your well-being while allowing selective connection.

Create Your Own Resonance Network

Your family of origin isn't your only source of family-like connection. Cultivate deep relationships with those who appreciate your authentic self. These chosen connections can provide the understanding and acceptance you might not fully receive from biological family. This doesn't mean abandoning family ties but rather expanding your circle of meaningful relationships.

Practice Radical Acceptance

Much family dissonance comes from trying to change others or wishing the family system were different. Practice accepting your family members exactly as they are—not as you wish they would be. This doesn't mean condoning harmful behavior but rather releasing the exhausting effort of trying to transform others. From this place of acceptance, you can make clearer choices about how to engage authentically.

Contribute What Only You Can

Your difference is your gift. Perhaps your outsider perspective helps the family see blind spots. Maybe your independence models new possibilities for younger generations. Your courage to walk a different path might inspire others who feel constrained by family expectations. Look for ways to contribute from your unique strengths rather than trying to conform to roles that don't fit.

REMEMBER: THE ORCHESTRA NEEDS EVERY INSTRUMENT

In music, the instruments that stand apart—the oboe's haunting tone, the trumpet's bright call, the bass drum's deep resonance—often provide the most memorable moments in a symphony. Without these distinct voices, the music would lose its richness and complexity. Your family needs your different note, even if they don't yet have the ears to hear it.

Resonance Instrument

FAMILY SYSTEMS MAPPING

Purpose: To understand your family dynamics and identify patterns of resonance and dissonance

Time Required: 45–60 minutes

Materials: Your Resonance Journal, colored pens or markers (optional)

Practice:

Create Your Map. Draw a diagram of your family system:

- Place yourself in the center of the page;
- Position immediate family members (parents, siblings, spouse, children) closer to you;

- Add extended family in outer rings as relevant;
- Use circles for females, squares for males, or other symbols that work for you;
- Write names inside each symbol.

Represent Relationships: Draw lines between family members to show connections:

- Solid lines: Strong, positive relationships
- Dashed lines: Distant or strained relationships
- Jagged lines: Conflicted relationships
- Double lines: Extremely close (possibly enmeshed) relationships
- Add arrowheads to show direction of energy/influence if relevant.
- Optional: Use different colors to represent emotional qualities of relationships.

Identify Patterns: Examine your map and note:

- Alliances. Who consistently sides with whom?
- Triangles. Where do three people form relationship triangles?
- Cut-offs. Where have relationships been severed?
- Generational patterns. What dynamics repeat across generations?
- Role assignments. Who plays which roles (peacekeeper, rebel, hero, etc.)?

Reflect Deeply: In your journal, respond to these questions:

- What surprised you about your family map?
- Where is the most resonance in your family system?
- Where is the most dissonance?
- How have family patterns influenced your approach to relationships?

- What one change might create more resonance in your family system?

Identify Leverage Points: Circle 1–3 relationships on your map where:

- You have influence to create positive change.
- Improving this relationship would benefit the whole system.
- You feel ready to invest energy.

Variations:

- **Historical Mapping:** Create maps showing your family at different time periods to see how dynamics have evolved.
- **Ideal State Mapping:** Create a second map showing how you'd like your family system to look.
- **Focused Mapping:** Create detailed maps of specific subsystems (e.g., sibling relationships).

Real-World Application: Use insights from your map to guide conscious choices about:

- Which relationships need more attention?
- What boundaries might need strengthening?
- Where you might need to step back from mediator roles?
- How you avoid repeating problematic patterns?

Remember that understanding is the first step toward transformation. This map is a tool for awareness, not judgment.

Resonance Instrument

FAMILY CONNECTION RITUALS

Purpose: To create intentional, regular opportunities for family connection

Time Required: Varies (from five minutes daily to several hours weekly)

Materials: Depends on chosen rituals

Practice:

First, assess the current state. In your journal, answer:

- What connection rituals already exist in my family?
- Which feel most meaningful? Which feel obligatory?
- What types of connection are missing?

Next, design new rituals. Create rituals at different time scales.

- **Daily Micro Rituals (5–15 minutes):** Morning check-ins, evening gratitude shares, bedtime story or reflection time, text check-ins with distant family members.
- **Weekly Rituals (30–120 minutes):** Family meals with phones away, game nights or movie nights, Sunday walks or outdoor activities, weekly family meetings to coordinate schedules and check in.
- **Monthly Rituals (2–4 hours):** Extended family gatherings, special outings or adventures, service projects done together, celebration of monthly achievements.
- **Annual Traditions (1–7 days):** Family vacations or retreats, holiday celebrations with unique family touches, anniversary

celebrations of important family milestones, birthday traditions that honor each person.

Then try implementing your rituals with these strategies:

- Start small, with one or two new rituals.
- Involve family members in planning them.
- Be consistent but flexible as everyone tries them out.
- Evaluate and adjust based on what works.

Keep these ritual design principles in mind:

- Make the ritual meaningful, connected to your values.
- Make it enjoyable, something to look forward to.
- Make it inclusive, allowing everyone to participate.
- Make it sustainable, a realistic goal for everyone involved.

Variations:

- **Two-Person Rituals:** Design specific rituals for important dyads within the family (parent-child, siblings, etc.).
- **Extended Family Connections:** Create rituals that include grandparents, aunts, uncles, cousins.
- **Digital Family Rituals:** Design virtual online rituals for geographically separated family members.

Real-World Application

The most powerful family rituals often combine multiple elements:

- Physical togetherness
- Emotional sharing
- Fun or play
- Purpose or meaning

THIRTY-DAY FAMILY RESONANCE CHALLENGE

Transform your family dynamics with this progressive monthlong practice. Each week builds on the previous one, creating a foundation for lasting resonance.

Week 1: Observation and Awareness

Day 1: Complete the Family Resonance Assessment.

Day 2: Notice one inherited pattern that creates dissonance.

Day 3: Identify your primary "instrument" in your family orchestra.

Day 4: Observe who plays which roles in family interactions.

Day 5: Notice one unspoken family rule that governs behavior.

Day 6: Identify a family strength that's often overlooked.

Day 7: Reflect on what you've learned about your family system.

Week 2: Personal Preparation

Day 8: Practice deep listening with one family member.

Day 9: Identify one boundary you need to establish or strengthen.

Day 10: Practice expressing a difficult emotion constructively.

Day 11: Reflect on your own trigger patterns in family interactions.

Day 12: Create a self-regulation strategy for challenging moments.

Day 13: Practice radical acceptance of a family member's limitation.

Day 14: Identify one relationship where you can initiate positive change.

Week 3: Connection Creation

Day 15: Express specific appreciation to a family member.

Day 16: Initiate a conversation about a family memory.

Day 17: Establish a small daily connection ritual.

Day 18: Plan a shared activity that everyone can enjoy.

Day 19: Ask a genuine question about a family member's experience.

Day 20: Share something vulnerable with a trusted family member.

Day 21: Create a weekly family check-in practice.

Week 4: Transformation and Growth

Day 22: Have a breakthrough conversation using the framework.

Day 23: Create a family mission statement or set of values.

Day 24: Address one small dissonant pattern with a new response.

Day 25: Introduce a new tradition that supports connection.

Day 26: Share your family systems insights with an appropriate family member.

Day 27: Celebrate a family win, no matter how small.

Day 28: Address an unresolved conflict using constructive communication.

Integration Days

Day 29: Create a "Family Resonance Maintenance Plan" with specific practices you'll continue.

Day 30: Reflect on changes you've observed, and set intentions for ongoing growth.

Tips For Success

Start where you are—not every family is ready for deep transformation.

Adapt exercises based on your unique family dynamics.

Remember that your changed behavior alone can shift the entire system.

Celebrate small wins rather than expecting overnight transformation.

Be patient with resistance—it's a natural response to change.

Focus on progress, not perfection.

The goal isn't to create a perfect family but to increase moments of genuine connection and gradually transform dissonant patterns into more harmonious interactions. Even small changes in the family system can create significant shifts over time.

FROM FAMILY OF ORIGIN TO FAMILY OF CHOICE

Creating family resonance isn't limited to biological or legal relationships. For many, "chosen family"—close friends who function as family—provides essential connection and belonging. The principles of resonance apply equally to these relationships, often with more freedom to intentionally design the relationship dynamics.

The beauty of chosen family lies in its deliberate nature. While we don't choose our family of origin, we actively select our chosen family based on shared values, mutual respect, and authentic connection. These relationships can provide healing for those whose family of origin relationships contain significant dissonance. They can also complement existing family bonds, expanding our network of meaningful connections.

Dr. Maya Angelou once observed: "Family isn't always blood. It's the people in your life who want you in theirs; the ones who accept you for who you are. The ones who would do anything to see you smile and who love you no matter what." This expanded definition of family allows us to create resonant connections even when biological family relationships are strained or absent.

The skills you've developed throughout this chapter—creating rituals, engaging in open communication, navigating conflict constructively, and celebrating each other's uniqueness—can be applied with even greater intentionality in chosen family relationships. Without the weight of generational patterns, these relationships can sometimes achieve resonance more readily, though they face their own unique challenges.

Resonance Instrument

THE GENERATIONAL HEALING PRACTICE

Purpose: To transform inherited patterns and heal family wounds across generations

Time Required: 60–90 minutes for initial practice; 15–30 minutes for follow-up reflections

Materials: Your Resonance Journal, quiet space for reflection, family photos or mementos (optional)

Practice:

1. **Identify Inherited Patterns:** In your journal, create three columns:
    - **Patterns I've Inherited:** List communication styles, emotional responses, relationship dynamics, or beliefs that have been passed down in your family.
    - **Impact on Me:** Note how each pattern has affected your life and relationships.
    - **Origin Story:** If known, note where and why this pattern might have originated in your family history.
2. **Sort for Resonance and Dissonance:** Review your list and mark each pattern as:
    - **Harmonious:** Creates positive connection and well-being (mark with a +)
    - **Dissonant:** Creates tension, disconnection, or suffering (mark with a –)
    - **Neutral:** Neither particularly harmful nor helpful (mark with a 0)
3. **Select One Pattern for Transformation:** Choose one dissonant pattern that has significant impact on your life and relationships, that you have some emotional readiness to address, and that is within your power to influence.
4. **Create an Alternative Pattern:** For your chosen pattern, answer:
    - What need was this pattern originally trying to meet (e.g., protection, connection, stability)?
    - What healthier pattern could meet this same need?
    - What would this new pattern look, sound, and feel like in practice?
5. **Design Your Transformation Practice:**

- Identify trigger situations where the old pattern typically appears.

- Design a new response that embodies your alternative pattern.
- Establish a reminder or cue that will help you pause before defaulting to the old pattern.
- Determine how you'll support yourself in moments when the old pattern feels overwhelming.

6. **Express Gratitude and Set Intention:** Write a brief letter (not necessarily to send) that:
    - Acknowledges the original purpose of the inherited pattern
    - Expresses gratitude for the protection or coping it provided in the past
    - Declares your intention to create a new pattern going forward
    - Affirms your commitment to healing for yourself and future generations

Variations:

- **Ceremony:** Create a simple ritual to mark your commitment to transformation (e.g., burning the letter, planting a seed, creating an altar).
- **Support Circle:** Share your insights and intentions with trusted friends who can witness and support your transformation.
- **Visual Representation:** Create an artwork, collage, or vision board that represents both the old and new patterns.

REAL-WORLD APPLICATION

This practice is not a one-time exercise but the beginning of ongoing transformation. Consider:

- Tracking instances of both old and new patterns in your journal
- Celebrating small shifts and moments of choosing differently
- Sharing your insights with family members when appropriate
- Extending compassion to yourself and others when old patterns resurface

Remember that changing generational patterns is profound work that unfolds over time. Each small choice to respond differently creates a ripple effect that can transform your family system for generations to come.

Resonance Instrument

THE FAMILY APPRECIATION PRACTICE

Purpose: To cultivate a culture of recognition and gratitude within your family

Time Required: 10–15 minutes per week initially; can become an ongoing habit

Materials: Note cards, journal, or digital platform; creative supplies (optional)

Practice:

1. **Set a Regular Schedule:** Choose a consistent time for this practice—for example, weekly during a family meal or gathering, monthly as part of a family celebration or check-in, or milestone based, around birthdays, achievements, or anniversaries.
2. **Create the Appreciation Format:** Select an approach that fits your family style:

- **Spoken circle.** Each person takes a turn sharing appreciation for others.
- **Written notes.** Family members write and exchange appreciation messages.
- **Appreciation jar.** Everyone adds notes to a communal container throughout the week.
- **Digital sharing.** Create group texts or a family chat channel dedicated to appreciation.

3. **Establish Clear Guidelines:**
   - Appreciation should be specific, not generic.
   - Focus on character qualities and actions, not just achievements.
   - Include how the appreciated behavior made you feel or impacted you.
   - Everyone gets to both give and receive appreciation.
4. **Model Effective Appreciation:** Put those guidelines into practice whenever you can. Instead of "Thanks for helping with dinner," for example, say something like "I appreciated your help with dinner tonight. I noticed how you stepped in without being asked when you saw I was overwhelmed. It made me feel supported and valued."
5. **Create Supportive Conditions:**
   - Ensure this practice doesn't become perfunctory or obligatory.
   - Allow authentic expression rather than demanding forced participation.
   - Adapt the format based on family feedback and engagement.
   - Protect this practice from criticism or sarcasm.

Variations:

- **Appreciation Albums:** Collect written appreciation in a book for each family member.
- **Video Messages:** Record appreciation videos for special occasions.
- **Appreciation Wall:** Designate a space in your home for posting appreciation.
- **Secret Appreciator:** Assign each person someone to secretly appreciate during the week.

Real-World Application: Research shows that relationships with at least five positive interactions for every negative one are significantly healthier and more resilient. This practice helps create that positive foundation by:

- Training attention to notice what's going well
- Building a vocabulary of specific appreciation
- Creating a repository of positive memories and acknowledgments
- Establishing appreciation as a family value and habit

For the greatest impact, encourage appreciation that recognizes growth areas, unexpected contributions, and the unique gifts each person brings to the family.

POWER PLAYLIST

GENERATIONAL HARMONY

Family is where we first learn the music of relationship—harmony and discord, solos and ensemble pieces, that teach us how to love and be loved. These songs explore the complex beauty of family bonds that shape our understanding of connection across generations.

- **"Father and Son" by Cat Stevens.** Listen for: Two distinct vocal parts representing different life perspectives—how generational tension can sound loving rather than divisive.
- **"The Circle Game" by Joni Mitchell.** Listen for: The circular melody that mirrors life's seasons; the inevitability of change sounds both melancholy and beautiful.
- **"We Are Family" by Sister Sledge.** Listen for: The disco rhythm that makes family connection feel like joyful celebration rather than obligation, with harmonized voices blending in natural support.

Listening Practice: This week, choose one song and listen while reflecting on a specific family relationship—perhaps with a parent, child, sibling, or extended family member. Notice what emotions arise—gratitude, longing, frustration, love. After listening, write in your Resonance Journal: What family story does this song bring to mind? How has my family shaped my understanding of connection and belonging?

Creating Your Personal Additions: Add songs that remind you of family gatherings, traditions, or moments of deep family connection.

Consider how these songs capture the unique rhythms and melodies of your own family's story.

Family bonds, despite their complexity, create the foundational melodies that echo throughout our lives. These songs remind us that the patterns we learn in our first relationships—both beautiful and challenging—become the templates for how we connect with everyone else.

A CALL TO RESONANT ACTION

As we conclude this exploration of family resonance, I invite you to take one significant action within the next forty-eight hours to create more harmony in your family system. This might be:

- Initiating a difficult but necessary conversation you've been avoiding
- Establishing a new family ritual that creates space for authentic connection
- Reaching out to a family member with whom your relationship has grown distant
- Taking the first step to break a destructive pattern you've identified in your family map
- Expressing appreciation to a family member whose contributions often go unrecognized
- Creating a boundary that protects your well-being while still allowing for connection

Remember that change takes time. Family patterns often develop over generations, and transforming them requires patience, persistence, and compassion—both for yourself and for other family members. Every small step toward greater resonance creates ripples that can ultimately transform the entire family system.

The work you do to create more harmonious family relationships reverberates far beyond your immediate circle. When you heal family wounds, you not only transform your own experience but potentially shift trajectories for generations to come. When you establish new, healthier patterns, you create a blueprint that others can follow. When you show up with authenticity and integrity, you demonstrate what's possible in family relationships.

Creating a resonant family environment is a powerful way to nurture our own well-being and to equip future generations with the skills and resilience they need to thrive. But the principles of resonance extend beyond the walls of our homes. In the next chapter, we'll explore how to cultivate these same principles in our intimate relationships, where the dance of connection takes on its most vulnerable and transformative form. After all, the partnerships we choose become the foundation for new family systems, carrying forward the resonance we've developed or creating it anew where it was absent before.

CHAPTER 9

Duet: Resonance in Your Personal Life

The most beautiful duets are between people who have learned to sing their own songs perfectly.

UNKNOWN

THE HARMONY OF TWO VOICES

We've journeyed inward, learning to tune our inner instruments and discover the authentic melodies of our true selves. We've explored the power of authenticity to attract resonant relationships and the importance of integrity as the foundation for trust. Now, we turn our attention to the realm of close personal relationships—the "duets" of our lives. This is where we learn to blend our unique song with another's, creating a harmony that is both beautiful and enduring.

What if the secret to a truly fulfilling relationship isn't about finding the "perfect" person but about becoming the kind of partner who can create a resonant connection? What if, instead of searching for a flawless melody, we focus on learning to harmonize, to blend our unique song with another's, creating a duet that is both beautiful and enduring? Fulfillment doesn't come from changing who you are to fit someone else's mold. It's the result of becoming the fullest, most authentic version of yourself—and attracting someone who resonates with that truth.

Resonance Session

PARTNERSHIP IN HARMONY

Artist Spotlight: Yo-Yo Ma and Kathryn Stott
Focal Point: The Evolution of a Musical Partnership

It began with a simple invitation over thirty years ago. Cellist Yo-Yo Ma, already renowned for his virtuosity and musical depth, invited British pianist Kathryn Stott to join him for a performance. On the surface, they came from different musical worlds—Ma trained at Juilliard and Harvard, with a foundation in classical repertoire and a growing interest in cross-cultural exploration; Stott was educated at the Royal College of Music, with deep roots in European musical traditions.

Their first rehearsals revealed their differences. Ma approached music with a powerful emotional immediacy, while Stott brought meticulous attention to structure and interpretative subtlety. Yet beneath these differences, they discovered a shared commitment to vulnerability and emotional honesty in performance.

Their musical partnership has evolved over decades, creating acclaimed recordings and performances across the globe. What makes their collaboration extraordinary isn't an absence of differences but their ability to transform those differences into creative strengths.

What audiences witness in their performances is the visible

manifestation of true resonance—two distinct voices creating something greater than either could achieve alone.

Reflection: Think about a significant relationship in your life—romantic or otherwise. How do your differences complement each other? What shared values or purposes form the foundation of your connection? How might viewing your relationship as a "duet" rather than a "solo" change how you approach challenges?

REVISITING PILLAR #1: BE GENEROUS OF TIME AND ENERGY, BE AN OFFERING (THE HANDS)

In this chapter, we'll revisit and expand upon Pillar #1: Be Generous of Time and Energy, Be an Offering, applying it specifically to the context of close, personal one-on-one relationships—romantic partnerships and deep friendships. While we've explored this principle in earlier chapters, here we dig into the nuances of what it means to be truly generous in the most intimate spheres of our lives.

Being an offering in a personal relationship means:

Prioritizing Presence: Making a conscious effort to be fully present with your partner or friend, putting aside distractions and giving them your undivided attention. This is about creating a space where they feel seen, heard, and valued.

Active Listening: Listening not just to the words being spoken but also to the underlying emotions, needs, and unspoken messages. This requires empathy, curiosity, and a willingness to truly understand the other person's perspective.

Emotional Support: Being there for your partner or friend during both good times and bad, offering a shoulder to lean on, a listening ear, and a compassionate heart. This means validating their feelings, offering encouragement, and celebrating their successes as if they were your own.

Unconditional Love and Acceptance: Accepting your partner or friend for who they are, flaws and all, and offering your love and support without judgment.

This doesn't mean condoning harmful behavior, but it does mean recognizing that everyone is on their own journey of growth and that we all make mistakes.

Vulnerability and Trust: Being willing to share your own thoughts, feelings, and vulnerabilities, creating a space for mutual openness and honesty. This requires courage, as it involves taking the risk of being seen and known, flaws and all.

The Dance of Intimacy: Recognizing that intimacy is a delicate dance, a give-and-take between two individuals. It's about finding a rhythm that works for both partners, allowing each person to shine while also creating something harmonious together.

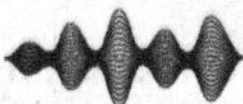

BRIDGE NOTE: THE DUET METAPHOR

The duet offers a perfect metaphor for intimate relationships. Consider what makes a musical duet successful:

Distinct Voices: Each performer maintains their unique sound and style. In a great duet, you don't hear one voice disappearing into the other—you hear both, distinct yet harmonious.

Complementary Qualities: Often, duet partners have different vocal ranges or timbres that complement each other. The contrast creates interest and depth that neither could achieve alone.

Responsive Listening: Duet performers must listen intently to each other, adjusting in real time to stay in harmony. This active listening requires both self-awareness and other awareness.

Shared Interpretation: Though singing different parts, duet partners must share an understanding of the song's meaning and emotional landscape.

Momentary Leadership: In most duets, the lead passes back and forth—sometimes one voice dominates while the other supports, then they switch.

Synchronized Breathing: Perhaps most subtly, successful duet partners often breathe together, creating a physical synchrony that allows for perfect timing.

In our intimate relationships, these same qualities create resonance. We maintain our individual identities while creating something neither could create alone.

We listen and respond to each other. We share a vision while trading the lead based on our strengths. And sometimes, in moments of deep connection, we find ourselves literally and figuratively "breathing together."

What would change in your closest relationships if you approached them as a duet rather than a solo performance?

THE SCIENCE OF INTIMATE CONNECTION

The importance of these qualities in building resonant personal relationships is not just based on intuition or anecdotal evidence; it's supported by a wealth of scientific research:

Gottman Institute Research: Dr. John Gottman, through decades of research on couples, has identified specific behaviors that contribute to strong and lasting relationships. His work highlights the importance of "bids for connection," the small, everyday interactions where partners reach out to each other for attention, affection, or support. Resonant relationships are characterized by a high rate of turning toward these bids, demonstrating a willingness to engage and connect.

Gottman's research also underscores the destructive power of the "Four Horsemen of the Apocalypse"—criticism, contempt, defensiveness, and stonewalling—which erode trust and create dissonance. Being an offering, in Gottman's terms, means actively turning toward your partner, responding to their bids for connection, and fostering a culture of appreciation and respect.

Empathy and Emotional Intelligence: Empathy, the ability to understand and share the feelings of another, is a cornerstone of resonant relationships. Studies have shown a strong correlation between empathy, emotional intelligence, and relationship satisfaction. Emotional intelligence, which encompasses the ability to recognize, understand, and manage our own emotions and the emotions of others, allows us to navigate the complexities of relationships with greater skill and sensitivity. When we can empathize with our partners, understanding their emotional landscape, we can respond to their needs more effectively and build deeper connections.

Attachment Theory: Attachment theory, developed by John Bowlby and

Mary Ainsworth, provides a framework for understanding how early childhood experiences shape our capacity for intimacy and connection in later life. Secure attachment, characterized by trust and emotional responsiveness, is fostered by consistent caregiving and a sense of being seen and valued. In adult relationships, being an offering can help create a secure attachment style, providing the emotional safety and support needed for deep connection to flourish. By consistently offering our time, attention, and empathy, we create a secure base from which our partners can explore the world and grow.

Neuroscience: The research on oxytocin that we explored in earlier chapters, as well as the phenomenon of "mirror neurons" (brain cells that are activated when we perform an action are also activated by observing another person performing that action), have particular relevance for intimate relationships. These biological mechanisms help explain why being generous with our attention and affection creates such powerful bonds. When we consistently engage in positive, supportive interactions with our partners, we create neural and chemical patterns that strengthen our connection over time.

Resonance Session

REDEMPTIVE LOVE

Artist Spotlight: Johnny and June Carter Cash
Focal Point: Transformation Through Partnership

He was a legend, the "Man in Black," known for his deep voice and songs about hardship and redemption. She was a member of country music royalty, a talented singer and performer in her own right. Their paths crossed many times in the world of music, but it wasn't until they started touring together that a deeper connection began to form.

When they met, Johnny Cash was struggling with addiction, his personal and professional life spiraling out of control. June Carter saw beyond the darkness, recognizing the good heart and the brilliant artist beneath the surface. In her autobiography, she wrote: "I found myself thinking about him even when I didn't want to."

Johnny later credited June with saving his life. Her steadfast support became his anchor during his journey to sobriety.

When they finally married in 1968, their partnership blossomed into one of country music's greatest love stories. Their duets, like "Jackson" and "It Ain't Me Babe," showcased their musical chemistry—two distinct voices creating something greater together than either could alone.

What made their relationship extraordinary wasn't romantic perfection; it was commitment through imperfection. When Johnny relapsed, June stood by him without enabling. When challenges arose, they faced them together. Their partnership wasn't built on idealized love but on day-by-day choice and presence.

Reflection: Consider a relationship that has weathered significant challenges. What qualities allowed it to endure? How might the Cashes' story of imperfect but committed love inform your approach to your own relationships?

THE ART OF THE RELATIONSHIP DUET

Just like a musical duet, resonant personal relationships require a delicate balance of individual expression and harmonious blending. Resonance occurs when we find a rhythm that works for both partners, allowing each to shine while also creating something beautiful together. Let's take a look at what this involves.

DEEP LISTENING: BEYOND THE WORDS

What It Is: Truly hearing and understanding your partner's perspective, even when it differs from your own. Listening not just to their words, but also to their tone, body language, and the emotions they're expressing (or not expressing).

How to Achieve It:

- Practice empathy by making a conscious effort to see the world through your partner's eyes.
- Note nonverbal cues like body language, facial expressions, and tone of voice.
- Ask open-ended questions that encourage deeper sharing.
- Reflect back what you hear to confirm understanding.
- Avoid interrupting or preparing your response while the other person is speaking.
- Create space for silence, allowing thoughts and feelings to emerge.

Mutual Respect: Celebrating Differences, Finding Harmony

What It Is: Valuing each other's unique contributions, perspectives, and personalities, even when they differ from your own. Recognizing that you are both essential parts of the whole, like two instruments in a duet.

How to Achieve It:

- Regularly acknowledge and appreciate your partner's strengths and talents.
- Reframe differences as complementary rather than contradictory.
- Avoid criticism and contempt, focusing instead on constructive communication.
- Express appreciation daily for specific actions or qualities.
- Defend your partner's perspective when they're not present.
- Create spaces where each person's unique interests can flourish.

Flexibility and Adaptability: Finding the Shared Rhythm

What It Is: Being willing to adjust your own "volume" and "tempo" to create harmony with your partner. This means being open to compromise, negotiation, and stepping outside your comfort zone. It's about recognizing that relationships are dynamic and require ongoing adjustments.

How to Achieve It:

- Practice compromise that honors both people's core needs.
- Remain open to change as individuals and the relationship evolve.
- Communicate your needs clearly while remaining receptive to theirs.
- Approach disagreements as collaborative problem-solving opportunities.
- Take turns accommodating each other's preferences.
- View flexibility as strength rather than weakness.

Shared Purpose: Creating a Common Melody

What It Is: Having a common goal or vision that unites you, even amid your differences. This could be a shared dream for the future, a commitment to raising a family, a passion for a particular cause, or simply a desire to grow and evolve together.

How to Achieve It:

- Engage in ongoing conversations about individual and shared dreams.
- Identify and articulate the values that unite you.
- Create explicit agreements about your shared vision.
- Support each other's individual goals while nurturing collective ones.
- Celebrate milestones along your shared journey.
- Revisit and refine your shared vision as you both grow.

Resonance Instrument

THE RELATIONSHIP CHECK-IN

Purpose: To create a regular space for deepening connection and addressing potential issues before they create dissonance

Time Required: 30–45 minutes weekly

Material: A quiet, private space free from distractions

Preparation:

- Choose a consistent time when you're both relatively relaxed.
- Agree that this is a safe space for honest communication.
- Turn off phones and other distractions.
- Consider having a "talking object" that designates whose turn it is to speak.

Practice:

1. **Opening Appreciation** (Five minutes):
   Take turns sharing something specific you appreciate about each other from the past week. Be detailed and authentic in your appreciation. Example: "I really appreciated how you listened to me after my difficult meeting on Tuesday. You didn't try to fix it—you just made space for me to process."
2. **Personal Check-in** (Ten minutes):
   Each person takes five minutes to share:
   - How they're feeling in general
   - How they're feeling about your relationship specifically

- What's been on their mind that they haven't had a chance to share

The listening partner practices active listening without interrupting.

3. **Relationship Questions** (Fifteen minutes):
   Take turns asking and answering these questions:
   - "What's one thing I did well as a partner this week?"
   - "What's one thing I could do better next week?"
   - "Is there anything you need from me that you're not getting?"
   - "What can we do to feel more connected in the coming week?"
4. **Issues and Elephants** (Ten minutes):
   Each person should briefly address any issues that need attention. Use "I" statements and focus on feelings and needs rather than blame. For bigger issues—the elephants in the room—acknowledge them and schedule a separate time to discuss.

   Example: "I notice I've been feeling disconnected when we're both on our phones in the evening. Could we talk about creating some screen-free time?"
5. **Future Planning** (Five minutes):
   Each of you shares something you're looking forward to doing together. Make specific plans for connection in the coming week.

   Example: "I'd love to take a walk with you this weekend and catch up without distractions."

Variations

- **Written Prelude:** Before meeting, write your thoughts to gather clarity.

- **Themed Check-ins:** Focus on specific areas (intimacy, parenting, finances, etc.).
- **Quarter/Annual Reviews:** Supplement weekly check-ins with deeper seasonal conversations about larger goals and visions.

Real-World Application

These check-ins serve as preventative maintenance for your relationship. They create a regular space for issues to be addressed before they grow into resentments and for appreciation to be explicitly expressed rather than assumed. Over time, they build a culture of open communication and intentional connection.

The most successful relationship check-ins maintain a ratio of at least 5:1 positive to negative interactions. Even when discussing challenges, approach the conversation with an attitude of "us against the problem" rather than "me against you."

THE POWER OF AUTHENTIC ACKNOWLEDGMENT

One of the most powerful tools in creating resonant relationships is the practice of authentic acknowledgment. When we truly see our partners—their strengths, their efforts, their growth, their essence—and express that seeing, we create a profound sense of connection. Unlike generic compliments, authentic acknowledgment is specific, heartfelt, and targeted to the unique qualities of the individual.

Why acknowledgment matters:

- **It validates identity.** When we acknowledge specific qualities in our partners, we validate their sense of self and affirm their value.
- **It creates safety.** Knowing we are seen and appreciated for who we truly are creates psychological safety, allowing for greater vulnerability and intimacy.

- **It reinforces positive behaviors.** What gets acknowledged tends to get repeated. When we acknowledge the behaviors we appreciate, we're likely to see more of them.
- **It builds resilience.** A foundation of positive acknowledgment creates a reservoir of goodwill that helps relationships weather inevitable conflicts and challenges.

Moving Beyond Surface Appreciation

There's a profound difference between casual appreciation and deep acknowledgment. Compare these examples:

Surface Level: "Thanks for making dinner."

Deep Acknowledgment: "I noticed how you incorporated my favorite ingredients into dinner tonight, even though they required extra preparation. That thoughtfulness means so much to me."

Surface Level: "You're a good listener."

Deep Acknowledgment: "When I was struggling to express myself earlier, you put aside what you were doing, gave me your full attention, and asked questions that helped me clarify my own thoughts. I felt truly heard and understood."

The difference lies in specificity, connection to values, and emotional impact. Deep acknowledgment requires attentiveness and a willingness to articulate what we notice and value in others.

Resonance Instrument

THE ACKNOWLEDGMENT PRACTICE

Purpose: To develop the habit of specific, authentic acknowledgment that strengthens connection

Time Required: Five minutes daily

Materials: None required, though a journal for reflection is helpful

Practice:

1. **Daily observation.** Each day, intentionally observe your partner with fresh eyes. Notice:
    - Specific actions that demonstrate their character strengths
    - Efforts they make that might otherwise go unnoticed
    - Qualities that you value but may take for granted
    - Growth or changes you've observed over time
2. **Crafting acknowledgment.** Create an acknowledgment that includes:
    - The specific behavior or quality you noticed
    - The impact it had on you or others
    - The character strength it represents
    - Your appreciation for this aspect of who they are
3. **Authentic delivery.** Share your acknowledgment:
    - Choose a moment when you both can be present.
    - Make eye contact and speak from the heart.
    - Use a tone that conveys your genuine feelings.
    - Allow space for them to receive your words.

Try following this blueprint: When you ________ (specific action/behavior), I felt/noticed ________ (impact). This showed me ________ (character quality), and I appreciate this about you because ________.

Example: When you remembered to ask about my presentation today, I felt truly cared for. This showed me your thoughtfulness and how you hold space for the things that matter to me, even in the midst of your own busy day. I appreciate this quality in you because it makes me feel valued and reminds me that we're truly partners in each other's lives.

Reflection Questions:

- How did it feel to offer this acknowledgment?
- How did your partner respond?
- What did you learn about what matters to you in this relationship?
- How might regular acknowledgment shift the atmosphere of your relationship?

Variations:

Written Acknowledgments: Leave notes, texts, or emails with your observations.

Acknowledgment Jar: Write acknowledgments on slips of paper and collect them in a jar to read together during difficult times.

Public Acknowledgment: When appropriate, acknowledge your partner's qualities in front of others.

Photographic Acknowledgment: Capture moments that exemplify qualities you value and share them with a specific acknowledgment.

Remember that acknowledgment is distinct from praise. Praise focuses on achievements and performance, while acknowledgment recognizes the person's inherent qualities and efforts regardless of outcome. Both have their place, but acknowledgment often creates deeper connection because it communicates: "I see you, not just what you do."

NAVIGATING DISSONANCE: WHEN HARMONY BREAKS DOWN

Even the most resonant relationships experience periods of dissonance—moments of conflict, misunderstanding, or disconnect. These challenging times don't necessarily indicate failure; they're often opportunities for growth and deeper understanding, if navigated consciously. Just as musical dissonance can add depth and interest to a composition when resolved skillfully, relationship dissonance can lead to greater intimacy when approached with wisdom.

Understanding Relationship Dissonance

Dissonance in relationships typically stems from several sources:

Unmet needs. Each person has fundamental needs for connection, autonomy, significance, and security. When these go unmet, tension arises.

Different values or priorities. What matters deeply to one person may not hold the same significance for another.

Communication styles. Differences in how people express themselves, process information, or handle conflict can create misunderstanding.

External stressors. Pressures from work, family obligations, health challenges, or financial concerns can strain even strong relationships.

Wounded history. Past hurts, either from childhood or previous relationship experiences, can be triggered in current interactions.

The key is not to avoid dissonance altogether—that's neither possible nor desirable—but to learn to move through it constructively, allowing it to deepen rather than damage your connection.

The Repair Sequence: Transforming Dissonance into Growth

Research by relationship experts like Dr. Sue Johnson and Dr. John Gottman highlights the importance of effective repair after conflict. Here's a framework for navigating dissonance:

1. **Pause and self-regulate.** Before attempting to resolve conflict, take time to calm your nervous system. Deep breathing, movement,

or brief solitude can help you return to a state where productive conversation is possible.

2. **Reconnect with compassion.** Remind yourself of your care for the other person and your commitment to the relationship. Approach the conversation with curiosity rather than defensiveness.
3. **Name the pattern.** Often, relationship conflicts follow predictable patterns. Identify what's happening: "I notice we're in that cycle where I pursue and you withdraw," or "We seem to be talking past each other again."
4. **Share underlying feelings.** Move beyond surface anger to the more vulnerable feelings beneath: hurt, fear, sadness, or longing. "Beneath my frustration, I'm feeling scared that I don't matter to you."
5. **Express needs clearly.** Identify what you need, framed positively: "I need reassurance about your commitment" rather than "I need you to stop being so distant."
6. **Listen to understand.** Truly hearing your partner's perspective doesn't mean you agree with it—only that you're willing to see the situation through their eyes.
7. **Co-create solutions.** Brainstorm approaches that honor both people's needs, looking for the "third way" that isn't simply compromise but true innovation.
8. **Celebrate the repair.** Acknowledge the work you've done together to move through difficulty. This reinforces your ability to handle future challenges.

DISSONANCE NOTE: THE VULNERABILITY PARADOX

One of the most challenging aspects of intimate relationships is what therapists call the "vulnerability paradox": The times when we most need connection are often the times we're least able to ask for it skillfully.

When we feel hurt, rejected, or insecure, our instinct is often to protect ourselves through defensive behaviors—criticism, withdrawal, contempt, or stonewalling. Yet these very behaviors push away the connection we crave.

The vulnerability paradox invites us to do the opposite of what feels natural: to move toward connection when we feel like withdrawing, to express our needs directly when we feel like attacking, to remain open when we want to shut down.

This requires tremendous courage and self-awareness. It means saying, "I'm feeling hurt and I need your reassurance" instead of "You always ignore me." It means acknowledging, "I'm feeling overwhelmed and need space to process" instead of simply going cold and distant.

The path through the vulnerability paradox is paved with small acts of brave authenticity—moments when we choose to reveal our true feelings rather than acting them out. Each time we navigate this successfully, we build not only a stronger relationship but also greater personal resilience.

Reflection: Think about a recent conflict in a close relationship. What were you really feeling beneath your words or actions? What would it have looked like to express that vulnerability directly? What might have happened differently?

CREATING YOUR RELATIONSHIP SYMPHONY

As we conclude this exploration of duets—the intimate one-on-one relationships that form the core of our personal lives—let's return to our central theme: Resonance isn't found; it's created. The quality of your closest relationships isn't determined by luck or circumstance but by the consistent choices you make and the practices you cultivate.

The most beautiful duets emerge when both partners commit to ongoing growth, both individually and together. Each person continues to develop their own "voice"—their authentic self-expression—while simultaneously learning to blend harmoniously with their partner. This dual commitment creates relationships that are both deeply fulfilling and remarkably resilient.

YOUR RESONANCE REFLECTION

Take a moment to consider:

1. Which aspects of your current close relationships feel most resonant? Where do you experience that sense of harmonious connection?
2. Where do you notice dissonance? Which patterns or dynamics create disconnect rather than harmony?
3. What one practice from this chapter could you implement this week to create greater resonance in your most important relationship?
4. How might becoming more fully yourself—more authentic, more present, more generous—transform your capacity for intimate connection?

Remember that creating resonance is not a destination but a journey. Even the most skilled musicians continue to practice, refine, and deepen their art throughout their lives. The same is true for the art of relationships. Each day offers new opportunities to listen more deeply, to offer yourself more generously, to harmonize more beautifully with those you love.

POWER PLAYLIST

THE DUET, WHEN TWO VOICES BECOME ONE SONG

These songs demonstrate how two distinct voices can create something more beautiful together than either could achieve alone, while maintaining their individual authenticity.

- **"It Ain't Me Babe" by Johnny Cash and June Carter.** Listen for: How two people can disagree and still harmonize—notice the playful tension that strengthens rather than threatens their bond.
- **"Shallow" by Lady Gaga and Bradley Cooper.** Listen for: The moment when vulnerability becomes shared courage and emotional honesty creates space for deeper intimacy.
- **"Islands in the Stream" by Dolly Parton and Kenny Rogers.** Listen for: Perfect complementarity without losing individuality, with different vocal qualities enhancing, rather than competing with, each other.

Listening Practice: This week, if you're in a relationship, listen to one song together with your partner. Pay attention to how you each respond differently to the music—what moves them that you hadn't noticed? If you're single, listen while reflecting on past relationships or future hopes. After listening, write in your Resonance Journal: What does it mean to maintain my authentic voice while creating harmony with another? How do I balance independence with interdependence?

Creating Your Personal Additions: Add songs that represent significant relationships in your life—whether current partnerships, past loves, or future dreams. Consider sharing these with someone close to you, explaining what these songs reveal about your approach to intimate connection.

The duet teaches us that love is not about becoming the same person, but about becoming better versions of ourselves through the alchemy of authentic connection. These songs remind us that the most beautiful partnerships honor both individual voices and their combined harmony.

LOOKING AHEAD: FROM DUETS TO ENSEMBLES

As we continue our journey of resonant relationships, we'll expand our focus from the intimate duets explored in this chapter to the larger ensembles that enrich our lives—friendship circles and community connections. We'll discover how the principles of resonance scale from one-on-one relationships to more complex social networks, creating ever-widening circles of connection and meaning.

In chapter 10, we'll focus specifically on friendships—those chosen connections that provide support, growth, joy, and meaning throughout our lives.

CHAPTER 10

Resonance in Bonds of Friendship

You can make more friends in two months by being interested in them than in two years by making them interested in you.

DALE CARNEGIE

Each friend represents a world in us, a world possibly not born until they arrive, and it is only by this meeting that a new world is born.

ANAÏS NIN

A friend is one soul abiding in two bodies.

ARISTOTLE

THE CHOSEN CONNECTIONS

We've explored the dynamics of resonance within the family and intimate partnerships, learning how to create harmonious and supportive environments with those to whom we are bound by commitment or circumstance. Now, we turn our attention to a different kind of family—the family we choose for ourselves. Our friends.

Friendships, those vital relationships that provide companionship, support, and a sense of belonging throughout our lives, are another fertile ground for cultivating resonance. Just as a band relies on the unique talents and contributions of each member, so, too, do we rely on our friends to enrich our lives, challenge us to grow, and help us create a symphony of shared experiences.

Resonance Session

THE HARMONY OF FRIENDSHIP

Artist Spotlight: Elton John and Bernie Taupin

They met through a newspaper ad in 1967, two young men responding to the same call for songwriters at Liberty Records. Elton John was a gifted pianist and performer searching for lyrical inspiration. Bernie Taupin was a poet with vivid imagery but no musical training. Neither got the job they applied for, but they found something far more valuable—each other.

Their creative process was unlike most songwriting partnerships. Bernie would write lyrics in isolation, crafting stories and emotions into verse, then mail or hand them to Elton. Without discussion or collaboration, Elton would sit at his piano and set these words to music, often completing entire songs in minutes. They rarely wrote in the same room.

What made their partnership extraordinary wasn't similarity but complementarity. Bernie's lyrics painted cinematic stories—rocket ships, yellow brick roads, tiny dancers—while Elton's melodies transformed these images into anthems that moved millions.

Their friendship has endured for over fifty years, surviving Elton's struggles with addiction, Bernie's reclusiveness, changes in the music industry, and the natural evolution of two very different personalities. They've created over thirty albums together, with Bernie writing lyrics for nearly all of Elton's biggest hits.

What sustained their partnership wasn't constant agreement but mutual respect, clear roles, and shared commitment to the music.

Reflection: Consider a friendship or partnership in your life where differences create strength rather than conflict. How do your distinct qualities complement each other? What shared purpose or commitment helps you navigate the inevitable challenges of any long-term relationship?

REVISITING PILLAR #4: ADD VALUE WITHOUT EXPECTATION OF RETURN

This chapter expands upon Pillar #4: Add Value Without Expectation of Return, applying it specifically to the context of friendship. In friendships, adding value means being a source of support, encouragement, and genuine care for our friends, without keeping score or expecting something in return. It's about celebrating their successes, offering a listening ear during challenging times, and simply being present in their lives. It's about recognizing that true friendship is not a transaction but a bond built on mutual respect, shared experiences, and a genuine desire to see each other thrive.

Practices for Adding Value in Friendship

Being a Battery: As we discussed in earlier chapters, we all encounter "batteries" and "black holes" in our lives. In friendships, striving to be a battery means bringing positive energy, enthusiasm, and support to the relationship. It's about being someone who lifts your friends up rather than dragging them down.

Celebrating Successes: Genuinely celebrating your friends' accomplishments, both big and small, without jealousy or envy. This means sharing in their joy and acknowledging their achievements, creating a culture of mutual celebration and support.

Offering Support: Being there for your friends during difficult times, offering a listening ear, a shoulder to cry on, or practical help when needed. It's about showing up consistently, especially when things are tough.

Sharing Experiences: Creating shared memories through activities, adventures, and meaningful conversations. These shared experiences form the foundation of lasting friendships and provide a rich tapestry of connection.

Being Present: Giving your friends your undivided attention, putting away distractions, and truly engaging in the moment. In a world full of distractions, the gift of presence is increasingly rare and valuable.

Honest Feedback: Offering honest and constructive feedback when needed, always with kindness and respect. True friends help each other grow by providing thoughtful perspectives and challenging each other in healthy ways.

Unconditional Acceptance: Accepting your friends for who they are, flaws and all, and offering your love and support without judgment. This creates a safe space for authentic expression and deep connection.

THE SCIENCE OF FRIENDSHIP

The importance of friendship in our lives is not just a matter of subjective experience; it's supported by a substantial body of scientific research.

Health and well-being. Research has consistently demonstrated the profound impact of friendship on our well-being. Studies have shown that having strong social ties, particularly close friendships, is associated with increased happiness, reduced stress, improved physical health, and even a longer lifespan. Friends provide a buffer against life's challenges, offer a sense of belonging, and contribute to our overall sense of purpose and meaning.

Social support and resilience. Research on social support highlights the crucial role of friends in helping us cope with stress and adversity. Friends offer emotional support, practical assistance, and a sense of belonging that can help us navigate difficult times. Knowing that we have people we can rely on, who will stand by us no matter what, gives us the strength and resilience to overcome challenges.

Reciprocity in friendship. While Pillar #4 emphasizes giving without expectation, research also shows that reciprocity is a natural and important aspect of healthy friendships. Studies on the evolution of cooperation found that reciprocity—the tendency to return favors and respond in kind to acts of generosity—is a fundamental aspect of human social behavior. In friendships, this translates to a balanced give-and-take, where both individuals feel supported and valued.

Just as a jam session requires each musician to listen to the others, contribute their unique talents, and find a common groove, so, too, do friendships require a balance of give-and-take, a willingness to both offer and receive support, and a shared commitment to creating something beautiful together.

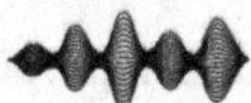

BRIDGE NOTE: THE GIFT OF DISAGREEMENT

True friendship isn't about always agreeing; it's about being able to disagree respectfully and still maintain a strong connection. Disagreements, when handled with empathy and a willingness to understand, can deepen friendships and lead to greater intimacy.

Think of it as two different instruments playing contrasting melodies that ultimately create a richer, more complex harmony. The most interesting music often incorporates elements of tension and resolution, and the same is true for our most meaningful relationships.

When we can express different viewpoints and navigate conflicts with respect and care, we create a relationship environment where authenticity can flourish. We demonstrate that the bond is strong enough to withstand differences, that our connection transcends perfect agreement.

This doesn't mean seeking conflict or being contrary for its own sake. Rather, it means having the courage to express your true thoughts and feelings, even when they differ from your friend's, and creating space for them to do the same.

The next time you find yourself disagreeing with a close friend, try viewing it not as a threat to your relationship but as an opportunity for growth and deeper understanding. What might you learn from their perspective? How might navigating this disagreement actually strengthen your bond?

THE QUALITY QUOTIENT: YOUR INNER CIRCLE (BEYOND DUNBAR'S NUMBER)

We've established that friendships are vital for our well-being, and that adding value without expectation is a key principle for cultivating these bonds. But in a world obsessed with social media followers and sprawling networks, it's easy to lose sight of a crucial distinction: the difference between quantity and quality in our friendships.

Anthropologist Robin Dunbar's research, as mentioned in chapter 2, offers a compelling perspective on this. Dunbar proposed that our brains are structured to handle a limited number of meaningful relationships, with a cognitive limit of around 150 stable social connections, which has become known as "Dunbar's number." Recall that this number breaks down into layers of increasing intimacy. The innermost layer, our closest circle, typically consists of about five people. Then, we have expanding layers of approximately 15, 50, and 150. We have a limited capacity for deep connection.

This is where the concept of batteries and black holes, introduced earlier, becomes particularly relevant. Think of your friendships through this lens. Who are the people who consistently energize you, who support your authentic self, who lift you higher? These are your batteries, the relationships that nourish your soul and contribute to your overall well-being. And who are the people who drain you, who leave you feeling depleted or unfulfilled? These are your black holes—the relationships that, while perhaps not inherently negative, may be taking up valuable space in your limited social capacity.

"Lots of people want to ride with you in the limo, but what you want is someone who will take the bus with you when the limo breaks down." This quote (often attributed to Oprah Winfrey) speaks to the importance of identifying our true friends, the people who are there for us not just during the good times but also during the challenging ones. These are the relationships that deserve our priority, our time, and our energy. These are the relationships that form the core of our resonant "band."

DISCERNING TRUE FRIENDS: QUALITIES OF RESONANT FRIENDSHIP

How do we discern these true friends, the batteries in our lives? While every friendship is unique, there are some common qualities that characterize resonant connections:

Authenticity. True friends allow you to be yourself, without judgment or pretense. They appreciate your unique song and encourage you to express it fully.

Mutual support. They are there for you during both good times and bad, offering encouragement, understanding, and practical assistance when needed. They celebrate your successes and offer a shoulder to lean on during setbacks.

Shared values. While you don't have to agree on everything, true friends share core values and a similar outlook on life. This creates a foundation of mutual respect and understanding.

Growth-oriented feedback. They challenge you to grow, to step outside your comfort zone, and to become the best version of yourself. They are not afraid to offer honest feedback, always with kindness and support.

Reciprocity. While we emphasize giving without expectation, healthy friendships are characterized by a natural flow of reciprocity. Both individuals feel valued, supported, and appreciated.

Joy and laughter. True friends bring joy and laughter into your life. They are the people you can have fun with, be silly with, and simply enjoy being around.

Learning to identify and cultivate these qualities in our friendships is an ongoing process. It requires us to be mindful of our own needs and desires, to be honest with ourselves about which relationships are truly nourishing, and to be willing to invest our time and energy in the connections that matter most.

Resonance Instrument

THE FRIENDSHIP CHECK-IN

Purpose: To assess and strengthen your friendships by bringing conscious attention to their quality and dynamics

Time Required: 20–30 minutes of reflection

Materials: Your Resonance Journal or a dedicated notebook

Practice:

1. **Choose a friendship** (5 minutes). Select a close friendship you'd like to focus on. Take a moment to bring this person clearly to mind, recalling meaningful moments you've shared.
2. **Reflect** (15–20 minutes). In your journal, reflect on the following prompts:
    - What specific qualities make this friendship special?
    - How does this friend add value to your life?
    - How do you add value to theirs?
    - Are there any areas of dissonance or unmet needs in this friendship?
    - How well do you communicate with each other?
    - Do you feel you can be your authentic self with this friend?
    - How often do you express appreciation for this friendship?
    - What patterns or habits have developed in this friendship? Which serve you both, and which might need attention?

3. **Choose an action** (5 minutes). Based on your reflections, identify one specific action you can take to strengthen your connection. This could be scheduling quality time together, expressing appreciation, addressing an unresolved issue, or simply reaching out to reconnect. Write down when and how you'll take this action.
4. **Follow up with reflection.**
   After taking your action step, return to your journal and note how it impacted your friendship.
   - What did you notice about your friend's response?
   - How did it make you feel?
   - What insights did you gain about your friendship?

Variations:

- **Friendship Portfolio Assessment:** Instead of focusing on one friendship, briefly assess three to five of your closest friendships to gain perspective on your overall friendship network.
- **Shared Check-in:** For very close friendships, consider doing a version of this check-in together, where you both share what you value about the friendship and how it might grow.
- **Regular Practice:** Schedule this check-in quarterly for your most important friendships as a form of "relationship maintenance."

Real-World Application

This practice helps you become more intentional about the quality of your friendships rather than letting them develop on autopilot. By regularly assessing your close friendships, you can nurture what's working well, address emerging issues before they become problems, and ensure that these vital relationships receive the care and attention they deserve.

The most valuable friendships often benefit from this kind of conscious attention. Just as a garden needs regular tending to flourish, our friendships benefit from mindful care and occasional pruning.

THE CHANGING SEASONS OF FRIENDSHIP

One of the most challenging aspects of friendship is understanding and accepting its seasonal nature. Just as musicians might play together intensely for a period and then pursue different projects, our friendships naturally ebb and flow throughout our lives. Some friends are with us for a season, some for a reason, and some for a lifetime.

Understanding the natural seasons of friendship can help us navigate these changes with grace and wisdom.

The Spring of Friendship: New Beginnings

In the spring phase, friendships are fresh and filled with discovery. There's excitement about finding common interests, sharing experiences, and getting to know each other. This phase is characterized by:

- High levels of engagement and curiosity
- Frequent communication and interaction
- Mutual discovery and enthusiasm
- The establishing of shared rituals or patterns

Resonant Approach: Embrace the energy of new connection, remain open and authentic, and enjoy the process of discovery without forcing intimacy or making premature judgments.

The Summer of Friendship: Deep Connection

Summer friendships are in full bloom—comfortable, rich, and deeply rewarding. These are the friendships that feel solid and reliable, where both people feel secure and understood. This phase features:

- Deep mutual understanding and acceptance
- A comfortable rhythm of connection
- Shared memories and inside jokes
- Reliable support and presence

Resonant Approach: Invest in these friendships while they're thriving, express appreciation regularly, and create meaningful shared experiences that strengthen your bond.

The Autumn of Friendship: Transition and Change

Autumn represents a time of transition, when external circumstances or internal changes create distance or shifting dynamics. This might occur when:

- One or both friends enter new life phases (marriage, parenthood, career change)
- Geographic distance creates separation
- Interests or values begin to diverge
- Time and attention are claimed by other priorities

Resonant Approach: Acknowledge the changes openly, communicate about shifting needs and expectations, find new ways to connect that honor current realities, and adjust expectations with compassion.

The Winter of Friendship: Dormancy or Completion

Some friendships naturally enter a winter phase—a period of dormancy or, in some cases, completion. This doesn't necessarily indicate failure but may be a natural conclusion to a relationship that has served its purpose. Winter phases include:

- Significantly reduced communication or connection
- Feeling like you've grown apart or no longer have much in common
- Relationships that have become strained or painful
- Friendships that have fulfilled their purpose in your life

Resonant Approach: Discern whether this friendship is in a temporary dormancy (to be rekindled later) or has naturally completed its cycle. Honor what the friendship has meant to you, release guilt about changed circumstances, and if appropriate, allow the relationship to transform or conclude with gratitude.

The Miracle of Perennial Friendships

Some rare and precious friendships transcend the seasonal cycle, recurring or persisting throughout our lives. These "perennial friendships" may go through periods of distance or lesser contact but always return to bloom again. They are characterized by:

- The ability to pick up where you left off, even after long absences
- A sense of timelessness when you reconnect
- Mutual understanding of life's ebbs and flows
- Acceptance of each other's changing circumstances

Resonant Approach: Treasure these rare connections, nurture them without clinging too tightly, and trust in the resilience of your bond even through periods of distance.

Resonance Session

FRIENDSHIP ACROSS DISTANCES

Artist Spotlight: Randy Newman, "You've Got a Friend in Me"
Focal Point: The Enduring Power of Friendship

In 1995, composer Randy Newman created what would become one of the most beloved friendship anthems of modern times. Originally written for the animated film *Toy Story*, "You've Got a Friend in Me" captures the essence of unconditional friendship—the kind that persists through changes, challenges, and the passage of time.

Newman, known for his sophisticated compositions and often satirical lyrics, tapped into something universally recognizable with this song: the powerful certainty that comes from knowing someone has your back, no matter what.

As Newman explained in interviews, he wasn't writing about the idealized, perfect friendship but about the messy, real connections that sustain us—the friends who stand by us "when the road looks rough ahead," who help us remember our worth "when the other folks might be a little bit smarter than I am."

What makes the song particularly poignant is its recognition that friendship isn't about grand gestures but about reliable presence. It's a celebration of the friend who shows up, who offers support without being asked, who sees our value even when we can't see it ourselves.

Newman's composition reminds us that true friendship isn't about physical proximity—it's about emotional presence. Even when circumstances change, even when distance separates us, the essence of profound friendship remains: "You've got a friend in me."

Reflection: Think about a friendship that has endured despite physical distance, changing circumstances, or the passage of time. What qualities have allowed this friendship to persist? How do you maintain connection across distance? What might this teach you about the essence of true friendship?

CREATING YOUR FRIENDSHIP SYMPHONY: BUILDING A DIVERSE PORTFOLIO

Just as an orchestra consists of different sections—strings, woodwinds, brass, and percussion—each contributing unique tones and textures to the overall sound, a rich friendship portfolio includes different types of connections, each serving important functions in our lives. Rather than seeking one or two friends to meet all our needs (an impossible task), we can cultivate a diverse "friendship symphony" that collectively enriches our lives.

The Elements of a Balanced Friendship Portfolio

Anchor Friends: These are your closest confidants, the people who know you most deeply and with whom you share your most vulnerable self. They provide stability, acceptance, and a sense of being truly known. While these relationships require the most investment, they also offer the deepest rewards.

Growth Friends: These friends challenge you to evolve, try new things, and step outside your comfort zone. They might introduce you to new ideas, activities, or perspectives. They serve as catalysts for personal development and expansion.

Joy Friends: These connections center around play, humor, and lightheartedness. They remind you not to take life too seriously and create space for fun and recreation. These friendships might be less emotionally intense but provide essential balance and rejuvenation.

Purpose Friends: These relationships form around shared goals, causes, or interests. They might be colleagues working on meaningful projects, fellow volunteers, or people with whom you share a passion or mission. They connect you to something larger than yourself.

Wisdom Friends: These might be mentors, older friends, or simply wise souls who offer perspective, guidance, and the benefit of their experience. They help you see the bigger picture and navigate life's complexities with greater wisdom.

History Friends: These are the people who have known you through different phases of life and hold pieces of your story. They provide continuity and a sense of your evolving identity over time, even if they're not actively in your day-to-day life.

Developing awareness of your current friendship portfolio allows you to identify areas of richness and potential gaps. Are you surrounded by joy friends but lacking wisdom friends? Do you have purpose friends but few anchor friends with whom you can be vulnerable? This awareness can guide your intentions as you cultivate new connections and deepen existing ones.

CULTIVATING NEW FRIENDSHIPS IN ADULTHOOD

While many of us found it relatively easy to make friends during childhood and early adulthood, forming new meaningful connections can become more challenging as we age. Structured environments like school and college naturally facilitate friendship formation, but as adults, we often need to be more intentional. Here are strategies for cultivating new friendships:

Lead with curiosity. Approach potential friendships with genuine interest in the other person. Ask thoughtful questions and listen deeply to their responses. Curiosity signals that you value the other person and opens the door to meaningful connection.

Follow up consistently. When you meet someone you connect with, take the initiative to suggest a follow-up interaction. Be specific: "I'd love to continue our conversation about photography. Would you like to grab coffee next Tuesday?" Consistency in follow-up demonstrates that you value the potential friendship.

Create regular touchpoints. Look for ways to establish regular contact, whether through shared activities, scheduled meetups, or recurring events. Consistent interaction provides the foundation for deepening connection over time.

Share incrementally. Friendship develops through gradual, reciprocal self-disclosure. Share aspects of yourself authentically, but build intimacy progressively rather than overwhelming new friends with immediate intensity.

Embrace vulnerability. At appropriate moments, be willing to share challenges, doubts, or struggles. Vulnerability, when met with empathy, creates powerful bonds. Start with smaller disclosures and deepen as trust develops.

Connect others. Become someone who thoughtfully connects people. Hosting gatherings or introducing compatible friends to each other creates a web of connection that enriches everyone involved.

Be patient. Meaningful friendships take time to develop. Unlike romantic relationships, which often have a clear trajectory, friendships often grow gradually through accumulated shared experiences. Trust the process and don't rush intimacy.

Resonance Instrument

THE FRIENDSHIP CULTIVATION PRACTICE

Purpose: To intentionally nurture both new and established friendships through regular, meaningful contact

Time Required: Varies; approximately 30–60 minutes per week

Materials: Calendar or scheduling system, communication tools

Practice:

1. **Friendship Triage** (one-time setup, 30 minutes):
   Create three lists: "Active Nurture" (5–8 close friends you want to actively maintain connection with), "Periodic Check-In" (10–15 friends you want to stay connected to less frequently), and "Rekindling Candidates" (2–3 friendships you'd like to revitalize). For each person, note one thing you particularly value about them and one way they prefer to connect.
2. **Schedule Regular Connections** (10 minutes weekly):
   Set aside regular time in your schedule specifically for friendship cultivation. Each week, select one friend from your "Active Nurture" list for meaningful connection. Every 2–4 weeks, reach out to someone from your "Periodic Check-In" list. Every 1–2 months, extend an invitation to someone from your "Rekindling Candidates" list.

3. **Meaningful Outreach** (10–30 minutes per connection): Choose connection methods that match the friendship's nature and the person's preferences:
   - Voice/video calls that allow for real conversation
   - Personalized messages that show you're thinking of them specifically
   - Sharing content (articles, music, etc.) tailored to their interests
   - In-person meetings for coffee, walks, or activities you both enjoy
   - Group gatherings that bring compatible friends together
4. **Quality over Quantity** (ongoing):
   - Focus on the quality of interaction rather than frequency.
   - Be fully present during connections rather than multitasking.
   - Ask thoughtful questions that invite meaningful sharing.
   - Follow up on previous conversations to show you remember what matters to them.
   - Express specific appreciation for aspects of them you value.
5. **Seasonal Review** (quarterly, 30 minutes):
   - Reflect on the state of your friendships: Which are thriving? Which need attention?
   - Update your three lists based on changing circumstances and relationships.
   - Note any patterns in your friendship cultivation that you'd like to adjust.

Variations:

- **Friendship Focus Months:** Dedicate certain months to intensified focus on friendship (similar to what people do with fitness or creative challenges).
- **Theme-Based Connection:** Center connections around shared interests or activities (book clubs, hiking groups, cooking exchanges).
- **Celebration-Oriented Practice:** Use celebrations (birthdays, achievements, holidays) as anchors for meaningful connection.

Real-World Application:

This practice transforms friendship cultivation from a haphazard process to an intentional practice. By creating systematic touchpoints while maintaining authentic connection, you ensure that the important relationships in your life receive the care they deserve. The practice acknowledges both the importance of deep, individual connections and the reality of limited time and energy.

The most resonant friendships typically combine consistent attention with genuine presence. This practice helps you provide both, creating a sustainable approach to nurturing meaningful connections throughout your life.

THE CONSTRUCTIVE POWER OF FRIENDSHIP DISSONANCE

While harmony in friendship is valuable, moments of dissonance—disagreement, conflict, or tension—often hold the greatest potential for growth and deepened connection. When navigated with wisdom and care, these challenging moments can become catalysts for greater understanding, respect, and intimacy.

The Value of Constructive Friction

Think of two musical instruments playing slightly different interpretations of the same melody. The initial dissonance might sound jarring, but as the musicians listen to each other and adjust, they often discover new, more interesting expressions that neither would have found alone. Similarly, when friends with different perspectives engage in respectful dialogue, they often reach deeper understanding and more creative solutions than either would achieve independently.

Constructive dissonance in friendship offers several important benefits:

Growth through different perspectives. Friends with different viewpoints can help us see beyond our own limitations and biases. They expand our thinking and challenge us to consider new possibilities.

Development of conflict resolution skills. Learning to navigate disagreements respectfully with friends builds skills that serve us in all relationships. We develop patience, empathy, and the ability to separate people from their positions.

Deeper understanding and intimacy. When we work through conflict successfully, we often develop deeper understanding of each other and greater appreciation for the complexity of the relationship. Navigating difficulties together can strengthen bonds.

Reality testing. Friends who care enough to disagree with us when necessary provide valuable reality testing. They help us avoid the echo chambers that can lead to poor decisions or one-dimensional thinking.

Navigating Friendship Dissonance Skillfully

When dissonance arises in friendship, these approaches can help transform it from a threat to an opportunity:

Lead with curiosity, not judgment. When a friend expresses a view that differs from yours, approach it with genuine curiosity rather than immediate judgment. Ask questions that help you understand their perspective more fully.

Seek understanding before agreement. The goal in navigating differences isn't necessarily to agree but to understand each other's viewpoints. Sometimes, deepened understanding alone resolves tension; other times, it allows you to "disagree better."

Use "I" statements rather than accusations. Express your own feelings and needs rather than attributing motives or flaws to your friend. "I felt hurt when you canceled our plans" opens conversation more effectively than "You're so unreliable."

Maintain perspective. Ask yourself, "Will this matter in five years?" Many disagreements that seem momentous in the present become insignificant in the longer view of a valued friendship.

Focus on shared values and goals. Even in disagreement, remind yourselves of the values and goals you share. This creates common ground from which to navigate differences.

Know when to pause. Sometimes, the wisest response to escalating tension is a thoughtful pause. Taking space to process emotions before continuing the conversation often leads to more productive outcomes.

Repair actively. After difficult interactions, take initiative in repair. Acknowledge any hurt you may have caused, express appreciation for the relationship, and recommit to understanding each other better.

When to Hold, When to Fold

While constructive dissonance can strengthen friendships, not all dissonance is constructive. Some patterns of interaction are consistently damaging rather than producing growth. Learning to discern the difference requires wisdom and self-awareness.

Consider these questions when evaluating challenging friendship dynamics:

Does this relationship consistently leave me feeling valued, even amid disagreements?

Is there a pattern of mutual respect, even when we differ?

Do we both take responsibility for our contributions to problems?

Is there a genuine commitment to understanding each other?

Does this person respect my boundaries?

Do I feel safe expressing my authentic thoughts and feelings?

If you consistently answer no to these questions, the dissonance may be destructive rather than constructive. In such cases, it may be appropriate to establish firmer boundaries or, in some cases, to allow the friendship to transition to a different phase.

LOOKING AHEAD: FROM PERSONAL TO PROFESSIONAL RESONANCE

As we conclude our exploration of friendship, we've discovered how these chosen connections enrich our lives, challenge us to grow, and provide essential support throughout life's journey. We've explored how the principle of adding value without expectation creates the foundation for meaningful, resonant friendships; and we've examined practices for cultivating, maintaining, and sometimes releasing these vital bonds.

In the chapters ahead, we'll expand our focus from personal relationships to professional ones, exploring how the principles of resonance can transform our work lives, our creative collaborations, and our impact in the world. We'll discover how the skills we've developed in creating resonance in our personal relationships—deep listening, authentic expression, intentional connection, and adding unique value—translate powerfully into professional contexts.

Just as a musician might move from intimate chamber performances to playing in a full orchestra, we'll explore how to maintain our authentic voice while harmonizing with a wider range of people and systems. The journey of resonance continues to unfold, offering ever-expanding opportunities for connection, contribution, and meaning.

POWER PLAYLIST

THE SACRED CIRCLE OF FRIENDS

- **"You've Got a Friend" by Carole King.** Listen for: Friendship as sacred promise—the unwavering commitment that transcends distance and time.

- **"Stand By Me" by Ben E. King.** Listen for: How companionship becomes courage—notice how friendship transforms fear into strength.
- **"Count on Me" by Bruno Mars.** Listen for: The simple joy of mutual dependability as reliable presence becomes life's greatest gift.

Listening Practice: This week, reach out to a friend you haven't spoken to recently. Before calling or texting, listen to one of these songs and let it remind you why this person matters to you. After your conversation, reflect in your Resonance Journal: What makes this friendship sustaining? How do I show up as the kind of friend these songs celebrate?

Creating Your Personal Additions: Add songs that remind you of specific friends—perhaps a song you sang together, heard at a meaningful moment, or that simply captures their spirit. Consider sending one of these songs to a friend with a note about why they matter to you.

Friendship teaches us that family is not just what we're born into, but what we consciously create through loyalty, laughter, and love. These songs remind us that the friends who truly see us become the mirrors in which we discover our best selves.

CREATING A FRIENDSHIP SYMPHONY

We began this chapter by exploring how friendships, like all relationships, are enhanced by the principle of adding value without expectation. We've examined the science behind friendship's importance, the distinction between quality and quantity in our social connections, and the practices that help us cultivate and maintain meaningful bonds. We've also acknowledged the seasonal nature of friendships and the constructive potential of dissonance when navigated skillfully.

As you reflect on your own friendship symphony, consider these questions:

1. Who are the true batteries in your life—the friends who consistently energize and support your authentic self?
2. How might you become a more intentional battery for the people in your life, adding value without expectation?
3. What patterns or habits have developed in your friendships? Which serve you well, and which might benefit from conscious adjustment?
4. How balanced is your friendship portfolio? Are there types of friends or qualities of friendship that are currently missing?
5. How comfortable are you with navigating friendship dissonance? Are there skills you'd like to develop to transform conflict into opportunity?

Remember that creating resonant friendships, like all aspects of resonance, is not a destination but an ongoing practice. Each day offers new opportunities to listen more deeply, to show up more fully, to add value more generously, and to receive the gift of connection with greater appreciation.

In the next chapter, we'll expand our focus to the world of professional relationships, exploring how the principles of resonance can transform our work lives and enhance our impact in the broader world. We'll discover how the skills we've developed in creating resonant personal relationships translate powerfully into professional contexts, creating opportunities for meaningful collaboration and contribution.

Friendship is a priceless gift that cannot be bought nor sold,
but its value is far greater than a mountain made of gold.

MUHAMMAD ALI

PART 4

Building Your Band

The most profound revolutions begin with a single resonant note, are amplified through authentic connection, and culminate in the symphony of collective creation.

In part 1, you discovered how genuine connection forms the antidote to our modern epidemic of isolation.

In part 2, you developed your authentic voice—that unique note only you can contribute to the world.

Part 3 guided you to apply these principles to your most intimate circles.

Now, standing on this foundation of personal resonance, you face your next frontier: extending these principles into the professional realm—the arena where most adults spend the majority of their waking hours yet often experience the greatest disconnection.

This section marks your evolution from musician to conductor, from soloist to bandleader, from individual practitioner to architect of collaborative environments. You'll discover how the seven pillars of resonance—generosity, deep listening, integrity, adding value, finding uncommon common ground, creating connection opportunities, and standing for something bigger—transform business from transactional to transcendent.

In chapter 11, you'll learn how entrepreneurship becomes not just a vehicle for personal achievement but a powerful instrument for creating resonant communities.

Chapter 12 will reveal how workplace dynamics transform when approached through the lens of resonance.

Throughout history, the most enduring impacts rarely emerged from solo genius but from harmonious collaboration. Darwin had his correspondence network, spreading across continents. Marie Curie partnered with Pierre to discover radioactivity. Martin Luther King Jr. orchestrated a movement of thousands. Even Mozart, often portrayed as the quintessential solo genius, collaborated intimately with librettists, patrons, and performers.

In your hands now lies the conductor's baton—the power to orchestrate connections that create something far greater than you could achieve alone.

Are you ready to build your band and compose the symphony that will echo beyond your lifetime?

CHAPTER 11

The Entrepreneur's Edge: Resonance in the World of Business

The currency of real networking is not greed but generosity.

KEITH FERRAZZI

What if the most successful entrepreneurs weren't just skilled at building businesses but at building resonant relationships? What if their edge wasn't just their product or their strategy but their ability to create a magnetic field of connection, attracting the right people—investors, partners, clients, and team members—who shared their vision and amplified their impact?

This is the power of resonance in the world of business. Entrepreneurship, at its core, is not a solitary pursuit but a collaborative symphony. The most innovative and impactful ventures are born out of The More—that exponential potential that emerges when authentic connections are aligned with a shared purpose. It is about building a business that is also a movement.

In this chapter, we're going to apply the principles of resonance to the specific challenges and opportunities of building and growing a business. Your venture, like a band, needs a unique sound, a clear vision, and a group of talented individuals who can work together harmoniously. It's about moving beyond transactional networking to cultivate genuine connections with those who resonate with your values and your vision for The More.

The most powerful tool you have is not your business plan but your ability to create resonance—to attract the people who will help you make your vision a reality. The profound truth is that businesses don't just succeed based on what they do but on who they attract to do it with them. It is resonance that will bring the right people to your door.

The principles of resonance offer a powerful framework for entrepreneurs seeking to build not just successful businesses but also meaningful and impactful ones. By prioritizing authentic connection, fostering a culture of generosity, and aligning with a purpose that extends beyond profit, entrepreneurs can create a magnetic field that attracts the right people and unlocks exponential potential. This is where the art and science of resonance converge to create a unique entrepreneurial edge.

This is not simply a nice idea—it is a strategy that works, and one increasingly supported by research. The traditional model of the hard-nosed, lone-wolf entrepreneur is being challenged by a new paradigm, one that recognizes the power of collaboration, empathy, and authentic connection in driving entrepreneurial success.

MUSICAL METAPHORS FOR THE ENTREPRENEURIAL JOURNEY

Collaboration: A business, like a band, needs a rhythm, a harmony, a shared purpose to create something truly extraordinary.

Finding Your Audience: An entrepreneur is like a musician searching for their audience—you need to find the people who resonate with your "song," your unique offering.

Playing in Tune: In business, as in music, success comes not just from playing your own instrument well but from playing in tune with others.

THE SCIENCE OF CONNECTION IN BUSINESS

Studies have consistently shown that entrepreneurs with diverse networks are more likely to succeed. Sociologist Martin Ruef found that entrepreneurs with networks composed of varied, nonredundant contacts were three times more likely to innovate than those with homogenous networks. These diverse connections are the ones most likely to spark new ideas, challenge your assumptions, and help you see your venture in a new light.

Research on trust in business relationships underscores the importance of authenticity and integrity in attracting investors, partners, and clients. When entrepreneurs act with integrity and build trust with their stakeholders, they create a foundation for long-term success. Investors and partners are more likely to support ventures led by individuals they perceive as genuine, trustworthy, and aligned with their values.

Leaders who are perceived as authentic are more likely to inspire trust, foster commitment, and create a positive work environment. By being true to themselves, entrepreneurs can attract team members, partners, and customers who resonate with their authentic message, creating a powerful brand identity that sets them apart.

Finally, research on purpose-driven organizations demonstrates that companies with a clear and compelling mission, one that extends beyond profit, tend to outperform their competitors. A shared purpose creates a strong sense of meaning and motivation, attracting and retaining top talent, fostering innovation, and building a loyal customer base.

These findings underscore a fundamental truth about entrepreneurship in the twenty-first century: It's no longer enough to have a great product or a clever strategy. Success today requires a new kind of leadership, a leadership based on resonance, authenticity, and a commitment to creating The More—building businesses that are not just profitable but also purposeful, businesses that attract the right people because of the values they embody and the impact they seek to make.

It's time to discover how you can apply the principles of resonance to transform your business from a transaction into a movement, from a product into a purpose, and from a company into a community.

BE EXPONENTIAL: MULTIPLYING YOUR IMPACT THROUGH RESONANT CONNECTION

Creating resonance in the world of business is not just about one-on-one interactions. It requires understanding the power of exponential connection, the power of becoming a node through which others connect and flourish. It's about recognizing that your network is not just a collection of individuals but a living, breathing ecosystem with the potential to create The More—that amplified impact that extends far beyond your own efforts.

This is where we can truly embody Pillar #6: Create Exponential Opportunities for Connection.

Think of it this way: A traditional, linear approach to networking might involve having coffee with one person at a time. While this can be valuable, it's inherently limited by the number of hours in a day. But what if, instead of one-on-one coffee meetings, you hosted a hike for five people? Or a small dinner party for eight? Suddenly, you're not just building individual relationships, you're creating a space for multiple connections to occur simultaneously. You're becoming a catalyst for resonance, not just within your own life but within the lives of others. This is the essence of being exponential—leveraging your time and energy to create a far greater impact.

This principle has been central to my own journey, from building Global Citizen to hosting His Holiness the Dalai Lama. In both cases, the impact was amplified exponentially by creating experiences that brought people together around shared values and a common purpose. This wasn't a matter of collecting contacts; it was about curating connections, fostering a sense of community, and igniting a spark that could spread far beyond the initial gathering. It is also how I have built multiple communities and continue to foster them to this day.

Being exponential in your approach to connection offers numerous benefits:

- **Efficiency.** You can connect with more people in less time.
- **Synergy.** Group settings often lead to more dynamic and creative interactions than one-on-one meetings.
- **Amplified impact.** By connecting others, you create a ripple effect, extending your reach and influence far beyond your immediate circle.
- **Stronger bonds.** Shared experiences, especially those that are unique or memorable, create stronger bonds between people.
- **Reciprocity.** When you become known as a connector, a facilitator of resonant experiences, people will naturally start to reciprocate, inviting you to their events and introducing you to their networks. This is the subtle power of the law of reciprocity in action. You become a magnet for opportunity, simply by creating opportunities for others.

How to Be Exponential

- **Host events.** Don't just attend networking events; host your own. This could be anything from a small dinner party to a larger gathering focused on a specific topic or interest. The key is to create an experience that is both enjoyable and meaningful, something that people will remember and talk about.
- **Curate your guest list.** Be intentional about whom you invite. Think about people who might benefit from knowing each other, who share similar values, or who have complementary skills and interests.
- **Create a resonant atmosphere.** Set the stage for authentic connection by creating a welcoming and inclusive atmosphere. Think about the music, the lighting, the food, and the overall vibe of the event. You want to create a space where people feel comfortable being themselves and engaging in meaningful conversations.
- **Facilitate connections.** Don't just throw people together and hope for

the best. Actively facilitate connections by introducing people to each other, suggesting topics of conversation, and creating opportunities for interaction.

- **Follow up.** After the event, follow up with your guests. Thank them for coming, and, if appropriate, suggest further ways to connect or collaborate.

WOLF CONNECTION: THE POWER OF UNCONVENTIONAL EXPERIENCES

One experience that profoundly shaped my understanding of resonance in a professional context began with a simple, yet unconventional, invitation. It wasn't an invitation to another industry conference or networking event but to a place called the Wolf Connection, a sanctuary for rescued wolves and wolf dogs nestled in the mountains north of Los Angeles.

Intrigued, I accepted, not knowing that this simple act would lead to a profound shift in my professional life. On the day of the event, I found myself hiking under the moonlight with a pack of wolves, their howls echoing through the canyons. I was surrounded by a diverse group of people—entrepreneurs, artists, executives—all drawn together by this unique experience.

Later, gathered around a crackling campfire under a canopy of stars, I found myself engaged in deep conversations with people I might never have met in my usual professional circles. I learned about their passions, their challenges, and their dreams. I shared my own. Connections were forged, not through the exchange of business cards but through the shared experience of something extraordinary.

One of those connections was with a legendary music producer, a man known for his innovative approach to music and his keen eye for talent. We talked for hours that night, not about business but about life, about creativity, about the importance of connection. A seed of an idea was planted.

That music producer was Moby. The invitation to the Wolf Connection, extended to a diverse group of influential individuals, wasn't a calculated networking tactic but an offering, a chance to share a unique and meaningful experience. This encounter, sparked by a willingness to connect in an unconventional setting, ultimately led to valuable collaborations and a lasting friendship. It was a testament to the power of resonance in the professional realm, demonstrating that authentic connection can open doors to opportunities that would otherwise remain closed. It also became a defining element of my work, as I later went on to interview hundreds of the world's most successful individuals, including many I had shared that experience with.

This incident, and many others throughout my career, have taught me that one of the most powerful Resonance Instruments at our disposal is the ability to create unique and shareable experiences. These occasions, like the one at the Wolf Connection, act as catalysts for connection, drawing people together around shared values and creating a space for authentic interactions to unfold. They are the antithesis of traditional networking events, where the focus is often on self-promotion and transactional exchanges. Instead, they are about offering something of value—an experience that is memorable, meaningful, and perhaps even transformative.

Being exponential is not just about maximizing your impact; it's about creating a more connected and resonant world. It's about recognizing that we are all part of a larger ecosystem, and that by fostering connections between others, we contribute to the overall harmony of the whole. It is about creating the conditions for The More to emerge, not just in our own lives but in the lives of everyone we touch. It is about recognizing that true leadership lies not in hoarding connections but in sharing them, in becoming a conduit for resonance to flow freely and powerfully. This very principle is embodied in a song that emerged from a unique collaboration, fusing together different voices for a common cause.

Resonance Instrument

THE RESONANT NETWORKING EXERCISE

This instrument helps you apply the principles of resonant networking to your professional life, transforming transactional interactions into authentic connections. It's about building a network based on shared values, mutual support, and a genuine desire to contribute to each other's success. The practice draws inspiration from Keith Ferrazzi's "Relationship Action Plan" but reframes it through the lens of resonance.

How to Play It:

1. **Identify key connections.** In your Resonance Journal, make a list of five to ten people in your professional network (or people you'd like to connect with) who align with your values and resonate with your vision for The More. These could be potential investors, partners, mentors, collaborators, or clients.
2. **Assess the relationship.** For each person, briefly assess the current state of the relationship. How well do you know them? What is the level of trust and rapport?
3. **Define your intention.** For each person, define your intention for the relationship. How can you add value to their lives or careers? How can you support their goals? Think beyond what you can get from them and focus on what you can offer.
4. **Create a plan.** Develop a simple plan for connecting with each person over the next three to six months. This could involve scheduling a coffee meeting, sending them a relevant article, offering to make an introduction, or simply checking in with a personalized email. Consider applying Ferrazzi's "pinging" concept—staying in touch regularly with brief, meaningful interactions.
5. **Focus on giving.** Approach each interaction with a genuine desire to give, to be an offering, without expecting anything in return.
6. **Track your progress.** Use your Resonance Journal to track your progress and reflect on the impact of your efforts. Note any responses you receive, any new opportunities that arise, and any insights you gain about the power of resonant networking.

Tuning Tips:

Be authentic. Focus on building genuine relationships, not just collecting contacts, and let your true self shine through in your interactions.

Be patient and don't expect immediate results. Building resonant relationships takes time and effort. Make networking a regular practice, not just something you do when you need something.

Be generous and look for opportunities to help others, make introductions, and share your knowledge and resources.

And **take opportunities to go beyond email.** While email can be a useful tool, explore other ways to connect, such as handwritten notes, thoughtful gifts, or attending events where you can meet people in person. Offer to take someone to lunch or coffee, embodying the spirit of "never eat alone."

These techniques, while powerful, are simply tools. The real magic happens when we approach networking with the intention of creating resonance, of building relationships based on shared values and a genuine desire to contribute to each other's success. This is how we unlock The More in the entrepreneurial world.

THE MORE IN ENTREPRENEURSHIP

For entrepreneurs, The More is not just a goal of achieving financial success; it's an accomplishment of creating something of lasting value, something that makes a positive impact on the world. It's about building a business that is aligned with your purpose, that reflects your authentic self, and that attracts a team of collaborators who share your vision.

When you build your venture on a foundation of resonant relationships, you create the potential for exponential growth, amplified impact, and a deeper sense of fulfillment. You attract people who are not just looking for a job or an investment opportunity but who are drawn to your vision and want to be part of something bigger than themselves. This is how you build a business that is not just successful but truly meaningful.

Resonance Session

ARTIST SPOTLIGHT: U2

It was 1976, in Dublin, Ireland. A fourteen-year-old drummer posted a notice on his high school bulletin board. It wasn't an advertisement for a typical rock band. He wasn't looking for the most technically proficient musicians, the flashiest guitarists, or the singers with the widest vocal range. He was looking for something else, something more intangible. He was looking for connection.

He envisioned a band built on shared values, on a collective vision that transcended individual ego. He wanted bandmates who were committed to something bigger than themselves, who saw music not just as a means to personal fame but as a way to connect with others, to express themselves authentically, and to make a difference in the world.

The response to the notice was modest, but the musicians who showed up for that first meeting in the drummer's kitchen were a diverse bunch. There was a guitarist who was more interested in textures and soundscapes than in flashy solos. There was a bassist who was solid and reliable, providing a steady foundation for the music. And there was a singer, a charismatic front man with a powerful voice and a penchant for writing lyrics that were both poetic and politically charged.

They weren't the most technically skilled musicians in Dublin. Far from it. But they had something more important: a shared passion, a common purpose, and a deep connection that resonated from the very first note they played together.

They chose a name that reflected their ambition and their commitment to unity: U2. And over the next four decades, they would go on to become one of the biggest bands in the world, selling millions of albums, filling stadiums across the globe, and using their platform to advocate for social justice and human rights.

Reflection: One of U2's most iconic songs, "With or Without You," captures the complexities of relationships, the tension between individual needs and collective commitment. But it also speaks to the enduring power of connection, the yearning for something deeper than fleeting fame or fortune. As you listen, consider the "band" you're building in your own entrepreneurial journey. Are you prioritizing technical skill over shared values? Are you seeking connections that are merely transactional, or are you striving to create a resonant ensemble, a group of individuals united by a common purpose and a commitment to creating something truly extraordinary?

THE ART OF THE PITCH

Just as a musician uses their voice and instrument to convey emotion and connect with an audience, entrepreneurs can use the principles of resonance to craft a compelling pitch. Consider it an opportunity to not just present data and projections but to tell a story, share your passion, and create an emotional connection with potential investors and partners. Think of your pitch as a performance, a chance to share your unique song with the world. How can you make it resonate?

Building a resonant network is not a quick fix or a shortcut to success. It's an ongoing process of cultivating authentic connections, nurturing relationships, and aligning your professional life with your values and your vision for The More. But the rewards are immeasurable. By embracing the principles of resonance, entrepreneurs can create businesses that are not only profitable but also deeply fulfilling, businesses that attract the right people, that foster innovation, and that make a positive impact on the world. In the next chapter, we'll delve deeper into the power of shared purpose, exploring how to align your relationships with a larger vision and create a symphony of impact that reaches far beyond your individual efforts. It's about recognizing that even the most ambitious dreams are achievable when we find our band—the people who share our passion and are committed to creating something extraordinary together.

FROM THE CONCERT TO THE SYMPHONY: UNLOCKING EXPONENTIAL CREATIVITY

The principles of resonance apply to any endeavor where human beings come together to create something new, something meaningful, something that transcends their individual capabilities. Just as a skilled band can create music that is far greater than the sum of its individual members, we can, in any area of life, unlock exponential creativity and achieve extraordinary results when we learn to collaborate in a truly resonant way.

The Beatles, arguably the most influential band in music history, provide a powerful case in point. John Lennon was a brilliant songwriter, a visionary artist with a rebellious spirit and a gift for crafting lyrics that were both poetic and provocative. Paul McCartney was a master melodist, a craftsman with an innate sense of harmony and a knack for writing songs that were both catchy and enduring. George Harrison, often referred to as the "quiet Beatle," brought a spiritual depth and a unique musical sensibility to the group, while Ringo Starr's solid drumming provided the rhythmic backbone that held it all together.

Each of these musicians was exceptionally talented in his own right. But it was when they came together, when they learned to blend their individual voices and musical styles, that something truly magical happened. They created a sound that was greater than anything they could have achieved on their own, a sound that resonated with millions around the world and continues to inspire and influence musicians today. The Beatles were transcendent not in spite of their differences but because of them. They were not just four individuals playing music together; they were a band, a unified entity where each member's unique talents were amplified and harmonized to create something extraordinary. They found a way to turn their creative differences, their individual "songs," into a symphony of sound that changed the course of music history.

What can we learn from the Beatles about the power of resonant collaboration? How can we apply these same principles to our own lives, to our own creative endeavors, to our own dream projects?

RESONANT NETWORKING: BEYOND THE BUSINESS CARD

Research underscores the profound impact that resonance can have in the professional sphere. It's a reminder that even in the most results-driven environments, human connection remains paramount. A workplace, like an orchestra, is made up of individuals, each with their own unique talents, needs, and aspirations. With resonance, we strive to create a culture where those individuals can thrive, both individually and collectively. But how do we move beyond the transactional nature of traditional networking to create these kinds of resonant professional relationships?

While the traditional model of networking often focuses on transactional exchanges and collecting business cards, resonant networking is about building authentic relationships based on shared values and mutual benefit. It's an intent to move beyond superficial interactions to create genuine connections that can lead to both professional success and personal fulfillment. Resonant networking recognizes that our professional lives, like a well-orchestrated concert, require collaboration, coordination, and a shared sense of purpose.

One of the most influential voices in the field of relationship building is Keith Ferrazzi, author of the bestselling book *Never Eat Alone*. Ferrazzi argues that the key to success lies in building a strong network of relationships, not through calculated manipulation but through genuine generosity and a proactive approach to connecting with others.

Ferrazzi's philosophy aligns remarkably well with the principles of resonance we've been exploring. His core principle, "Never eat alone," is essentially an invitation to be more intentional about creating opportunities for connection in our daily lives. He encourages us to use mealtimes, social gatherings, and even chance encounters as opportunities to build relationships, to learn from others, and to offer our own support and expertise.

But how do we connect with those who inspire us, those who may seem out of reach? Here is a technique, inspired by the work of author and entrepreneur Tim Ferriss, that can help you break through the noise and make a genuine connection.

Resonance Instrument

THE FIVE-MINUTE CONNECTION

This instrument helps you reach out to influential people in your field, even those who seem out of reach. It empowers you to craft a concise, compelling, and respectful message that demonstrates your genuine interest in another's work and offers value whenever possible. Think of it as composing a brief but powerful overture, an invitation to a potential mentorship or collaboration.

How to Play It

1. **Identify your subject.** Choose one person you admire and would like to connect with. This could be someone in your industry, a potential mentor, or someone whose work has inspired you.
2. **Do your research.** Thoroughly research the person's work, background, and interests. Read their books, articles, or blog posts. Listen to their interviews. Identify specific areas where your interests and their expertise overlap.
3. **Craft your message.** Write a concise and personalized email.

- **Subject Line:** Short and to the point. Mention a specific topic related to their work or, if applicable, a mutual connection.
- **Greeting:** Address the person by name.
- **Introduction:** Briefly introduce yourself and your connection to their work.
- **Specific Compliment/Question:** Mention something specific you admire about their work or ask a focused question related to their area of expertise.
- **Value Proposition (optional):** If possible, offer something of value—a relevant resource, an introduction, or a genuine offer to help.
- **Clear Ask:** Clearly and concisely state your request (if any). Keep it simple and easy to fulfill.
- **Respect Their Time:** Acknowledge that they are busy and express your gratitude for their time and consideration.
- **Closing:** End with a professional closing and your contact information.

4. **Send and track.** Send the email and keep a record of your outreach in your Resonance Journal. Note the date you sent it and any response you receive.

Five-Minute Connection Email Template

Subject: [Their Name]—Question about [Specific Topic]

Dear [Name],

My name is [Your Name] and I'm [brief, relevant description of yourself—e.g., a writer working on a book about resonant relationships]. I've been following your work on [their specific area of expertise] for some time now, and I particularly enjoyed [mention a specific article, book, or project]. [Optional: Briefly mention a mutual connection, if applicable.]

I'm reaching out because I have a question about [specific topic related to their work]. [Clearly and concisely state your question or request. Be as specific as possible. For example, instead of asking "Can I pick your brain about publishing?" you might ask: "I'm struggling to craft a compelling book proposal. Based on your experience with {their book}, do you have any advice on how to best position a book for success in the current market?"].

[Optional: Briefly offer something of value. For example, "I recently came across this article on {related topic} that I thought you might find interesting. I've also shared your work with my network, as I believe it could be very helpful to them."]

I know you're busy, so I've kept this brief. I completely understand if you're unable to respond, but any insights would mean the world to me.

Thank you for your time and consideration.

Best regards,

[Your Name]
[Your Website/Social Media Link (optional)]

Tuning Tips:

Generic emails are less likely to be effective, so tailor each email to the specific person you're reaching out to. Be genuine and let your true admiration for their work shine through. Approach this as an opportunity to build a relationship, not just to get something from the person, focusing on the connection rather than the transaction. If you don't hear back within a week or two, you can send a polite follow-up email. But don't be pushy or persistent. Always lead with value. Use your Resonance Journal to track your outreach efforts and note any responses you receive. This will help you refine your approach over time.

Community Building
Recruit some friend to try this exercise along with you. Share your experiences, offering feedback on email drafts and providing support and encouragement. You can also brainstorm potential people to reach out to and share connections within their networks.

BEYOND THE INBOX: CREATIVE WAYS TO CONNECT

While email can be an effective way to reach out, it's important to recognize that inboxes are often overflowing, and it can be challenging for your message to stand out from the crowd. Fortunately, there are other, often more impactful, ways to connect with people who inspire you. The key is to be creative, authentic, and to always lead with generosity. Consider these options:

- **The power of snail mail.** In an age of digital communication, a handwritten note or a small, thoughtful gift can have a surprising impact. It demonstrates that you've taken the time and effort to create something personal and tangible. Consider sending a thank-you note to someone whose work has influenced you or sending a copy of your favorite book with a personalized inscription. The key is to be genuine and to choose something that you believe the recipient will truly appreciate.
- **The art of the video message.** A short, personalized video message can be a powerful way to connect with someone on a more human level. It allows you to convey your enthusiasm and personality in a way that's difficult to achieve through text alone. Platforms like Loom or Bonjoro

make it easy to create and send personalized video messages. Keep it brief, authentic, and focused on the recipient.

- **Social media engagement.** Engage with people you admire on social media, but do so in a meaningful way. Don't just like their posts; leave thoughtful comments, ask questions, and share their work with your own network. Be genuine, be respectful, and focus on building a relationship over time.
- **The gift of an introduction.** One of the most valuable things you can offer someone is an introduction to someone else in your network who could be a valuable connection for them. This demonstrates that you understand their work and are invested in their success.
- **Create a unique experience.** This is where you can truly let your creativity shine. Think about what unique experiences you can offer that might resonate with the people you want to connect with. This could be anything from inviting them to a small, curated dinner party to organizing a private tour of a local museum or gallery. The key is to create an experience that is both memorable and meaningful, something that goes beyond the typical networking event. This is a tactic that I embraced. The story I shared of my experience at the Wolf Connection is a prime example of how creating a unique and shareable experience can lead to unexpected and resonant professional connections. It wasn't about networking in the traditional sense; it was about offering something of value—a chance to connect with nature, with animals, and with other like-minded individuals—and letting the connections unfold organically.

FINDING THE SIGNAL IN A NOISY WORLD

The digital age has given us unprecedented access to information and connections. A few clicks, and we can reach out to almost anyone, anywhere in the world. Yet this very accessibility has created a new challenge: the overwhelming noise of constant communication. Our inboxes overflow, our social media feeds are saturated, and our attention is constantly being pulled in a thousand different directions.

How, in this environment, do we cut through the clutter and build genuine, resonant connections? How do we find the signal amid the noise?

The answer, often, lies in going where others aren't. It's about moving beyond the crowded, predictable spaces of online networking and seeking out opportunities for authentic interaction in less conventional places. It's about recognizing that resonance is not just about finding people who share your interests; it's about finding people who share your values, your energy, and your willingness to connect on a deeper level.

While email and LinkedIn have their places, relying solely on these platforms can limit your ability to create truly resonant connections. Here's why:

- **Impersonality.** Digital communication, by its very nature, can feel impersonal and transactional.
- **Competition.** Everyone is vying for attention online. Your message is likely competing with hundreds of others.
- **Superficiality.** Online profiles often present a curated, idealized version of reality. It's difficult to get a true sense of someone's authenticity and values.

Finding Resonance in Unexpected Places

To find truly resonant connections, consider venturing beyond the digital realm and exploring these less conventional avenues.

Industry-adjacent events. Don't limit yourself to events directly related to your industry. Consider attending conferences, workshops, or seminars in related fields. This can expose you to new perspectives, new ideas, and new people who share your broader interests. For example, if you're in marketing, consider attending a design conference or a psychology seminar.

Volunteer opportunities. Volunteering for a cause you care about is a fantastic way to meet like-minded individuals who share your values. The shared purpose and collaborative effort create a natural environment for building genuine connections. Consider joining a local cleanup group or soup kitchen—finding where your time can be of the best use.

Community groups and clubs. Join groups that align with your personal interests, whether it's a hiking club, a book club, a cooking class, or a music ensemble. These activities provide a natural context for conversation and shared experiences, making it easier to connect with people on a deeper level.

Mastermind groups. Join or create a mastermind group with people who share your goals and aspirations. These groups provide a supportive environment for sharing ideas, receiving feedback, and holding each other accountable.

Unconferences and retreats. These events often emphasize informal networking and collaboration, creating a more relaxed and authentic atmosphere for building relationships.

Travel and cultural experiences. Stepping outside your comfort zone and immersing yourself in new cultures can lead to unexpected connections and broaden your perspective.

Acts of service. Offer your skills and expertise to help others, without expecting anything in return. This can be a powerful way to build trust and create meaningful relationships.

The art of the handwritten note. In our email world, sending a note becomes a standout act of intention.

THE PRINCIPLE OF "GOING WHERE OTHERS DON'T"

The underlying principle here is to be intentional and strategic about where you invest your time and energy. Don't just follow the crowd; seek out environments and activities that align with your values and your desire for authentic connection. Be open to serendipity and be willing to step outside your comfort zone.

Building resonant relationships is not about collecting contacts; it's about cultivating genuine connections. It's about quality, not quantity. A single meaningful conversation in an unexpected place can be far more valuable than a hundred superficial interactions online.

CALL TO ACTION

This week, challenge yourself to step outside your usual networking routine. Explore one of the unconventional avenues listed above or come up with your own creative way to connect with others. Be open to the unexpected and be willing to invest the time and energy required to build truly resonant relationships. The most meaningful connections often emerge from the places we least expect.

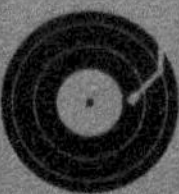

POWER PLAYLIST

THE ENTREPRENEUR'S SYMPHONY

- **"With or Without You" by U2.** Listen for: The way the song builds from a simple bass line to a full, resonant sound—much like how businesses grow from a single idea to a collaborative venture that requires both personal dedication and team unity.
- **"Come Together" by The Beatles.** Listen for: How four distinct musical personalities blend to create something greater than the sum of their parts—the essence of building high-performing entrepreneurial teams.
- **"Rise Up" by Andra Day.** Listen for: The emotional journey from struggle to triumph through collective support, and how the gospel influences make perseverance feel like a spiritual calling rather than mere stubbornness.

Listening Practice: Choose one song and listen while reflecting on your current entrepreneurial challenge or aspiration. Notice what emotions arise—excitement, fear, determination, isolation. After listening, write in your Resonance Journal: What entrepreneurial vision stirs my soul? Who are the collaborators I need to make this real? What would success look like if it included not just profit, but genuine positive impact?

Creating Your Personal Additions: Add songs that remind you of breakthrough moments in your career, successful partnerships, or times when business felt like a calling rather than just work. Consider how these songs capture the unique rhythm of your entrepreneurial journey.

The most successful entrepreneurs aren't just skilled at building businesses—they're masterful at creating resonant relationships that transform their ventures from mere enterprises into movements that matter. These songs remind us that entrepreneurship, at its best, is a collaborative symphony where individual vision harmonizes with collective impact to create something beautiful and lasting.

KEY INSIGHTS FOR YOUR RESONANCE JOURNAL

As we conclude this exploration of resonance in the world of entrepreneurship, take a moment to capture these key insights in your Resonance Journal:

1. **The resonant advantage.** Businesses built on authentic connection create magnetic fields that naturally attract aligned collaborators, customers, and opportunities.
2. **From linear to exponential.** Moving beyond one-on-one networking to creating environments where multiple connections flourish simultaneously amplifies your impact without depleting your energy.
3. **The power of unique experiences.** Unconventional settings often create more meaningful connections than traditional networking environments.

4. **Quality over quantity.** A few deep, resonant connections can be more valuable than hundreds of superficial ones.
5. **The music of purpose.** Companies with missions that extend beyond profit attract more committed teams and loyal customers.
6. **Authentic leadership.** Being true to yourself creates a distinct "sound" that draws others who resonate with your values and vision.
7. **The unseen orchestra.** Your business success depends not just on your vision but on the harmonious collaboration of diverse talents united by shared purpose.

THE BRIDGE TO WORKPLACE RESONANCE

We've explored how entrepreneurs can build ventures founded on resonant relationships. But what about those working within established organizations? How can you apply these same principles if you're not the founder or CEO?

In the next chapter, we'll discover how resonance transforms traditional workplace dynamics regardless of your formal position. You'll learn how to become what I call a "resonant leader"—someone who creates harmonious, high-performing environments through authentic connection rather than hierarchical control.

The journey we've begun doesn't end with entrepreneurship. It extends into every professional context, offering a path to more fulfilling, impactful, and harmonious work experiences for everyone.

Reflection: Think about your current workplace. Where do you see opportunities to create more resonance? What instrument are you playing, and how might you help others find their unique voice in the organizational symphony?

CHAPTER 12

Concert: Resonance in Your Professional Life

No matter how brilliant your mind or strategy, if you're playing a solo game, you'll always lose out to a team.

REID HOFFMAN

The virtuoso violinist stands alone onstage, bow poised, waiting. In that moment, talent means nothing without the orchestra. The true magic emerges not from isolated brilliance but from the harmonious blend of diverse instruments—each with its unique voice, yet all playing in concert.

This is the essence of resonant professional relationships.

We've seen how entrepreneurs can leverage resonance to build ventures that are both successful and meaningful. But these principles extend far beyond startups. They apply to *every professional setting*—from small businesses to multinational corporations, from the boardroom to the factory floor. Success is never a solo performance but a collaborative symphony where each individual's talents contribute to the overall harmony.

What's stopping your workplace from becoming an extraordinary orchestra? Is it truly external constraints, or is it a failure of imagination and courage?

THE WORKPLACE AS ORCHESTRA

Imagine stepping into a workplace where the air vibrates with positive energy; where conversations flow openly; where ideas circulate freely; and where every person feels valued, respected, and empowered. This isn't utopian fantasy; it's the reality of a resonant workplace—an environment where connection, empathy, and shared purpose aren't just talked about but embodied in daily interactions from CEO to newest intern.

What if you could create this environment regardless of your formal role? What if you could transform your workplace from a collection of individuals into a cohesive, high-performing orchestra playing in perfect harmony?

The question isn't whether this transformation is possible—it's whether you're willing to be the catalyst.

Make This Real: Think about your current workplace. On a scale of 1–10, how would you rate its "resonance factor"? What specific behaviors or conditions contribute to that rating? Choose one area where you personally could increase resonance, regardless of your formal position.

THE SCIENCE OF WORKPLACE RESONANCE

The impact of resonant relationships in professional settings isn't just a feel-good philosophy—it's backed by compelling research that demonstrates direct connections between workplace culture and measurable outcomes.

Psychological Safety: The Foundation

Amy Edmondson's groundbreaking research shows that high-performing teams aren't necessarily those with the smartest individuals but those where members feel safe to take risks, express ideas, and admit mistakes without fear. Like a skilled conductor, resonant leaders create spaces where every person feels safe to play their part—even if it means occasionally hitting wrong notes. When people feel psychologically safe, they share creative ideas, challenge assumptions, and contribute unique perspectives.

Google's extensive Project Aristotle research, which studied more than 180 teams over multiple years, reached a startling conclusion: The number one factor in team effectiveness wasn't individual talent, experience, or even clear goals—it was psychological safety. Teams where members felt safe to take risks outperformed all others, regardless of composition.

BRIDGE NOTE

Psychological safety is the organizational expression of Pillar #3: Be at Integrity in Word and Action. When leaders demonstrate consistent alignment between what they say and what they do, they create environments where others feel safe to be authentic.

Emotional Intelligence: The Instrument

Daniel Goleman's research demonstrates that emotional intelligence is as crucial as technical proficiency for effective leadership. Leaders who accurately read emotions, communicate with empathy, and build trust-based relationships inspire and motivate their teams. They create environments where people feel valued and empowered to contribute their best work. This isn't about being "nice"—it's understanding emotional dynamics to create more productive environments.

Recent research by Richard Boyatzis and his colleagues at Case Western Reserve University reveals how "resonant leadership" triggers positive neurological responses that enhance cognitive function and creativity. Their work shows that when leaders create positive emotional states, they literally change the brain chemistry of their teams, improving problem-solving abilities and boosting innovation.

Dissonance Note: Beware of "performance empathy"—feigning emotional intelligence to manipulate outcomes. People have remarkably sensitive radar for detecting inauthentic behavior. True emotional intelligence flows from genuine care and interest in others, not from calculated techniques.

The Neuroscience of Trust: The Harmony

Paul Zak's fascinating research on oxytocin demonstrates that when leaders show trustworthiness and empathy, it triggers oxytocin release in team members, fostering connection and promoting collaboration. His studies show that compared to low-trust organizations, people at high-trust companies report:

- 74 percent less stress
- 106 percent more energy at work
- 50 percent higher productivity
- 13 percent fewer sick days
- 76 percent more engagement

Resonance isn't just social—it's biological, influencing our brain chemistry in ways that fundamentally transform our experience of work and our capacity for innovation.

Purpose and Performance: The Score

Companies with strong, positive cultures consistently outperform competitors. Research by Deloitte shows that mission-driven companies have 30 percent higher levels of innovation and 40 percent higher retention. Similarly, a study by Imperative and LinkedIn found that purpose-oriented employees are 54 percent more likely to stay at a company for five-plus years and 30 percent more likely to be high performers.

These findings underscore what we've been exploring throughout this book: Resonance isn't just about feeling good—it's about doing good, both for people and for organizational outcomes.

Reflection: Recall a time when you were part of a highly resonant team or project. What made that experience different from others? How did it affect your creativity, commitment, and overall performance? What elements from that experience could you bring to your current professional environment?

The Resonant Leader: Conducting the Symphony

A conductor doesn't make music. They create the conditions for music to emerge. Similarly, resonant leadership is about cultivating environments where connection flourishes. It's being a conductor, not a dictator—guiding the collective energy rather than controlling individual expression.

And here's the crucial insight: You can be a resonant leader regardless of your formal position. Leadership isn't about titles—it's about influence. And influence stems from resonance.

Resonant leaders at any level:

- **Are Generous with Time and Energy (Pillar #1):** They invest in others' growth and development, offering support, mentorship, and learning opportunities. They're an "offering" to their team, not just a taskmaster.
- **Listen Deeply (Pillar #2):** They tune in to the needs and aspirations of team members. They practice active listening, creating space for diverse perspectives and honest communication.
- **Act with Integrity (Pillar #3):** They align words with actions, building trust and psychological safety through consistent behavior.
- **Add Value Without Expectation (Pillar #4):** They recognize and celebrate individual contributions, creating cultures of appreciation rather than scarcity.
- **Find Uncommon Common Ground (Pillar #5):** They break down silos and encourage teamwork, creating spaces where diverse perspectives blend into innovative solutions.
- **Create Opportunities for Connection (Pillar #6):** They actively build bridges between team members, nurturing community and belonging.
- **Stand for Something Bigger (Pillar #7):** They articulate inspiring visions and shared purposes that connect daily work to meaningful impact.

Make This Real: Identify one person in your organization who embodies resonant leadership (regardless of their formal position). What specific behaviors make them resonant? How do they affect the people around them? Choose one quality you admire in them that you could begin cultivating yourself.

DIFFERENT INSTRUMENTS, SAME SCORE: HONORING DIVERSITY

A great orchestra doesn't force every musician to play the same instrument. The beauty emerges from the diversity of sounds—the deep resonance of the cello, the bright clarity of the trumpet, the ethereal quality of the flute. Similarly, resonant workplaces don't demand uniformity; they celebrate the distinct contributions each person brings.

This is where Pillar #5: Find Uncommon Common Ground becomes especially powerful in professional settings. It's about discovering the shared purpose (the score) while honoring the unique talents, perspectives, and approaches (the instruments) each person brings.

Research by Scott Page at the University of Michigan demonstrates that diverse teams consistently outperform homogeneous ones on complex problems. The key isn't just demographic diversity (though that matters) but cognitive diversity—different ways of thinking, different life experiences, different approaches to problem-solving.

Four Practices for Orchestrating Diversity

1. **Create dialogue, not debate.** Dialogue seeks understanding; debate seeks victory. In resonant teams, people speak to discover, not to dominate. Practice asking, "What am I not seeing?" and "Can you help me understand your perspective?" These questions transform contentious discussions into collaborative explorations.
2. **Recognize different types of intelligence.** Harvard professor Howard Gardner's multiple intelligence theory reminds us that brilliance manifests in many forms. Some team members excel at

logical analysis, others at interpersonal dynamics, others at big-picture visioning. Resonant leaders recognize and value these diverse types of intelligence, creating roles that leverage people's natural strengths.

3. **Seek cognitive friction.** When ideas rub against each other, they create the heat that sparks innovation. Cultivate constructive disagreement by explicitly inviting diverse perspectives: "What would be a completely different approach to this problem?" or "Who sees this differently and why?"
4. **Build decision-making bridges.** When diverse perspectives lead to different conclusions, the goal isn't to determine who's "right" but to build bridges between viewpoints. Ask, "What elements of each perspective could we incorporate?" and "What shared values or goals unite us despite different approaches?"

Dissonance Note: Diversity without inclusion creates dissonance, not resonance. It's not enough to bring different instruments into the orchestra; you must ensure everyone has the opportunity to play. Watch for subtle patterns that might silence certain voices, and actively create space for all perspectives to be heard.

THE STORY OF THE ORPHEUS CHAMBER ORCHESTRA

In 1972, a group of classical musicians in New York City formed something revolutionary: an orchestra without a conductor. The Orpheus Chamber Orchestra was founded on the radical idea that musicians could collaboratively interpret and perform complex classical works without a single authoritative leader.

Many predicted failure. How could dozens of talented musicians, each with their own interpretations and artistic sensibilities, possibly create coherent, world-class performances without someone waving a baton?

Fifty years later, Orpheus has become one of the world's most respected chamber orchestras, winning Grammy Awards and performing in the most prestigious concert halls globally. Their secret? A system they call the "Orpheus Process"—a set of principles for collaborative leadership and creative problem-solving.

At the heart of this process is rotating leadership. For each piece, different musicians take on core leadership roles, guiding interpretation and making key artistic decisions. Ideas come from everywhere in the orchestra, not just the designated leaders. All musicians are encouraged to speak up, offer suggestions, and participate actively in refining their collective performance.

The results aren't just artistically impressive; they're economically sound. Orpheus musicians report higher job satisfaction, greater commitment, and deeper engagement than their peers in traditional orchestras. They've proven that shared leadership can create both extraordinary art and sustainable organizations.

Reflection: In what areas of your professional life could you experiment with more distributed leadership? What might emerge if you stepped back from controlling outcomes and instead focused on creating conditions where collective wisdom could flourish?

Resonance Instrument

THE RESONANT LEADER SELF-ASSESSMENT

This instrument helps you evaluate your current approach to leadership through the lens of resonance. It identifies your resonant strengths and opportunities for growth, providing a foundation for becoming more intentional about how you influence your professional environment.

How to Play It:

Rate yourself on a scale of 1 (rarely) to 5 (consistently) for each of the following statements.

Generosity (Pillar #1):

1. I freely share knowledge, resources, and opportunities with colleagues.
2. I invest time in helping others develop their skills and capabilities.
3. I give credit generously and publicly recognize others' contributions.
4. I make myself available when others need support or guidance.
5. I offer help without being asked when I see a need I can address.

Listening and Presence (Pillar #2):

1. I give others my full attention when they're speaking, without planning my response.
2. I ask thoughtful follow-up questions that deepen understanding.
3. I notice and respond appropriately to emotional cues and nonverbal communication.
4. I create space for quieter voices to be heard in group settings.
5. I seek feedback about my own behaviors and receive it without defensiveness.

Integrity and Trust (Pillar #3):

1. I follow through on commitments, even small ones.
2. I speak honestly and directly, avoiding politics and manipulation.
3. I admit mistakes and take responsibility for my actions.
4. I maintain confidentiality when appropriate and don't engage in gossip.
5. My words and actions consistently align, even when under pressure.

Adding Value (Pillar #4):

1. I look for ways to contribute beyond my formal role or job description.

2. I offer constructive ideas and solutions rather than just identifying problems.
3. I build on others' suggestions instead of immediately critiquing them.
4. I bring positive energy to interactions and projects.
5. I help create conditions where others can do their best work.

Bridge Building (Pillar #5):

1. I actively connect people who could benefit from knowing each other.
2. I look for common ground when conflicts or differences arise.
3. I help translate between different functions, departments, or viewpoints.
4. I'm curious about perspectives that differ from my own.
5. I help build consensus without forcing artificial agreement.

Connection Making (Pillar #6):

1. I create opportunities for people to interact outside formal meetings.
2. I facilitate meaningful conversations that go beyond surface-level small talk.
3. I help establish rituals and traditions that foster community.
4. I notice when people feel excluded and take action to bring them in.
5. I share appropriate personal stories that invite authentic connection.

Purpose Alignment (Pillar #7):

1. I connect day-to-day tasks to larger meaning and impact.
2. I talk about values and principles, not just metrics and outcomes.

3. I help others see how their work contributes to something meaningful.
4. I make decisions based on long-term purpose, not just short-term gains.
5. I embody the values I talk about, even when it's difficult.

Scoring and Interpretation:

Total your scores for each pillar (maximum 25 points per pillar).

- **20–25 points:** This is an area of resonant strength. You consistently embody these behaviors and likely inspire others through your example.
- **15–19 points:** You demonstrate these behaviors frequently but have room to become more consistent and intentional.
- **10–14 points:** These behaviors appear occasionally in your leadership approach but need more conscious development.
- **5–9 points:** This represents a significant growth opportunity. Focusing here could dramatically increase your resonant impact.

Tuning Tips:

Choose the two lowest-scoring pillars as your primary growth areas. For each, select one specific behavior to focus on developing over the next thirty days. Create a simple daily practice that will help you strengthen this behavior.

For example, if "I create space for quieter voices to be heard in group settings" scored low, you might establish a personal rule to ask, "Who hasn't shared their perspective yet?" in every meeting you attend.

Record your progress in your Resonance Journal, noting specific situations where you practiced these behaviors and the impact they had.

Make This Real: Complete the assessment now. What patterns do you notice? Which pillar represents your greatest strength? Which offers the most significant opportunity for growth? Choose one specific behavior to focus on developing in the coming week.

FROM DISSONANCE TO HARMONY: NAVIGATING WORKPLACE CHALLENGES

Even the world's greatest orchestras occasionally hit sour notes. What distinguishes resonant workplaces isn't the absence of problems but the way they're addressed. Let's explore common workplace challenges through the lens of resonance.

The Toxic Colleague

We've all encountered them—the colleague whose negativity, gossip, manipulation, or hostility creates dissonance throughout the workplace. The traditional approaches—avoidance or confrontation—often amplify the problem.

The Resonant Approach:

- **Start with listening** (Pillar #2). Most difficult behavior stems from unmet needs or fears. Create space for the person to express their concerns.
- **Find uncommon common ground** (Pillar #5). Beneath conflicting behaviors often lie shared values or goals. Identify what you both care about.
- **Set clear, kind boundaries** (Pillar #3). Integrity includes honoring your own needs. Clearly communicate which behaviors you can and cannot accept.
- **Offer specific support** (Pillar #1). Where appropriate, generously offer resources, information, or assistance that might address underlying issues.

- **Expand the context** (Pillar #7). Connect your interactions to larger shared purposes that transcend personal differences.

The Silo Mentality

When departments or teams operate in isolation, protecting their turf and information, organizational effectiveness suffers. Innovation stalls, duplicate efforts waste resources, and a culture of competition replaces collaboration.

The Resonant Approach:

- **Create cross-functional experiences** (Pillar #6). Organize events, projects, or learning opportunities that bring different departments together.
- **Establish "translation" roles** (Pillar #5). Identify individuals who can bridge different functional languages and perspectives.
- **Celebrate collaborative wins** (Pillar #4). Publicly recognize and reward cross-silo cooperation to reinforce its value.
- **Share stories, not just data** (Pillar #2). Help teams understand each other's challenges, priorities, and contributions through narrative.
- **Align around shared impact** (Pillar #7). Focus on how different functions contribute to common organizational purpose.

The Innovation Drought

When organizations prioritize efficiency and predictability over experimentation and learning, creativity withers. People stop suggesting new ideas, instead focusing on safe, incremental improvements that won't rock the boat.

The Resonant Approach:

- **Create psychological safety** (Pillar #3). Establish environments where people feel safe to take risks and share untested ideas.
- **Reward learning, not just success** (Pillar #4). Celebrate experiments that yield valuable insights, even when they don't succeed as planned.
- **Diversify input sources** (Pillar #2). Actively seek perspectives from different levels, functions, and backgrounds to spark creative friction.

- **Provide innovation resources** (Pillar #1). Generously offer time, space, funding, and support for exploring new possibilities.
- **Connect innovation to purpose** (Pillar #7). Frame creativity as essential to fulfilling the organization's deeper mission.

Dissonance Note: Beware of viewing resonance as a technique for getting what you want. If you approach these challenges thinking, "How can I use resonance to make this person behave differently?" you're still operating from a manipulative mindset. True resonance starts with genuine openness to connection and shared understanding.

LEADING FROM ANY CHAIR: CREATING RESONANCE WITHOUT AUTHORITY

One of the most powerful stories from the orchestral world comes from renowned conductor Benjamin Zander. During a rehearsal with a youth orchestra, he noticed a young violinist in the back row looking disengaged. After the session, Zander asked him what was wrong.

"I've been playing in orchestras for years," the young man replied, "and I've never played a single note that made a difference."

Zander realized that the musician felt powerless—just one of many violinists, following the conductor's direction, with no sense of personal contribution or impact. This insight led Zander to develop what he calls "leading from any chair"—the idea that every orchestral member, regardless of position, can be a leader by playing with purpose, passion, and presence.

This concept applies powerfully to organizational life. Regardless of your formal role or position, you can create resonance through how you show up each day. Let's see how.

Be a Microclimate Creator

While you may not control the organization's overall culture, you can create a "microclimate" around you—a space where resonant principles flourish. Your immediate sphere of influence might include your team, your project collaborators, or even just those you interact with regularly.

Within this sphere, you can:

- Practice deep listening
- Demonstrate genuine care
- Maintain impeccable integrity
- Add value consistently
- Build bridges across differences
- Create connection opportunities
- Embody shared purpose

These behaviors create a resonant field that naturally expands over time as others experience their benefits and begin adopting similar approaches.

Master Influential Communication

Resonant communicators don't rely on formal authority to make their voices heard. They understand that how you communicate matters as much as what you communicate. They:

- **Ask powerful questions** that shift perspectives and open new possibilities: "What if we approached this differently?" "What are we not seeing?" "How might we . . . ?"
- **Frame ideas in terms of shared values** rather than personal preferences: "Given our commitment to customer experience, what if we . . ." rather than "I think we should . . ."
- **Offer observations without judgment,** creating space for mutual exploration: "I've noticed that our meetings tend to focus on immediate problems rather than long-term opportunities. What do others think about that balance?"
- **Connect suggestions to larger context,** helping others see the why behind the what: "If we made this change, it could help us better deliver on our promise of sustainability while also improving efficiency."

Build Strategic Relationships

Resonance isn't just about how you behave in the moment; it's about intentionally cultivating relationships that create positive change throughout the organization. This doesn't mean political networking—it means authentic connection with purpose. Consider:

- **Identifying resonant allies** across different departments, levels, and functions who share your values and vision
- **Creating informal communities of practice** where like-minded colleagues can support each other's growth
- **Establishing mentoring relationships** in both directions—being both mentor and mentee
- **Building bridges to key decision-makers** through genuine value-adding rather than self-promotion

Make This Real: Identify one area where you could create more resonance without needing more authority. What specific behavior could you begin practicing tomorrow that would create a more resonant environment in your immediate sphere?

FROM CONCERT TO SYMPHONY: AMPLIFYING YOUR IMPACT

As you develop your capacity to create resonance in your professional life, your impact naturally expands. What begins as individual behaviors becomes team norms. What starts as team culture ripples outward to influence entire departments. What emerges in one department can ultimately transform organizations.

This is the true power of resonance in professional contexts—it's inherently contagious and expansive. When people experience environments characterized by trust, belonging, purpose, and respect, they naturally want to create more of these conditions.

The journey from dissonant to resonant workplaces isn't a single transformation but a progressive expansion of resonant fields.

1. **Personal Resonance:** Cultivating your own authentic presence and resonant behaviors
2. **Interpersonal Resonance:** Creating one-on-one connections based on trust and mutual respect
3. **Team Resonance:** Fostering environments where diverse talents harmonize around shared goals
4. **Organizational Resonance:** Building cultures and systems that embody resonant principles at scale
5. **Ecosystem Resonance:** Extending resonant practices to relationships with clients, partners, suppliers, and communities
6. Each stage builds on the previous one, creating concentric circles of impact that can ultimately transform entire industries and societies.

Reflection: Where do you currently have the greatest resonant impact? At which level would focusing your energy create the most positive change in your professional context?

POWER PLAYLIST

THE WORKPLACE SYMPHONY

- **"9 to 5" by Dolly Parton.** Listen for: The tension between human potential and constraining systems. Authentic leadership requires changing structures that diminish people.
- **"Air on the G String" by The Orpheus Chamber Orchestra.** Listen for: A conductor-less orchestra creating perfect harmony through deep listening and mutual respect—the model for collaborative leadership.

- **"Working Man" by Rush.** Listen for: The pride and strength found in honest contribution. Meaningful work becomes an expression of authentic self.

Listening Practice: Choose one song and listen while reflecting on your professional relationships. After listening, write in your Resonance Journal: How do I contribute to my workplace's "symphony"? Where do I create harmony versus discord? What would change if I brought more authenticity to my professional interactions?

Work becomes meaningful when it serves as an extension of our authentic selves rather than a mask we wear. These songs remind us that professional excellence emerges not from performance but from bringing our genuine gifts to shared endeavors.

KEY INSIGHTS FOR YOUR RESONANCE JOURNAL

As we conclude this exploration of resonance in professional settings, capture these key insights in your Resonance Journal.

1. **The orchestra principle.** Professional success isn't a solo performance but a collaborative symphony where diverse talents harmonize around shared purpose.
2. **Safety before brilliance.** Psychological safety—the foundation of trust and authentic expression—precedes innovation and high performance.
3. **Neurological resonance.** Positive workplace relationships create measurable changes in brain chemistry that enhance creativity, problem-solving, and well-being.
4. **Leadership without authority.** Creating resonance doesn't require

formal position—it flows from how you show up, communicate, and connect.

5. **The contagion effect.** Resonant behaviors naturally spread, creating expanding circles of positive impact throughout organizations.
6. **Diversity as strength.** Like an orchestra needs different instruments, organizations thrive when they celebrate and integrate diverse perspectives.
7. **Purpose as amplifier.** Connecting work to meaningful impact transforms jobs into callings and groups into movements.

THE BRIDGE TO LASTING LEGACY

We've explored how resonance transforms both entrepreneurial ventures and established organizations. We've seen how these principles create not just more successful businesses but more fulfilling professional experiences for everyone involved.

In the next chapter, we'll discover how resonance principles can help align your relationships with larger purpose to create lasting impact and meaningful legacy. You'll learn how to amplify your symphony beyond time, ensuring that the music you create continues to resonate long after you've played your final note.

The journey we've begun extends beyond professional success to something far more significant: creating a life of meaning, connection, and contribution that echoes through generations. Are you ready to compose your symphony of lasting impact?

Reflection: As you think about your professional life and the impact you hope to have, what legacy do you want to leave? What kind of "music" do you want to continue playing in the world even after you've moved on?

PART 5

Sharing Your Song

The most powerful person in the world is the storyteller. The storyteller sets the vision, values, and agenda of an entire generation that is to come.

STEVE JOBS

THE FINAL MOVEMENT

You've journeyed far—from understanding the value of deep connection, to finding your authentic voice, to striking resonant chords in close relationships, to building your band in your professional life. Each step has been preparation for this final transformation—perhaps the most profound of all.

Now we ask: What symphony will you leave behind?

The relationships you've cultivated aren't just for your fulfillment. They're vessels for something larger—conduits through which your unique contribution flows into the world and beyond your time in it. This is where your personal journey transcends into legacy.

Think of the music that has moved you most deeply. Behind every transformative song lies not just individual talent but a constellation of relationships—between band members, producers, engineers, audiences, and generations of musicians who came before. The most enduring compositions arise from this web of connection, where individual notes become something greater than their sum.

Your life follows this same pattern.

THE RESONANCE REVOLUTION COMES FULL CIRCLE

When we began this journey, we faced a fundamental truth: Despite unprecedented technological connection, we've never been more isolated. The loneliness epidemic isn't just a personal tragedy—it's a collective wound.

Your growing mastery of resonant relationships offers healing not just for yourself but for our fragmented world. The ripples of your transformed relationships extend far beyond what you can see: the colleague whose life philosophy shifted after your genuine conversation. The friend who learned to trust again through your consistent presence. The family dynamics that will change for generations because you broke patterns of disconnection.

These are not minor effects. They are your living legacy.

FROM SOLO TO SYMPHONY: THE JOURNEY AHEAD

In the chapters that follow, we'll explore three dimensions of relationship as legacy.

Chapter 13: "Harmonic Legacy" examines how your network of relationships amplifies your impact beyond what you could achieve alone.

Chapter 14: "Eulogy Goals Over Résumé Goals" challenges you to measure your life not by external achievements but by the depth and impact of your connections.

Chapter 15: "Symphony: Resonance and Your Dream Projects" shows you how to orchestrate your unique collaboration of voices around shared vision, creating projects and movements that manifest your greatest contribution through resonant relationships.

More than techniques, these chapters offer a profound shift in perspective—from seeing your relationships as personal assets to recognizing them as vehicles for contribution beyond yourself. In these final chapters, you'll discover how to protect and project the soul of who you are through the lasting impact of your relationships.

The world is waiting for your song.

Let's begin.

CHAPTER 13

Harmonic Legacy: Orchestrating Your Impact Beyond Time

What lies behind us and what lies before us are tiny matters compared to what lies within us.

HENRY STANLEY HASKINS

THE ETERNAL MOMENT OF CREATION

Imagine the opening notes of Beethoven's Ninth Symphony, the "Ode to Joy." Those first tentative strings that rise and build toward a transcendent chorus . . . this is the sound of individual voices uniting in shared purpose, each contributing to something far greater than themselves.

The ancient Greeks had a concept they called *kairos*: a perfect moment when opportunity opens, when the membrane between what is and what could be grows thin. It's not chronological time but divine timing. The ideal moment to act, when your contribution can ripple outward with maximum impact. The Japanese have a similar concept: *ichi-go ichi-e*—one time, one meeting—acknowledging that each moment is unique and will never come again. These are the moments when our song can transcend mere melody and become a harmonic legacy that echoes across generations.

What if I told you that you are living in *kairos* right now? That this very moment of reading these words represents a thin place between who you've been and who you might become? That your relationship with this page might be *ichi-go ichi-e*—a singular, unrepeatable opportunity to transform your life's song into something that resonates far beyond yourself?

We've traveled far together through this journey of resonance. We've explored how to tune our inner instruments, find our authentic voices, and create harmonious connections with others. We've discovered how resonance transforms our families, friendships, and professional relationships. But our journey doesn't end with simply building better connections. The ultimate expression of resonance is using those relationships as instruments in a grand orchestra, playing a symphony dedicated to something greater than ourselves.

> *Music is indeed the mediator between the spiritual and sensual life.*
>
> LUDWIG VAN BEETHOVEN

THE GREAT INVERSION

What if the most profound impact we can have isn't measured by what we personally achieve but by how effectively we amplify the gifts of others? What if the true mark of a resonant life is the legacy that continues to vibrate long after we've played our final note?

This represents what I call "the great inversion," a fundamental shift in how we measure success and meaning. In a culture obsessed with individual achievement, personal branding, and self-promotion, this inversion feels radical, even counterintuitive. We've been conditioned to believe that our worth is determined by what we personally accomplish, the recognition we receive, the wealth we accumulate, or the influence we wield.

But what if this entire paradigm is backward? What if our greatest fulfillment—and our most lasting impact—comes not from building our own platform but from becoming a platform for others? Not from amplifying our own voice but from amplifying the voices of those who might otherwise go unheard? Not from claiming the spotlight but from becoming the spotlight that illuminates others?

This inversion isn't about diminishing your own gifts or denying your unique contribution. Rather, it's about recognizing that your gifts find their fullest expression when they serve something larger than yourself. It's about understanding that your voice becomes most powerful when it joins with others in harmony. It's about discovering that your greatest joy comes not from solo achievement but from collaborative creation.

Consider the humble bass line in a jazz quartet. While often less noticed than the soaring saxophone or the flashy piano solo, it's the bass that provides the foundation, the heartbeat that allows others to shine. In its steady presence, it creates the space for others to explore, improvise, and express. This is the power of supportive resonance—finding joy in creating the conditions for collective brilliance.

> ***In the sweet territory of silence we touch the mystery. It's the place of reflection and contemplation, and it's the place where we can connect with the deep knowing, the deep wisdom, the deep stillness that resides within us.***
>
> **ANGELES ARRIEN**

THE SYMPHONY OF PURPOSE

When I reflect on the most transformative moments of resonance in my own life, they all share a common thread: alignment with something larger than myself. The experience of hosting His Holiness the Dalai Lama for his eightieth birthday wasn't merely about organizing an event or gaining recognition. It was about creating a vessel for connection, inspiration, and the amplification of compassion in the world.

The challenges were immense—complex logistics, securing funding, and bringing together a diverse coalition of individuals and organizations. There were moments of doubt and dissonance when the undertaking felt overwhelming. Yet through it all, we remained anchored to our purpose: creating an experience that would not only honor His Holiness but inspire attendees to live more compassionate, purposeful lives.

What made this possible wasn't my individual effort but the resonant relationships we forged—with volunteers, sponsors, attendees, and His Holiness's team. It was a powerful demonstration of how shared purpose unites people from all walks of life, creating a symphony of collective effort that achieves far more than any individual could alone. The event became a testament to The More—that exponential potential that emerges when we align our individual energies with a larger vision.

THE ALCHEMY OF SHARED PURPOSE

There's a mysterious alchemy that occurs when people unite around a shared purpose. Something happens that transcends the mere addition of individual efforts. It's as if one plus one no longer equals two but something infinitely greater. A multiplication rather than an addition, an exponential expansion rather than a linear progression.

I've witnessed this alchemy in action countless times: in community organizing efforts, in creative collaborations, in business ventures driven by purpose rather than profit alone. There's a palpable energy that emerges, a collective intelligence that surpasses the capabilities of any single participant. Ideas flow more freely, solutions emerge more readily, and obstacles that might seem insurmountable to an individual become manageable for a united group.

This alchemy isn't mystical or supernatural; it's deeply human. It's what happens when we step out of isolation and into connection, when we move from competition to collaboration, when we shift from self-interest to shared interest. It's the manifestation of what Dr. Martin Luther King Jr. called the "beloved community"—a society based on justice, equal opportunity, and love of one's fellow human beings.

This kind of purpose-driven leadership—rooted in service, connection, and commitment to something greater than oneself—isn't limited to grand public gestures. It can manifest in quiet acts of courage that transform lives and inspire movements.

Picture a gospel choir, where dozens of distinct voices blend into one powerful sound that fills a cathedral. Each singer contributes their unique tone and timbre, yet something magical happens in their unity—a resonance that can literally move the physical space and the hearts within it. This is the sound of The More—individual gifts coalescing into something transcendent that could never exist in isolation.

> ***If I have seen further, it is by standing on the shoulders of giants.***
>
> ISAAC NEWTON

LEADERSHIP OVER CIRCUMSTANCE

Consider the extraordinary example of Nelson Mandela, a man who spent twenty-seven years in prison yet emerged as a global icon of peace and reconciliation. Nelson Mandela's life embodied what I call "leadership over circumstance." Imprisoned for his fight against apartheid, he could have surrendered to bitterness and despair. Instead, even within his prison cell, Mandela created resonance, led with principle, and lived the very values we've explored throughout this book.

He practiced deep listening, making the effort to understand his jailers by learning Afrikaans and studying their culture. He recognized that lasting change couldn't be achieved through hatred but through empathy and acknowledging the humanity in even his adversaries.

Mandela lived with unwavering integrity, refusing to compromise his values even when offered freedom in exchange for renouncing his political beliefs. Perhaps most powerfully, Mandela stood for something bigger than himself. He recognized that his personal freedom was inseparable from his people's liberation.

His capacity to forgive his oppressors after decades of imprisonment remains his greatest legacy—a profound demonstration of the transformative power of resonant relationships.

THE LIBERATION PARADOX

Mandela's story illuminates what I call "the liberation paradox"—the counterintuitive truth that our greatest freedom often comes through commitment rather than through unbounded choice.

Mandela found freedom even within the confines of a prison cell through his unwavering commitment to a cause greater than himself. His physical liberty was restricted, yet his spirit remained unbound because he had aligned himself with principles that transcended his individual circumstances.

This paradox applies to all of us, though perhaps in less dramatic circumstances. We find our greatest freedom not in keeping all options open, not in avoiding commitment, not in prioritizing our own comfort and convenience above all else. Rather, we find freedom in committing ourselves wholeheartedly to people, principles, and purposes that align with our deepest values.

In your own life, where might this paradox apply? Where might deeper commitment—rather than more options—be the path to greater freedom? Where might your song find its fullest expression through deliberate constraints rather than unlimited possibilities?

Musical Interlude: Listen to the disciplined structure of Bach's fugues—how the rigid mathematical patterns and precise counterpoint don't restrict the music but rather create the very conditions for transcendent beauty. This is the sound of the liberation paradox—how voluntary constraints, when aligned with purpose, don't limit expression but exponentially expand it.

THE SCIENCE OF PURPOSE AND CONTRIBUTION

This commitment to something larger than ourselves, this willingness to serve, isn't just inspiring—it's profoundly beneficial for both individuals and communities. The emerging science of purpose confirms what wisdom traditions have taught for millennia: that a life oriented toward contribution rather than acquisition, toward service rather than self-interest, leads to greater well-being, resilience, and fulfillment.

Altruism and happiness. Research consistently shows a strong link between altruism (selfless concern for others) and happiness. Studies have found that people who engage in acts of kindness and generosity report higher levels of life satisfaction and positive emotions. The neural pathways activated when we give are the same ones associated with receiving rewards, suggesting that generosity is hardwired into our very biology. The "helper's high" isn't just a poetic notion but a neurochemical reality—the brain's reward system responds more strongly to giving than to receiving.

Compassion and well-being. Cultivating compassion for ourselves and others yields numerous psychological and physical health benefits. Research demonstrates that compassion reduces stress, improves immune function, and promotes greater emotional resilience. When we open our hearts to others' suffering and respond with kindness, we don't deplete ourselves—we become more resilient. Practices like loving-kindness meditation have been shown to reduce inflammation, improve heart rate variability, and enhance overall emotional well-being.

Purpose and longevity. Having a sense of purpose has been linked to increased longevity and reduced risk of chronic diseases. Studies have found that individuals with a strong sense of purpose live longer, healthier lives, regardless of socioeconomic status or other factors. Purpose quite literally extends our lifespan, allowing our song to play longer. Research from "Blue Zones"—regions where people commonly live past one hundred—consistently identifies purpose as a key factor in exceptional longevity.

Meaning and resilience. A sense of meaning protects against depression, anxiety, and burnout. People who perceive their lives as meaningful demonstrate greater resilience in the face of adversity, recover more quickly from illness and trauma, and maintain higher levels of functioning even in challenging circumstances. Meaning serves as a psychological buffer, helping us navigate life's inevitable hardships with greater equanimity and courage.

Connection and health. Strong social connections—the kind fostered by purpose-driven collaborative efforts—have been shown to be as important to health as not smoking, maintaining a healthy weight, and regular physical activity. Isolation and loneliness, by contrast, are significant risk factors for early mortality. When we unite with others around shared purpose, we not only create greater impact but also foster the very connections that keep us alive and well.

Just as a symphony orchestra comprises many different instruments each playing its unique part, the world consists of diverse individuals with unique talents and contributions. Living a resonant life means recognizing that we're all part of this larger orchestra, and our individual actions contribute to the world's overall harmony or dissonance. We must play our part to the best of our ability while supporting others in doing the same.

THE SHADOW SIDE OF PURPOSE

While purpose brings tremendous benefits, it also carries potential pitfalls if misunderstood or misapplied. In the quest for meaning and impact, some fall into what psychologists call "purpose anxiety"—the stress that comes from feeling inadequate in the face of grand ambitions or comparing one's contribution to that of others. Some become so focused on future impact that they miss the present moment, trading mindful presence for ceaseless striving.

Some confuse purpose with perfection, believing that meaningful work must be flawless, grand in scale, or universally acclaimed. This perfectionism leads to burnout, disappointment, and a constriction of creative flow. Still others become attached to specific outcomes, forgetting that true purpose lies in the quality of effort and intention rather than in results alone.

Perhaps most insidiously, purpose can become a subtle form of ego aggrandizement—a way of seeking importance, recognition, or a sense of specialness. When this happens, service becomes self-serving, and the authentic joy of contribution gives way to the hollow pursuit of significance.

True purpose avoids these traps. It's humble yet confident, ambitious yet patient, visionary yet present. It recognizes that meaning comes not just from grand achievements but from small acts of kindness, daily practices of presence, and consistent alignment between values and actions. It understands that purpose isn't about leaving a mark but about being a channel through which something larger can flow.

Musical Interlude: Imagine a simple wooden flute being played by a master musician. The flute itself is nothing—just hollow space surrounded by material. Its entire purpose is to be empty, to be a vessel through which breath can flow and be transformed into music. This is the essence of purpose without ego—becoming a clear channel through which The More can express itself.

Resonance Instrument

VISUALIZING THE SYMPHONY OF THE MORE

This instrument helps you connect personal aspirations with a larger sense of purpose, creating a powerful vision for a resonant life. It's about recognizing that your individual song forms part of a larger symphony, and your contribution, however small, makes a difference.

How to Play It:

1. **Find a quiet space** where you can relax and focus without distractions. Create an environment that feels sacred or special—perhaps lighting a candle, playing soft instrumental music, or sitting in a natural setting.

2. **Close your eyes** and take several deep breaths, allowing your body and mind to settle. With each inhale, imagine drawing in inspiration and possibility; with each exhale, release tension, doubt, and limitation.
3. **Imagine your ideal life as a symphony.** Each relationship, passion, and project is an instrument contributing to the overall composition. Visualize the interplay of these connections, the shared melodies, and the collective crescendo. See the colors, hear the sounds, feel the vibrations of this symphony as it plays.
4. **See yourself as the conductor** of this symphony, guiding different sections, shaping the overall sound, and creating a beautiful, meaningful composition. Notice how it feels to stand in this position of creative leadership—not controlling but facilitating, not dominating but harmonizing.
5. **Connect to The More.** Now connect this vision to something bigger than yourself—a cause, purpose, or contribution to the world. How does your symphony contribute to humanity's greater harmony? What larger impact do you want to create? Visualize the ripple effect of your actions extending outward and touching the lives of others. See these ripples extending beyond your lifetime, influencing future generations in ways you may never witness.
6. **Feel the resonance.** As you visualize your symphony, allow yourself to feel the emotions that arise. Experience the joy, fulfillment, and purpose that comes from living a resonant life. Notice where you feel these emotions in your body. Let them expand and intensify, saturating every cell.
7. **Open your eyes.** In your Resonance Journal, describe the symphony you envision in vivid detail. What are the key instruments? What's the overall mood and message? How does

it make you feel? What specific actions can you take in the next twenty-four hours to begin bringing this symphony to life?

Tuning Tips:

- Be open to inspiration as you visualize, letting images and feelings flow freely without judgment. Your logical mind may try to edit or censor—gently set these thoughts aside and return to the flow of imagery.
- Pay attention to arising emotions. Your emotional response is a compass pointing toward authentic purpose. Notice which aspects of the visualization evoke the strongest feelings of expansiveness, joy, or peace.
- Ensure your vision aligns with core values. After completing the visualization, review your written description and check for alignment with the values you've identified as most important to you. Adjust as needed.
- Return to this visualization periodically, refining it as you gain new insights and experiences. Make it a regular practice—perhaps monthly on the new moon or quarterly as the seasons change.
- Share your vision selectively with trusted allies who can support and amplify it. Invite them to help you refine and expand your understanding of your unique contribution.

Advanced Practice: Once you've become comfortable with the basic visualization, try this variation: Imagine yourself at the end of your life, looking back on the symphony you've created. What do you see from this perspective? What matters most? What advice would your future self give to your present self about composing and conducting your life's symphony?

The best way to find yourself is to lose yourself in the service of others.

MAHATMA GANDHI

THE UNFINISHED SYMPHONY

Life is an unfinished symphony, a work in progress. There will always be new movements to compose, new harmonies to discover, new dissonances to resolve. Embrace the ongoing journey of creating resonance within yourself and in your relationships. The music never ends; it simply evolves.

THE HARMONIC LEGACY

The greatest musicians aren't remembered merely for technical prowess but for how their music touched souls and transformed lives. Similarly, our most profound impact comes not from personal achievements but from how we amplify and elevate others.

Consider the concept of a harmonic legacy—the resonant impact that continues to vibrate long after we've played our final note. It's about creating ripples that expand outward, touching lives we'll never meet and inspiring actions we'll never witness. It's about planting seeds that will bloom into forests long after we're gone.

This legacy isn't built through grand gestures alone but through consistent, authentic living that embodies the seven pillars of resonance:

Be Generous of Time and Energy, Be an Offering (the Hands): Give freely of yourself without expectation of return. Your generosity creates a momentum of giving that extends far beyond the initial act. When you share your resources, knowledge, attention, and care, you initiate a cascade of generosity that continues beyond your direct influence. The recipient of your generosity becomes more likely to give to others, creating a chain reaction of abundance that counteracts the scarcity mentality so prevalent in our culture.

Listen Deeply and Be Curious (the Ear): When you truly hear others, you validate their existence and worth. This gift of attention creates space for authentic connection that others will carry forward. Deep listening is revolutionary in a world of constant distraction and superficial interaction. When you listen with your full presence, you help others discover their own voices, clarify their thinking, and access their innate wisdom. This gift multiplies as they, in turn, learn to listen to others with the same quality of attention.

Be at Integrity in Word and Action (the Tuning Fork): Living with integrity creates trust. This trust becomes the foundation upon which others build their own resonant relationships. In a world where words and actions often diverge, consistent alignment creates a rare form of trustworthiness that inspires others. Your integrity becomes a reference point, a standard that elevates relationships around you and demonstrates what's possible when words and deeds harmonize. This integrity ripples outward as others witness its power and incorporate it into their own lives.

Add Value Without Expectation of Return (the Horn): When you contribute your unique gifts without attachment to outcome, you inspire others to discover and share their own talents. This generous contribution shifts the transactional paradigm that dominates many interactions. It creates an economy of abundance rather than scarcity, where value flows freely without constant calculation of cost and benefit. This spirit of unconditional contribution becomes contagious, inspiring others to bring their gifts forward with similar generosity.

Find Uncommon Common Ground (the Strings): Building bridges across difference creates models of connection that others can follow, expanding circles of understanding and empathy. In a world increasingly fractured by polarization, the ability to find connection across divides is revolutionary. Your willingness to seek understanding rather than merely proving your point creates pathways for dialogue that others can follow. These bridges of understanding multiply as others witness the power of connection across difference and apply the same principles in their own interactions.

Create Exponential Opportunities for Connection (the Conductor's Baton): By bringing people together in meaningful ways, you catalyze connections that will continue to flourish and multiply without your direct involvement. When you facilitate authentic connection between others, you create nodes in a network of relationships that extends far beyond your immediate circle. These connections generate new ideas, collaborations, and possibilities that would never have emerged in isolation. The web of relationships you help create continues to expand and evolve long after your direct involvement ends.

Stand for Something Bigger (the Drum): When you align your life with purpose, you inspire others to discover their own calling, creating a cascade of purpose-driven action. Your commitment to something larger than yourself demonstrates what's possible when we transcend self-interest and align with greater good. This inspiration doesn't clone your specific purpose but awakens others to their own unique contribution. The resulting ecosystem of purpose creates collective impact far greater than any individual effort.

A harmonic legacy isn't about being remembered personally; it's about contributing to the evolution of human consciousness and connection. It's about playing your unique note so beautifully that it inspires others to find and play theirs. It's about recognizing that we are all part of an intergenerational orchestra, our individual contributions merging into a grand symphony that transcends time.

Musical Interlude: Consider how a single note, played with perfect clarity and resonance, can linger in a concert hall long after the musician has stopped playing. This is the acoustic phenomenon of "sympathetic resonance"—how one vibration causes others to vibrate in harmony. Your life's work creates this same kind of resonance, continuing to vibrate in the lives of those you've touched long after your direct influence has ended.

> *Our deepest fear is not that we are inadequate. Our deepest fear is that we are powerful beyond measure. It is our light, not our darkness that most frightens us.*
>
> MARIANNE WILLIAMSON

FROM SUCCESS TO SIGNIFICANCE

This shift from personal achievement to collective impact represents a fundamental evolution in how we understand our lives' purpose. It's a movement from success to significance, from accumulation to contribution, from what we can get to what we can give.

This transition often unfolds naturally as we mature. In early adulthood, many focus primarily on establishing themselves—building careers, acquiring skills, securing resources, and achieving recognition. These pursuits aren't inherently selfish; they're natural stages of development that prepare us for more expansive contribution.

But at some point, a shift occurs. The achievements that once brought satisfaction begin to feel hollow. The accolades that once seemed important lose their luster. The material acquisitions that once brought pleasure become burdens rather than benefits. We find ourselves asking deeper questions: What's it all for? What truly matters? What will remain when I'm gone?

These questions mark the threshold between success and significance, between a life oriented toward personal gain and one oriented toward meaningful contribution. This threshold isn't crossed once and for all but represents an ongoing evolution, a continuous expansion of our circle of concern from self to others to community to world.

Where are you in this evolution? Are you still primarily focused on establishing yourself, or are you ready to shift toward greater contribution? What might this shift look like in your particular circumstances, with your unique gifts and constraints? How might your song evolve from a solo performance to a part in a larger symphony?

> *How wonderful it is that nobody need wait a single moment before beginning to improve the world.*
>
> ANNE FRANK

THE COURAGE TO PLAY YOUR SONG

> *Tell me, what is it you plan to do with your one wild and precious life?*
>
> MARY OLIVER

Creating a harmonic legacy requires courage—the courage to play your authentic song even when others might not understand or appreciate it. It requires resilience—the willingness to continue playing through dissonance and discord. And it requires vision—the ability to see beyond immediate circumstances to the potential for harmony that lies beneath the surface.

This courage, resilience, and vision constitute what I call "the resonant warrior"—an archetype that combines strength with sensitivity, conviction with compassion, and purposeful action with profound presence. The resonant warrior doesn't fight against others but against forces that diminish human potential and connection. This inner warrior battles not with weapons of destruction but with instruments of creation.

The resonant warrior faces fears that would silence their authentic voice: the fear of rejection, the fear of failure, the fear of success, the fear of standing out, the fear of not being enough, the fear of being too much. These fears are universal, part of the human condition rather than personal failings. Acknowledging them is not weakness but the first step toward transcending their limiting influence.

The path of the resonant warrior involves specific practices that cultivate courage:

Name your fears. Bring them into the light of awareness rather than allowing them to operate from the shadows. Write them down, speak them aloud to trusted allies, or express them through creative means. This naming begins to diminish their power.

Distinguish fear from intuition. Learn to differentiate between the constricting energy of fear and the expansive energy of intuition. Fear speaks in absolutes, catastrophizes, and fixates on worst-case scenarios. Intuition offers quiet guidance, opens possibilities, and provides a sense of rightness even amid uncertainty.

Take courageous micro actions. Break down intimidating leaps into small steps that stretch but don't overwhelm you. Each micro action builds confidence and momentum, gradually expanding your comfort zone without triggering overwhelming resistance.

Cultivate a courage community. Surround yourself with people who support your authentic expression, who see your potential even when you doubt it, who hold you accountable to your highest aspirations rather than colluding with your limitations.

Practice resilient self-talk. Develop an inner dialogue that acknowledges challenges without being defined by them. Replace catastrophizing ("This is terrible and will never improve") with realistic optimism ("This is difficult, and I have resources to navigate it").

Anchor to purpose. Connect your actions to something larger than your individual comfort or success. When your song serves something you deeply believe in, courage arises more naturally from commitment to that larger purpose.

These practices don't eliminate fear but transform your relationship with it. Fear becomes not an obstacle but a companion on the journey, a natural response to stretching beyond the familiar that signals growth rather than danger. The resonant warrior doesn't wait for fear to disappear before acting but learns to move forward with fear as a passenger rather than a driver.

Picture a street musician playing on a busy corner, exposed and vulnerable to criticism or indifference from passersby. Yet they play anyway, offering their authentic expression despite the risks. Some hurry past, some pause briefly, and occasionally someone stops, transfixed by the beauty they've encountered. This is the courage required of all who would share their unique gifts—the willingness to be seen, to be vulnerable, to offer without guarantee of reception.

> *It is not the critic who counts . . . The credit belongs to the man who is actually in the arena.*
>
> THEODORE ROOSEVELT

This journey isn't about finding people who are like us but those who complement us, challenge us, and inspire us to reach new heights. True creativity often emerges from the interplay of different perspectives, talents, and ways of seeing the world. Resonance includes learning to embrace dissonance not as an obstacle but as an opportunity for growth and innovation.

THE PARADOX OF GROWTH THROUGH DISSONANCE

The most beautiful music often incorporates dissonance that resolves into harmony. The tension creates a yearning for resolution, making the eventual harmony all the more satisfying. Similarly, the challenges we face in creating resonant relationships and building a harmonic legacy are not obstacles to be avoided but essential elements that give our life's symphony depth and meaning.

This paradox of growth through dissonance applies to all meaningful endeavors. The muscle grows stronger through the resistance of weights. The seed breaks open in the darkness of soil before pushing toward light. The butterfly emerges only after the caterpillar dissolves into formless potential within the chrysalis. Transformation requires disruption of what is before what could be can emerge.

In your own life, where are you encountering dissonance that might be the precursor to greater harmony? What challenges in your relationships might be invitations to deeper understanding rather than reasons to disconnect? What difficult emotions might be signals pointing toward important growth rather than problems to be eliminated? What apparent setbacks might be setting the stage for unexpected breakthroughs?

The willingness to stay present with dissonance—rather than immediately resolving it or fleeing from it—creates space for the emergence of more complex and beautiful harmonies. This doesn't mean passively accepting harmful situations but rather engaging with inevitable tensions and challenges as opportunities for evolution rather than merely as problems to be solved.

> ***Out of suffering have emerged the strongest souls; the most massive characters are seared with scars.***
>
> EDWIN HUBBELL CHAPIN

FINDING YOUR ORCHESTRA: THE COMMUNITY OF RESONANCE

As we conclude this chapter, remember that your harmonic legacy isn't created in isolation. It emerges through collaboration with others who resonate with your vision and values, who complement your strengths and compensate for your limitations, who challenge you to grow while supporting your authentic expression.

In the next chapter, we'll explore how to find and effectively collaborate with your band—the people who will help you create The More that wants to live, the transcendent music waiting to be born. We'll delve into principles of purpose-driven collaboration, exploring how to align relationships with a larger vision and create a symphony of impact that resonates far beyond ourselves. We'll learn to stand for something bigger and, in doing so, create a life that is both deeply meaningful and profoundly resonant.

POWER PLAYLIST

STANDING FOR SOMETHING BIGGER

- **"We Are the World" by USA for Africa.** Listen for: Distinct voices merging into unified purpose—notice how individual authenticity strengthens rather than weakens collective impact.
- **"People Get Ready" by Curtis Mayfield.** Listen for: The anticipation that makes positive change feel inevitable—shared vision creates unstoppable momentum.
- **"A Change Is Gonna Come" by Sam Cooke.** Listen for: Patient faith in the face of injustice—how personal struggle becomes universal hope when connected to larger purpose.

Listening Practice: This week, identify one issue or cause that stirs your soul. Choose one song and listen while reflecting on how your unique gifts could serve this larger purpose. Notice which emotions arise—excitement, fear, overwhelm, inspiration. After listening, write in your Resonance Journal: What cause or vision calls to my heart? How might my individual journey of authenticity serve something beyond myself?

Purpose transforms when it moves beyond personal achievement to shared service. These songs remind us that our individual journey toward authenticity finds its highest expression when it contributes to the healing and flourishing of our world.

CHAPTER 14

Eulogy Goals over Résumé Goals: Prioritizing the Music of Relationships

> *Strange is our situation here upon earth. Each of us comes for a short visit, not knowing why, yet sometimes seeming to divine a purpose. From the standpoint of daily life, however, there is one thing we do know: that man is here for the sake of other men.*
>
> ALBERT EINSTEIN

WHAT REALLY MATTERS IN THE END

The resonance of your life isn't measured in achievements framed on walls but in the hearts you've touched along the way.

David Brooks, in his book *The Road to Character*, makes a powerful distinction between "résumé virtues" and "eulogy virtues":

- **Résumé virtues** are the skills you bring to the marketplace—achievements, credentials, and capabilities that advance your career.
- **Eulogy virtues** are the qualities people will remember at your funeral—your kindness, bravery, honesty, and faithfulness in relationships.

Our culture fixates on résumé virtues. We obsess over productivity, status, and measurable outcomes. Social media celebrates visible achievements while the quiet work of relationship often goes unrecognized.

Yet at life's end, the calculus changes dramatically.

THE FINAL MEASURES

Bronnie Ware, an Australian nurse who spent years working in palliative care, wrote the book *The Top Five Regrets of the Dying: A Life Transformed by the Dearly Departing*. The most common regret wasn't about career achievements or wealth accumulation. It was: "I wish I'd had the courage to live a life true to myself, not the life others expected of me."

The second most common? "I wish I hadn't worked so hard"—with many patients expressing deep regret over missing their children's youth or their partner's companionship while pursuing career advancement.

Not a single patient mentioned wishing they had worked longer hours, earned more money, or accumulated more status symbols. Instead, their regrets centered almost entirely around relationships—connections not deepened, love not expressed, forgiveness not offered or received.

This perspective reveals a profound truth: What seems important through most of life often becomes trivial at its end, while what's easily overlooked—the quality of our connections—emerges as what truly mattered all along.

This insight brings us to Pillar #7: Stand for Something Bigger.

Musical Interlude: Imagine the plaintive notes of Leonard Cohen's "Hallelujah." The song captures life's beautiful imperfection—not a triumphant declaration but a broken hallelujah, acknowledging both joy and sorrow. Like our lives, it's not about perfect achievement but perfect expression of our humanity through connection with others. This is the music of eulogy values—raw, authentic, and profoundly resonant.

THE FUNERAL TEST

Imagine sitting in the back row at your own funeral. The people who knew you best have gathered to honor your memory. What would you want to hear them say?

No one delivers eulogies filled with quarterly sales targets, investment portfolios, or LinkedIn endorsements. Instead, they speak of how you made them feel, the wisdom you shared, the times you showed up, and the ways you transformed their lives through genuine connection.

Warren Buffett suggests that the ultimate measure of success is how many people love you. Steve Jobs, despite his legendary drive for perfection in products, has said that going to bed at night believing he's done something wonderful is more important to him than dying wealthy.

The ancient Stoics practiced *memento mori*—remembering death—not as a morbid exercise but as a clarifying perspective. When we confront our mortality, the trivial concerns fall away and what truly matters comes into focus. Our relationships. Our character. Our impact.

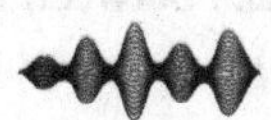

BRIDGE NOTE: THE SCIENCE OF LEGACY

Research from the field of positive psychology reveals that people who define their lives in terms of contribution to others report significantly higher levels of life satisfaction than those who define success primarily through achievement or acquisition. Studies by psychologist Emily Esfahani Smith show that meaning comes not from the pursuit of happiness itself but from commitments that transcend self-interest—particularly those involving close relationships and service to something beyond ourselves.

This research confirms what wisdom traditions have taught for millennia: Our deepest fulfillment comes not from what we accomplish but from how we connect.

THE SOUTH AFRICAN SYMPHONY

This profound shift from résumé to eulogy thinking was illuminated for me during a trip to South Africa with my father shortly after his dementia diagnosis.

One evening, as the African sun painted the savanna in gold and crimson, my father's face lit up with childlike wonder. "This is amazing, isn't it?" he whispered, gesturing toward the horizon. In that moment, I saw not the accomplished businessman he'd been but the essence of his being—his capacity for joy, his appreciation for beauty, his love for the natural world.

We weren't checking items off a bucket list. We were simply present, two souls sharing the miracle of existence. I realized that what mattered wasn't what we were doing but whom I was doing it with. This is what people remember—not your achievements but your presence.

The trip became a living manifestation of eulogy values—prioritizing connection over accomplishment, presence over production, and love over legacy building. It wasn't about creating memories to be captured and displayed; it was about being fully alive together in the sacred space between two hearts.

DISSONANCE NOTE: THE ACHIEVEMENT TRAP

Many high achievers fall into what psychologist Carol Dweck calls the "performance trap"—deriving identity and worth primarily from external recognition. This creates a cycle where accomplishments provide diminishing returns of satisfaction, requiring ever-greater achievements to maintain self-worth.

The achievement trap ultimately leads to what philosopher Kieran Setiya terms "midlife miseries"—the empty feeling that comes from climbing to the top of a ladder only to realize it was leaning against the wrong wall.

Signs you've fallen into the achievement trap include:

- Difficulty celebrating accomplishments before moving to the next goal
- Defining yourself primarily by what you do rather than who you are
- Sacrificing relationships for career advancement
- Persistent feelings of inadequacy despite objective success
- Anxiety when not working or being productive

The trap isn't the pursuit of achievement itself but making achievement the primary measure of your worth and success. The antidote isn't abandoning ambition but reorienting it around eulogy values—using your gifts in service of meaningful connection and contribution.

NAVIGATING THE RÉSUMÉ-EULOGY TENSION

The goal isn't to abandon résumé virtues entirely. Career achievement, financial stability, and skill development remain important. The question is one of primary orientation and ultimate purpose.

Resonance Instrument

THE PRIORITIES ALIGNMENT GRID

This matrix helps evaluate activities and commitments along two dimensions:

Vertical axis: Contribution to résumé goals (low to high)

Horizontal axis: Contribution to eulogy goals (low to high)

This creates four quadrants:

1: High Résumé/Low Eulogy	2: High Résumé/High Eulogy
3: Low Résumé/Low Eulogy	4: Low Résumé/High Eulogy

1. **High Résumé/Low Eulogy:** Activities to limit and clearly bound
2. **High Résumé/High Eulogy:** Ideal activities to maximize
3. **Low Résumé/Low Eulogy:** Activities to minimize or eliminate
4. **Low Résumé/High Eulogy:** Activities to protect and prioritize

The most fulfilling lives maximize Quadrant 2 activities—those that simultaneously build your résumé and eulogy by contributing to others through your unique gifts.

The Integration Principle

The résumé-eulogy tension isn't always a zero-sum game. Research by psychologist Adam Grant shows that "otherish givers"—those who contribute to others while maintaining healthy boundaries—often outperform both selfless givers (who burn out) and pure takers (who optimize for personal gain) in long-term career success.

This suggests the possibility of virtuous integration where eulogy priorities actually enhance résumé outcomes over time.

Musical Interlude: Consider John Coltrane's musical evolution. Early in his career, he was technically brilliant, but he struggled with addiction. As he healed and deepened his spiritual practice, his music transformed. Albums like *A Love Supreme* transcended mere virtuosity to express something profound about human connection and divine love. Technical mastery (résumé) merged with spiritual depth (eulogy) to create his most enduring work. This is the sound of résumé and eulogy values in perfect harmony.

> *Everyone has been made for some particular work, and the desire for that work has been put in every heart.*
>
> RUMI

THE SCIENCE OF WHAT MATTERS

This isn't sentimental philosophy; it's supported by decades of research:

The Harvard Study of Adult Development, spanning over seventy-five years, discovered that the quality of our relationships at age fifty predicts both happiness and physical health at eighty better than any other factor, including wealth, fame, or achievement.

As Robert Waldinger, the study's director, concludes: "Good relationships keep us happier and healthier. Period."

When we redirect our energy from résumé building to relationship nurturing, we aren't sacrificing success—we're redefining it. We're composing a life that will resonate long after we're gone, a symphony that will echo in the lives we've touched.

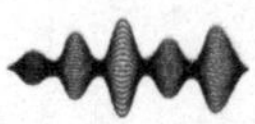

BRIDGE NOTE: THE NEUROSCIENCE OF SOCIAL CONNECTION

Neuroscience research reveals that our brains are fundamentally social organs, wired for connection. When we experience meaningful social connection, our brains release oxytocin and endorphins that reduce stress and increase well-being.

Conversely, social isolation activates the same neural pathways as physical pain, explaining why rejection or loneliness can feel physically painful. Our brains process social exclusion in the same region that registers physical suffering—the anterior cingulate cortex.

This biology suggests that prioritizing relationships isn't a luxury or a distraction from "real work"—it's honoring the fundamental design of our nervous system, which evolved to seek and maintain social bonds as essential to survival.

STANDING FOR SOMETHING BIGGER

The highest expression of relationship comes when we align our connections with purpose beyond personal gain. This doesn't require grand gestures or world-changing movements. It simply means orienting your relationships around contribution rather than acquisition.

True purpose isn't about public recognition or measurable impact. It's about aligning your unique gifts with authentic service to others. This might manifest in raising children with consciousness and care, supporting a friend through crisis, volunteering in your community, creating art that inspires, or bringing integrity to your workplace.

Whatever form it takes, standing for something bigger transforms relationships from means to ends—from what others can do for you to what you can do through each other.

THE RELATIONAL BUCKET LIST: COMPOSING YOUR SYMPHONY OF CONNECTION

Most bucket lists focus on personal achievements and experiences: climb Kilimanjaro, visit the Louvre, learn to play piano. They're about what we want to do, not who we want to become or who we want to connect with.

A relational bucket list inverts this paradigm. It asks: What experiences do I want to create with the people I love? What relationships do I want to deepen before I die? What bonds do I want to heal or strengthen?

Viktor Frankl, Holocaust survivor and psychiatrist, observed that "being human always points, and is directed, to something, or someone, other than oneself." Our most profound moments of meaning emerge not from isolated achievements but from shared experiences that forge deeper connection.

Consider these examples:

- Taking your child on a one-on-one adventure where they choose the destination
- Having the vulnerable conversation you've been avoiding with your parent
- Creating a regular ritual with your partner that deepens your bond
- Reconnecting with the mentor who shaped your early life
- Healing a fractured friendship through genuine reconciliation
- Teaching a skill or sharing wisdom with someone who could benefit from your experience

The power of a relational bucket list lies not in the experiences themselves but in their potential to create resonant connections that endure. They're opportunities to write beautiful passages in the symphonies of our relationships.

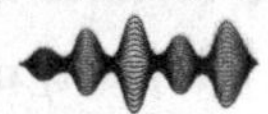

BRIDGE NOTE: THE NEUROSCIENCE OF SHARED EXPERIENCE

Research in neuroscience shows that shared experiences create stronger neural imprints than solo activities. When we engage in meaningful activities with others, our brains release oxytocin and dopamine, creating positive associations with both the experience and the relationship.

These shared moments literally wire our brains for connection, reinforcing the neural pathways of relationship and belonging.

REORDERING YOUR PRIORITIES

How do we shift from résumé goals to eulogy goals? Three essential practices:

1. Clarify What Truly Matters: The Eulogy Exercise

This powerful reflection helps reveal what truly matters by bringing mortality into sharper focus:

Imagine you've lived a rich, fulfilling life and passed away at age ninety. Four people will speak at your memorial service—a family member, a friend, a colleague, and someone from your community. Write the eulogy you would want each to give—not as fantasy but as an authentic reflection of a life well lived according to your deepest values.

What patterns emerge? What qualities and contributions appear across multiple eulogies? How do these priorities compare to where you currently invest your time, energy, and attention? The gaps revealed through this exercise offer invaluable guidance for realignment.

From your eulogy, extract two or three specific "eulogy goals"—intentions focused not on achievement but on the quality of connection and contribution you wish to create. Unlike traditional goals, these aren't about reaching endpoints but about embodying ways of being in relationship.

Examples:

- "To be fully present with my loved ones, creating space for their authentic expression"
- "To stand for others' highest potential, especially when they cannot see it themselves"
- "To build bridges of understanding across difference, creating connection where division once existed"

These eulogy goals become guiding stars for daily choices and priorities.

Dissonance Note: This exercise often produces emotional discomfort, as it reveals misalignment between stated values and actual priorities. Lean into this dissonance rather than avoiding it—it's the fertile ground for meaningful change.

2. Audit Your Time

Our calendars reveal our true priorities, not our stated values. As Annie Dillard writes: "How we spend our days is, of course, how we spend our lives."

Step 1: Track your time use for one week, categorizing activities as:

- **Résumé building** (career advancement, skills development)
- **Relationship building** (meaningful connection, contribution to others)
- **Renewal** (rest, reflection, recreation that restores you)

Step 2: Calculate percentage of time spent in each category.

Step 3: Compare these percentages to your eulogy priorities.

Step 4: Identify one specific adjustment to bring your time use into greater alignment with eulogy values.

This audit often reveals that what we say matters most actually receives the least time and attention, while what we claim to value least gets a disproportionate investment. The first step in realignment is seeing this gap clearly, without judgment but with honesty.

3. Create Relationship Rituals

Eulogy values only manifest through consistent practices. Creating relationship rituals—regular, intentional ways of connecting with others—ensures that what matters most doesn't get crowded out by what matters least.

For each key relationship domain (family, friends, community), design one ritual using these elements:

- **Purpose.** What deeper connection or value does this ritual serve?
- **People.** Who participates?
- **Place.** Where does it happen?
- **Process.** What specific actions occur?
- **Period.** How often and for how long?
- **Promise.** What makes this meaningful enough to prioritize?

Example: The Sunday Letter

Purpose: Express appreciation and maintain meaningful connection with distant loved ones

People: Extended family members and close friends living far away

Place: Written from my desk, sent electronically

Process: Handwritten letter (photographed and emailed) sharing meaningful reflections from my week and asking thoughtful questions

Period: Sunday mornings, thirty minutes

Promise: Creating an ongoing record of connection that transcends distance

Such rituals transform abstract values into concrete practices that shape your legacy one week at a time.

Resonance Instrument

THE RELATIONAL BUCKET LIST

Unlike traditional bucket lists focused on personal achievements, a relational bucket list centers on the connections you want to deepen and the shared experiences you want to create before you die. It shifts focus from what you want to do to who you want to be in relationship with others.

For each important relationship in your life, identify:

1. **Key Relationships:** The five or seven relationships that matter most to you
2. **Relationship Aspirations:** What you hope to create or experience together
3. **Meaningful Experiences:** Specific activities that would deepen each relationship
4. **Healing Opportunities:** Relationships that need reconciliation and what that might look like
5. **Timeline Intention:** When you hope to create each experience (next month, this year, within five years)
6. For each idea on your relational bucket list, ask:
    - How would this experience deepen our connection?
    - What unique gifts or qualities could each person bring to this experience?
    - What might we learn about each other that we don't already know?
    - How might this experience transform our relationship?

This process transforms your approach to both relationships and experiences, creating a life oriented around connection rather than achievement.

A man dies when he refuses to stand up for that which is right. A man dies when he refuses to stand up for justice. A man dies when he refuses to take a stand for that which is true.

MARTIN LUTHER KING JR.

FROM SUCCESS TO SIGNIFICANCE

The journey from résumé goals to eulogy goals often follows a predictable progression:

1. **Success Pursuit:** Building credentials, capabilities, and achievements
2. **Success Attainment:** Reaching external markers of accomplishment
3. **Success Questioning:** Wondering if these achievements truly satisfy
4. **Seeking Meaning:** Exploring deeper sources of fulfillment
5. **Significance Orientation:** Redirecting capabilities toward contribution
6. **Legacy Creation:** Building relationship structures around lasting impact

This evolution doesn't happen automatically. Many people get stuck at stages 2 or 3, continuing to pursue achievements long after they've stopped providing fulfillment.

The shift to significance requires conscious choice—a deliberate reorientation around contribution rather than acquisition.

Resonance Session

BRUCE SPRINGSTEEN'S TURN

After achieving unparalleled success as a rock star, Bruce Springsteen faced a profound internal crisis. As he writes in his autobiography *Born to Run*:

"I had achieved my dreams, but along the way I'd lost track of my personal life, my relationships, and my personal ties to the kind of community I'd grown up in."

Springsteen didn't abandon music. Instead, he reoriented his life and art around deeper connection—to his wife, children, bandmates, and the communities whose struggles informed his songwriting. His later work reflects this shift from pure achievement to meaningful contribution.

This reorientation transforms not just priorities but identity itself—from achievement-based worth to contribution-based purpose.

THE COURAGE TO PRIORITIZE WHAT TRULY MATTERS

Shifting from résumé goals to eulogy goals isn't simple. It requires courage to swim against powerful cultural currents that equate worth with achievement and status.

We live in a society that constantly reinforces résumé values. Social media celebrates visible achievements while the quiet work of relationship often goes unrecognized. Friends and family may question choices that prioritize connection over advancement. Employers may view relationship-oriented boundaries as lack of commitment.

Navigating these pressures requires both clarity and courage—the clarity to know what truly matters to you and the courage to organize your life accordingly.

Resonance Instrument

THE COURAGE CULTIVATION PRACTICE

When facing difficult priority choices, try this three-step practice:

1. **Future-self consultation.** Imagine your ninety-year-old self looking back on this decision. What would they advise?
2. **Values articulation.** Write a single sentence expressing the value that would guide your highest self in this situation.
3. **Commitment action.** Identify one small, concrete step that honors this value, regardless of external pressure.

This practice builds the courage muscle for larger alignment choices over time.

CREATING A LIFE ORIENTED AROUND RELATIONSHIP

Ultimately, prioritizing eulogy goals means designing your life with relationship at its center rather than its periphery. This doesn't require abandoning ambition but rather redefining it—from individual achievement to collective contribution.

Real-World Application: Three Shifts Toward Eulogy Living

1. **The Meeting Shift:** Begin team meetings with brief personal check-ins rather than diving straight into tasks.
2. **The Technology Shift:** Create phone-free zones and times to ensure technology serves relationship rather than displacing it.
3. **The Recognition Shift:** Celebrate relationship achievements (reconciliations, deepened connections, community contributions) with the same enthusiasm normally reserved for career milestones.

These small shifts create space for a relationship to move from the margins to the center of daily life.

TRANSFORMATIONAL PRACTICE: THE VALUES-TIME ALIGNMENT

1. List your top five eulogy values—the qualities you most want to be remembered for.
2. For each value, identify one relationship where this quality is most needed currently.
3. Schedule three specific "eulogy value" time blocks in your calendar for the coming week—protected time dedicated to expressing these values in key relationships.
4. After each time block, journal briefly about how it felt to prioritize eulogy values explicitly.

This practice bridges the gap between abstract values and concrete time allocation—the essential step in living toward your desired legacy.

Resonance Instrument

THE QUARTERLY REFLECTION

Understanding the distinction between résumé and eulogy goals is just the beginning. The real transformation comes through consistent action aligned with this new perspective.

Every ninety days, set aside time to assess your alignment with eulogy values:

1. Review your eulogy draft and relational bucket list.
2. Evaluate progress on your eulogy goals.
3. Identify relationships that need more attention.
4. Schedule specific relationship experiences for the coming quarter.
5. Adjust your calendar to reflect eulogy priorities.

This regular assessment prevents drift and ensures that daily choices align with ultimate priorities.

THE RELATIONSHIP INVESTMENT PORTFOLIO

Just as financial advisors recommend diversified investment portfolios, relationships require thoughtful allocation of your emotional and temporal resources. Create a relationship investment strategy that includes:

1. **Core Holdings:** Your most essential relationships that receive consistent, substantive investment

2. **Growth Investments:** Newer relationships with potential for meaningful connection
3. **Legacy Investments:** Mentoring and nurturing the next generation
4. **Maintenance Investments:** Valuable relationships that need occasional tending
5. **Relationship Pruning:** Courageous decisions about relationships that consistently deplete rather than nourish

This approach ensures intentional stewardship of your relational resources, maximizing their potential for both fulfillment and impact.

The purpose of life is not to be happy. It is to be useful, to be honorable, to be compassionate, to have it make some difference that you have lived.

LEO ROSTEN

POWER PLAYLIST

WHAT REALLY MATTERS

This playlist explores the tension between achievement and meaning, helping you reflect on what truly matters at life's end. Each song invites contemplation of the qualities and contributions that create lasting significance. As you listen, consider how these themes might guide your daily choices and long-term priorities.

- **"The Dance" by Garth Brooks.** Listen for: The choice to engage deeply despite life's brevity—how embracing vulnerability becomes the path to meaningful living.

- **"Cat's in the Cradle" by Harry Chapin.** Listen for: The painful recognition of misaligned priorities—the relationships we neglect can become our deepest regrets.
- **"Humble and Kind" by Tim McGraw.** Listen for: Simple virtues that echo through generations—the quiet acts of decency that outlive all our achievements.

Listening Practice: This week, imagine you're writing your own eulogy. Choose one song and listen while reflecting on what you'd want remembered about how you loved rather than what you accomplished. Notice which emotions arise—regret, gratitude, urgency, peace. After listening, write in your Resonance Journal: What would I want said about how I treated people? What small shift could better align my daily choices with these deeper values?

Creating Your Personal Additions: Add songs that remind you of people you've lost or moments when you felt most alive and present with others. Consider how these songs clarify what matters most when everything else falls away.

At life's end, our résumés become irrelevant, but our relationships remain eternal. These songs remind us that the love we give and receive creates the only legacy that truly matters—not what we achieved, but how we made others feel and how we chose to show up in the precious time we had together.

THE MUSIC THAT REMAINS

At life's end, what remains isn't the positions you held, the money you earned, or the possessions you accumulated. What remains is the impact you had on others—the love you expressed, the wisdom you shared, the bridges you built.

By consciously reorienting your priorities from résumé goals to eulogy goals—from what you achieve to how you relate—you create a life of deeper meaning and lasting significance.

Remember: The résumé-driven life asks, "How can I succeed?" The eulogy-driven life asks, "How can I matter?" The first leads to achievement; the second leads to fulfillment.

In our résumé-obsessed culture, choosing to prioritize eulogy values requires courage, clarity, and community. It means swimming against powerful currents of validation and status seeking. But as we've explored throughout this journey of resonance, the most meaningful music isn't played in isolation but in harmony with others.

As we move to our final chapter, we'll explore how to channel this reorientation into your most meaningful dream projects—creating collaborative symphonies that manifest your unique contribution through resonant relationships.

CHAPTER 15

Symphony: Resonance and Your Dream Projects

Coming together is a beginning, staying together is progress, and working together is success.

EDWARD EVERETT HALE

THE MAGIC OF CREATIVE COLLABORATION

In 1967, four young musicians—Aretha Franklin, her sisters Carolyn and Erma, and songwriter Carolyn White—gathered around a piano in Atlantic Records' New York studio. Together they transformed a song written by Otis Redding from a man's demand for respect into an anthem of female empowerment that would define a generation.

This moment exemplifies the magic of creative collaboration—what happens when diverse talents unite around shared vision to create something none could produce alone.

Your most meaningful contributions will likely follow this pattern. Your dream projects—whether artistic creations, business ventures, social movements, or community initiatives—achieve their highest expression not through solo brilliance but through collaborative genius.

This final chapter explores how to orchestrate your unique "symphony"—bringing together complementary talents around shared purpose to manifest your greatest contribution through resonant relationships.

Musical Interlude: Picture a jazz ensemble in full flow—each musician taking their moment to solo while others provide support, then seamlessly shifting roles as another voice takes center stage. No conductor dictates; the music emerges from mutual listening and responsive creativity. This is the sound of collaborative genius—individual excellence in service of collective creation, where the whole transcends the sum of its parts.

Alone we can do so little; together we can do so much.

HELEN KELLER

RESONANCE REFLECTION: YOUR SYMPHONY OF PURPOSE

Before we dive deeper, take a moment to connect with the music that wants to be born through your collaboration with others:

Close your eyes and envision your most ambitious dream project—a vision that excites you but feels impossible to achieve alone. Perhaps it's starting a community initiative, writing a book, launching a business with positive impact, or creating a movement for change.

Now imagine you've found your perfect collaborators—people whose skills complement yours, whose values align with your own, whose energy amplifies your vision. Feel the creative electricity that flows between you, the way your individual limitations dissolve in the power of your collective creativity.

Notice how your body responds to this vision. Is there a warming in your chest? An expansiveness in your breathing? A lifting of your spirit? This physical response is your body's recognition of resonance at scale—the symphony that emerges when we align our unique gifts with others around shared purpose.

Pause now to record in your Resonance Journal:

- What specific dream project emerged in your visualization?
- Who appeared as your ideal collaborators? What qualities did they embody?
- What physical sensations or emotions arose as you envisioned this collaboration?

Throughout this chapter, we'll return to this dream project as we explore how to transform individual notes into a magnificent symphony of purpose.

FROM SOLO TO SYMPHONY: THE COLLABORATION SPECTRUM

Creative work exists along a spectrum from solo performance to symphonic collaboration:

1. **Solo Performance:** Individual creation with minimal input from others
2. **Consultation:** Primary creation by an individual with targeted feedback from others
3. **Coordination:** Individual contributions combined under central direction
4. **Cooperation:** Shared creation with divided responsibilities

5. **Collaboration:** Fully integrated creative process where outcomes emerge from interaction
6. **Co-creation:** Boundary-dissolving partnership where individual contributions become inseparable

Most transformative projects operate at levels 4–6, where diverse perspectives generate solutions beyond any individual's conception.

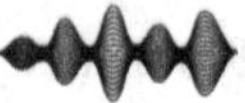

BRIDGE NOTE: THE SCIENCE OF COLLABORATIVE GENIUS

Research by psychologist Keith Sawyer reveals that breakthrough innovations rarely come from lone geniuses. Rather, they emerge from what he calls "group genius"—the dynamic interaction of diverse minds around shared challenges.

The key insight: Innovation happens not primarily within individual minds but in the spaces between them—through the resonant dialogue of different perspectives.

When we examine history's great innovations, we discover that they rarely sprang fully formed from isolated minds. Instead, they emerged from rich networks of interaction, where ideas could combine and recombine in novel ways. The light bulb, the internet, jazz music, and countless other innovations resulted not from individual brilliance alone but from collaborative ecosystems that allowed ideas to evolve through interaction.

This research challenges our cultural mythology of the lone genius and suggests that our most significant contributions may come not through solitary effort but through creating conditions for collective brilliance.

PILLAR #7: STAND FOR SOMETHING BIGGER (THE DRUM)

The drum is our metaphor for this final pillar because it represents the heartbeat of purpose that gives life to our relationships. In many musical traditions across cultures, the drum doesn't just keep time; it connects musicians to something primordial, to the very pulse of life itself. Similarly, when we align our relationships with larger purpose, we connect to something fundamental and essential—to the values, causes, and creative possibilities that give meaning to our existence.

Standing for something bigger means recognizing that our most fulfilling relationships aren't just about what we get from each other but about what we create together. It's about asking: What wants to be born through our connection? What becomes possible when we unite our gifts in service to something we both value deeply?

This pillar transforms relationships from ends in themselves to vehicles for impact. It elevates our connections from pleasant exchanges to partnerships of purpose. And paradoxically, when we align our relationships with something larger than ourselves, those relationships often become deeper, more resilient, and more fulfilling.

The scientific evidence for this is compelling. Research consistently shows that having a sense of purpose is strongly associated with greater happiness, life satisfaction, and even physical health. When we feel that our lives have meaning and that we're contributing to something larger than ourselves, we experience more fulfillment and deeper connection.

BUILDING YOUR IDEAL BAND FOR MEANINGFUL PROJECTS

Resonance Session

THE BEATLES' CREATIVE CHEMISTRY

The Beatles transformed music history not just through individual talent but through a specific collaborative chemistry. Each member brought distinct strengths:

- John Lennon: Conceptual visionary with cutting lyrical edge
- Paul McCartney: Melodic craftsman with commercial instincts
- George Harrison: Spiritual seeker with instrumental innovation
- Ringo Starr: Rhythmic anchor with unpretentious authenticity

Their magic came not from four brilliant musicians working separately but from the creative friction between their different approaches. As producer George Martin noted: "They sparked each other. John needed Paul's attention to detail and positivity; Paul needed John's anarchic wordplay and edge."

This exemplifies ideal creative collaboration—where diverse strengths create something beyond what any individual could conceive alone.

The Beatles' story teaches us several principles of resonant collaboration:

1. **Complementary strengths.** Each member brought different but harmonizing gifts.

2. **Creative tension.** Their differences created productive friction rather than destructive conflict.
3. **Shared vision.** Despite different approaches, they aligned around a common purpose.
4. **Mutual respect.** They recognized and valued each other's unique contributions.
5. **Continuous evolution.** Their willingness to experiment and grow together sustained creativity.

These principles apply whether you're creating music, launching a business, driving social change, or pursuing any meaningful collaborative project.

Dissonance Note: The Ego Trap

The eventual breakup of the Beatles also offers cautionary wisdom. When individual egos begin to overshadow collective purpose, even the most brilliant collaborations can fracture. As the band's success grew, so did tensions around creative control, outside influences, and diverging visions. Their story reminds us that sustaining collaboration requires ongoing attention to relationship health, shared purpose, and balanced contribution.

QUEEN AT LIVE AID: THE TRANSCENDENT MOMENT OF SHARED PURPOSE

On July 13, 1985, something extraordinary happened at Wembley Stadium in London. Among dozens of legendary performers at the Live Aid concert for Ethiopian famine relief, one band delivered a twenty-minute set that would be remembered as one of the greatest live performances in rock history.

Queen took the stage that afternoon not just as four musicians, but as a unified force of nature. Their front man, Freddie Mercury, commanded the stadium with such magnetic presence that 72,000 people moved as one body, clapping in unison, singing every word, responding to his every gesture with perfect synchronicity.

What made this performance transcendent wasn't just the band's technical brilliance or Mercury's charismatic presence. It was the perfect alignment of purpose, moment, and authentic connection—both among the band members and between the band and audience.

Queen's Live Aid performance exemplifies what becomes possible when we align our talents with a purpose greater than ourselves. They weren't just entertaining; they were channeling their gifts in service to a humanitarian cause that transcended national boundaries, political differences, and cultural divides. They became conductors of collective emotion, unity, and purpose.

FINDING YOUR SYMPHONY ORCHESTRA: BUILDING YOUR DREAM TEAM

Creating a resonant dream project requires finding the right collaborators—people who complement your strengths, share your values, and bring unique perspectives to the collective endeavor. Like a symphony orchestra that needs different instruments to create a rich, textured sound, your project will benefit from diverse talents united by shared purpose.

The Four Essential Roles

While every project has unique needs, most successful collaborations include these four fundamental roles:

1. **The Visionary:** This person holds the big picture, the inspiring "why" behind the project. They maintain connection to purpose and help the team navigate uncertainty by returning to fundamental values. Visionaries ask: "What's possible? Why does this matter? Where are we headed?"
2. **The Strategist:** This person translates vision into actionable plans, creating pathways from current reality to desired outcomes. They

think systematically about resources, timing, and approach. Strategists ask: "How will we get there? What's the most effective approach? What sequence of actions will create momentum?"

3. **The Implementer:** This person excels at execution, translating plans into consistent action. They manage details, maintain quality standards, and ensure progress toward goals. Implementers ask: "What needs to happen today? Who's responsible for each task? How do we maintain excellence in execution?"
4. **The Connector:** This person builds relationships both within the team and with external stakeholders. They foster team cohesion, navigate interpersonal dynamics, and create bridges to necessary resources. Connectors ask: "How are we working together? What relationships do we need to nurture? How can we leverage our network?"

These roles aren't rigid job descriptions but rather functions that must be fulfilled for a project to succeed. One person might embody multiple roles, or a role might be shared among several people. The key is ensuring all four functions are present and valued.

Creating Resonant Collaboration

Beyond filling essential roles, successful dream teams share certain characteristics:

Complementary strengths. Look for collaborators whose strengths complement yours. If you're a visionary but struggle with details, partner with strong implementers. If you excel at strategy but find relationship management challenging, bring in talented connectors.

Shared values, diverse perspectives. The most innovative teams combine alignment on fundamental values with diversity of experience and perspective. Find people who share your "why" but might see the "how" differently. This creative tension, when navigated with respect, generates breakthrough solutions.

Trust and psychological safety. For collaboration to flourish, team members must feel safe to express ideas, voice concerns, and take risks without fear of judgment or rejection. Build relationships where authenticity is valued and mistakes are treated as learning opportunities.

Clear agreements, flexible approach. Establish clear agreements about goals, roles, and decision-making processes, but remain flexible in your approach. The most successful collaborations balance structure with adaptability, principles with experimentation.

Celebration of contribution. Create a culture that acknowledges and celebrates each person's unique contributions. Recognition isn't just about achievements but about valuing the distinct qualities each person brings to the collective effort.

The Harmony of Differences

True resonance doesn't emerge from sameness but from the harmony of differences. The Beatles weren't powerful because they were identical; they were powerful because their distinct personalities and talents created something that none could have achieved alone.

In your own dream projects, resist the temptation to collaborate only with those who think exactly like you. Instead, seek out those whose different perspectives, experiences, and approaches will challenge and expand your own. The most extraordinary symphonies emerge not from uniformity but from diverse instruments finding harmony together.

Resonance Instrument

THE MANIFESTO DEVELOPMENT PROCESS

Your dream project needs more than a business plan; it needs a soul. This instrument helps you articulate the "why" behind your vision, creating a powerful tool for attracting and aligning resonant collaborators.

Purpose: To create a compelling declaration of purpose that helps you attract the right collaborators and maintain alignment during your project's evolution

Time Required: Two to three hours initially, with regular refinement

Materials: Your Resonance Journal, research notes, inspiration sources

Practice:

1. **Define Your Vision:** In your Resonance Journal, write a clear and concise statement of your dream project.
   - What specifically do you want to create or achieve?
   - What change do you hope to see in the world as a result?
   - What would success look like in one year? Five years? Ten years?
2. **Articulate Your Values:** Identify three to five core values that underpin your vision.
   - Why is this project important to you?
   - What principles are nonnegotiable in how you pursue this vision?
   - What kind of culture do you want to create within your collaborative effort?
3. **Identify The More:** Connect your project to something bigger than yourself.
   - Who will benefit from this work beyond yourself and immediate stakeholders?
   - What larger systems, challenges, or aspirations does your project address?

- How does this project contribute to human flourishing or planetary well-being?

4. **Describe Your Ideal Collaborators:** Envision the people who will help bring this vision to life.
   - What qualities, skills, and values are essential in your collaborators?
   - What kinds of diversity (perspective, experience, background) will strengthen the project?
   - What relationships will you need to cultivate for this project to succeed?
5. **Craft Your Manifesto:** Write a one- to two-page declaration that outlines your vision, values, and purpose.
   - Begin with a compelling "why" that communicates the deeper purpose.
   - Articulate clear principles that will guide the work.
   - Use language that inspires while remaining authentic to your voice.
   - Include a clear invitation for others to join the journey.
6. **Share Your Manifesto:** Release your declaration into the world, inviting others to join you.
   - Share it with potential collaborators, mentors, and supporters.
   - Use it to guide decision-making as your project evolves.
   - Revisit and refine it as your understanding deepens.

Variations:

- **Visual Manifesto:** Create a visual representation of your vision using images, colors, and symbols.
- **Audio Manifesto:** Record yourself speaking your manifesto with music that captures its spirit.

- **Collaborative Manifesto:** Develop the manifesto with early collaborators, creating shared ownership from the beginning.

Tuning Tips:
Focus on inspiration over information—a manifesto should move people emotionally. Use concrete language rather than jargon or abstraction, and keep it concise. A manifesto should be easily shared and remembered. Most of all, ensure your statement reflects your authentic voice rather than what you think others want to hear.

Real-World Applications: Use your manifesto to:

- Attract aligned collaborators who resonate with your vision;
- Guide decision-making when facing challenging choices;
- Maintain focus during the inevitable difficulties of bringing a dream to life;
- Inspire supporters to join your cause;
- Reconnect with your purpose when enthusiasm wanes.

FROM VISION TO REALITY: FOUR PHASES OF COLLABORATIVE CREATION

Bringing a dream project to fruition typically involves four distinct phases, each requiring different approaches and mindsets.

Phase 1: Conception

This initial phase focuses on clarifying vision, gathering resources, and building the core team. It's characterized by high energy, expansive thinking, and possibility.

Key Tasks:

- Articulating a compelling vision

- Attracting initial collaborators who share your purpose
- Securing foundational resources
- Conducting research and gathering insights

Common Challenges:

- Balancing vision with practical considerations
- Managing initial enthusiasm without becoming overcommitted
- Finding the right founding team members
- Refining the concept based on research and feedback

Phase 2: Development

This phase involves detailed planning, building systems, and preparing for implementation. It requires patience, thoroughness, and an eye for detail.

Key Tasks:

- Creating detailed implementation plans
- Establishing roles, responsibilities, and decision-making processes
- Developing necessary structures and systems
- Building additional partnerships and resources

Common Challenges:

- Maintaining inspiration during detail-oriented work
- Balancing thoroughness with forward momentum
- Navigating different working styles among team members
- Making decisions that will affect future flexibility

Phase 3: Implementation

This phase focuses on executing plans, managing operations, and addressing emerging challenges. It demands resilience, adaptability, and consistent effort.

Key Tasks:

- Launching initiatives and programs
- Managing day-to-day operations

- Solving problems as they arise
- Monitoring progress and making adjustments

Common Challenges:

- Adapting to unexpected developments
- Maintaining quality while managing growth
- Keeping team members engaged and energized
- Balancing operational demands with strategic vision

Phase 4: Evolution

This final phase involves evaluating impact, refining approaches, and considering expansion or replication. It requires reflection, learning, and strategic thinking.

Key Tasks:

- Assessing outcomes and impact
- Incorporating lessons learned
- Making strategic decisions about next steps
- Celebrating achievements and acknowledging contributions

Common Challenges:

- Objectively evaluating both successes and shortcomings
- Deciding whether to expand, replicate, or conclude
- Maintaining relationships through transitions
- Preserving core purpose while evolving methods

Throughout each phase, the pillars of resonance provide guidance. Generosity creates the foundation for collaboration, deep listening enables learning and adaptation, integrity builds trust during challenges, finding uncommon common ground bridges different perspectives, creating connection opportunities strengthens the collaborative web, and standing for something bigger maintains alignment with purpose.

FROM SOLO TO SYMPHONY: LEADING COLLABORATIVE PROJECTS

Leading a dream project requires a different approach than pursuing individual goals. Following are key mindset shifts and practices for creating resonant leadership.

Shift from Control to Cultivation

Traditional leadership often focuses on control—directing others to achieve predetermined outcomes. Resonant leadership focuses on cultivation—creating conditions where everyone can contribute their best while growing through the experience.

Practically, this means:

- Sharing ownership of both the vision and the process
- Inviting input on significant decisions
- Creating space for experimentation and learning
- Trusting others to fulfill their roles in their own way

Navigate Dissonance Constructively

Every meaningful collaboration encounters dissonance—differences in perspective, approach, or preference that create tension. Rather than avoiding these differences, resonant leaders navigate them constructively.

This involves:

- Treating disagreement as an opportunity for deeper understanding
- Distinguishing between values (which require alignment) and preferences (which allow for flexibility)
- Creating structured processes for addressing conflicts
- Modeling respectful engagement with different viewpoints

Balance Structure and Emergence

Dream projects require both structure (clear agreements, timelines, roles) and emergence (openness to unexpected opportunities, flexibility in approach). Finding this balance is essential for maintaining both progress and creativity.

Effective practices include:

- Establishing clear outcomes while remaining flexible about methods
- Creating regular rhythms for check-ins and coordination
- Balancing planning with space for spontaneity
- Reviewing and revising agreements as the project evolves

Maintain Connection to Purpose

As projects evolve, they often face challenges, setbacks, or unexpected difficulties. During these times, reconnecting with the underlying purpose—the "why" behind the work—becomes essential for maintaining momentum and cohesion.

Ways to sustain this connection include:

- Beginning meetings by revisiting the shared purpose
- Celebrating small wins and connecting them to larger impact
- Sharing stories of how the work affects beneficiaries
- Creating rituals that reinforce collective commitment

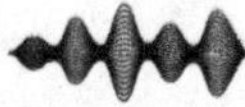

BRIDGE NOTE: THE CONDUCTOR'S BATON

Every great symphony needs a conductor—someone who brings different instruments together in harmony, who ensures that each voice is heard at the right moment, and who maintains the overall vision while attending to the details of execution.

When pursuing a dream project, you become the conductor of your own symphony. This doesn't mean controlling every aspect or micromanaging contributors. Rather, it means:

- **Holding the Vision:** Maintaining clarity about the overall purpose and direction
- **Creating Space:** Ensuring each person has room to express their unique gifts

- **Facilitating Connection:** Building bridges between different contributors
- **Managing Energy:** Knowing when to accelerate and when to rest
- **Navigating Dissonance:** Addressing conflicts constructively while maintaining momentum

Great conductors don't impose their will on the orchestra; they create conditions for collective brilliance to emerge. They understand that their primary role is to serve the music—to help bring forth what wants to be born through the collaborative effort.

As you build your dream projects, ask yourself: What kind of conductor do I want to be? How can I lead in a way that empowers others while maintaining a unified vision? How can I create a field of resonance where everyone feels both individually valued and collectively inspired?

CREATING YOUR SYMPHONY: FROM CONCEPT TO REALITY

The journey from initial concept to realized vision requires both inspiration and methodology. Here's a practical framework for bringing your dream project to life through resonant collaboration:

1. Clarify Your Vision

Begin by getting absolutely clear about what you're creating and why it matters. Write out your vision in detail, identifying both the tangible outcomes and the deeper purpose. Ask yourself:

- What specific change or creation am I working toward?
- Why does this matter to me and to others?
- What would success look like in concrete terms?
- How does this align with my core values?

This clarity becomes your North Star, guiding decisions and helping you communicate your vision to potential collaborators.

2. Map the Ecosystem

Before building your team, understand the broader landscape surrounding your project. Identify:

- Who is already working in this space?
- What related initiatives exist?
- Who might benefit from this project?
- Who might resist or oppose it?
- What resources, knowledge, and connections will be necessary?

This mapping helps you identify potential collaborators, anticipate challenges, and find your unique contribution within the existing ecosystem.

3. Build Your Core Team

With vision and ecosystem understanding in place, begin assembling your collaborative team. Look for people who:

- Share your fundamental values and purpose
- Bring complementary skills and perspectives
- Demonstrate reliability and follow-through
- Communicate openly and navigate conflict constructively
- Show genuine enthusiasm for the vision

Start small—a core team of three to five deeply committed people can accomplish far more than a larger group with lukewarm engagement.

4. Create Clear Agreements

Establish explicit agreements about how you'll work together. Document:

- The shared vision and values

- Each person's roles and responsibilities
- Decision-making processes (especially for difficult decisions)
- Communication expectations and methods
- How you'll address conflicts or disagreements
- Financial arrangements and resource allocation

These agreements prevent misunderstandings and provide a framework for navigating the inevitable challenges.

5. Develop an Iterative Plan

Create a plan that balances clear direction with adaptability. Rather than trying to map every step from beginning to end, focus on:

- Defining clear milestones and success criteria
- Breaking the project into manageable phases
- Identifying the first concrete steps for each team member
- Building in regular review points to assess and adapt

This approach provides structure while allowing for learning and evolution as the project unfolds.

6. Establish Rhythms and Rituals

Create regular practices that maintain connection, alignment, and momentum:

- Weekly check-ins to coordinate activities and address immediate issues
- Monthly deeper reviews to assess progress and make adjustments
- Quarterly strategic conversations to consider the bigger picture
- Celebrations that acknowledge achievements and strengthen relationships

These rhythms create the heartbeat of your collaborative effort, ensuring consistent progress while maintaining human connection.

7. Expand Your Network

As your project develops, systematically build relationships with stakeholders who can support your success:

- Advisors who offer expertise and guidance
- Advocates who amplify your message
- Partners who provide complementary resources or capabilities
- Beneficiaries who offer feedback on impact
- Funders or supporters who provide necessary resources

Remember that these relationships are not just transactional but opportunities for mutual value creation.

8. Navigate Challenges Constructively

Every meaningful project encounters obstacles. When they arise:

- Return to your fundamental purpose and values for guidance
- Address issues directly rather than avoiding uncomfortable conversations
- Focus on learning and adaptation rather than blame
- Be willing to adjust approaches while maintaining commitment to purpose
- Draw on the diverse perspectives in your team to generate solutions

These moments of challenge, when navigated with resonance principles, often become turning points that strengthen both your project and your collaborative relationships.

9. Maintain Personal Sustainability

Creating something meaningful requires sustained energy. Build practices that maintain your own well-being:

- Establish clear boundaries around time and availability.

- Develop renewal rituals that replenish your physical and emotional resources.
- Maintain perspective by connecting with supporters outside the project.
- Celebrate progress and acknowledge contributions, including your own.
- Stay connected to the joy and purpose that inspired you initially.

Remember that your capacity to lead and contribute depends on your own sustainability.

10. Amplify Impact Through Story

As your project creates value, share its story to inspire others and expand your impact:

- Document your journey, including both successes and lessons learned.
- Capture testimonials from those affected by your work.
- Share your methodology so others can build upon it.
- Connect with broader movements aligned with your purpose.
- Create opportunities for others to get involved.

This storytelling extends your impact beyond direct beneficiaries, creating ripples of influence throughout the ecosystem.

THE ENDURING POWER OF COLLABORATION

The history of music offers countless examples of collaborations that transcended what individuals could have created alone. Beyond the Beatles and Queen, consider these inspiring partnerships:

Ella Fitzgerald and Louis Armstrong brought together her precise, crystalline vocals with his warm, gravelly voice and innovative trumpet playing. Their differences created magical chemistry across three albums of duets that remain definitive recordings of classic American songs.

The Buena Vista Social Club united forgotten Cuban musicians in their seventies and eighties, recording an album that won a Grammy, spawned a documentary film, and revitalized not just their careers but worldwide appreciation for Cuban music. Their collaboration came from producer Ry Cooder's vision of reconnecting these master musicians with each other and the world.

Yo-Yo Ma's Silk Road Ensemble brings together musicians from across Asia, Europe, and America to create music that transcends cultural boundaries while honoring distinct traditions. Their work demonstrates how artistic collaboration can build bridges across differences and create new forms of cultural expression.

These musical partnerships remind us that true collaboration isn't about submerging individual gifts but about bringing them together in ways that create something greater than the sum of their parts. They show how differences, when approached with respect and shared purpose, become creative strengths rather than obstacles.

"WE ARE THE WORLD": A SYMPHONY OF UNIFIED VOICES

In 1985, responding to the devastating famine in Ethiopia, a remarkable collaboration unfolded. Some of music's biggest stars—spanning different genres, generations, and backgrounds—gathered in a Los Angeles studio to record a single song for African famine relief.

The project, USA for Africa, brought together forty-five American artists including Michael Jackson, Lionel Richie, Stevie Wonder, Bruce Springsteen, Tina Turner, Bob Dylan, and Ray Charles. What made this gathering extraordinary wasn't just the collection of musical talent but the spirit of unity that permeated the recording session.

The participants checked their egos at the door—producer Quincy Jones famously hung a sign outside the studio requiring exactly that—and came together not as individual stars but as a collective force for good. The artists recorded through the night, many standing for hours, working toward a single purpose that transcended individual recognition.

The resulting song became one of the best-selling singles in history. But its impact extended far beyond record sales. It raised over $63 million for humanitarian aid, helped spark a global movement addressing African famine, and demonstrated music's power to unite people across differences.

Most powerfully, it showed what becomes possible when talented individuals unite around shared purpose. These weren't just singers performing a charity song; they were using their gifts to amplify a message of global interconnection and responsibility. Their collaboration exemplifies the principle of standing for something bigger—showing how aligning relationships with purpose can create exponential impact, transforming individual voices into a global chorus for change.

THE SYMPHONY THAT CALLS YOU

Creating resonant relationships isn't just about enhancing personal happiness or building successful projects. It's about participating in something larger than ourselves—the ongoing symphony of human connection and creation that spans generations.

When we align our authentic gifts with others in service to meaningful purpose, we tap into a power that transcends individual limitation. We become part of a larger story, a continuing conversation, an unfolding symphony that began long before us and will continue long after.

What symphony is calling for your unique contribution? What music wants to be born through your collaboration with others? What purpose awaits your wholehearted engagement?

These questions aren't merely philosophical; they're practical invitations to live with greater meaning and impact. The world needs your authentic note, played in harmony with others, creating music that heals, inspires, and transforms.

As you close this chapter and prepare for the conclusion of our journey together, remember that you're not alone. You're part of a growing community of people committed to creating genuine connection and meaningful impact. Your efforts to build resonance—in your personal relationships, your professional endeavors, and your dream projects—contribute to a world where authentic connection flourishes.

The symphony awaits your unique contribution. The stage is set. The orchestra is gathering.

What music will you create?

POWER PLAYLIST

YOUR SYMPHONY AWAITS

The most meaningful projects bring together individual talents in service of something larger than ourselves. This playlist celebrates the power of working together toward shared vision and transformative impact.

- **"We Are the World" by USA for Africa.** Listen for: How distinct voices merge into one powerful message of hope and action. Notice how individual talents don't disappear but strengthen the collective impact, and how the simple melody allows each artist's unique style to shine while serving the greater good.
- **"Come Together" by The Beatles.** Listen for: The way that uniqueness strengthens rather than threatens unity—each instrument maintains its character while contributing to an unstoppable groove.
- **"Bohemian Rhapsody" by Queen.** Listen for: Four distinct talents creating a musical journey no single artist could achieve—the seamless transitions between rock, opera, and ballad that mirrors how diverse skills combine in dream projects.

Listening Practice: This week, identify one dream project that excites you but feels too big to tackle alone. Choose "We Are the World" and listen while envisioning the collaborators you'd need to make it real. Notice what emotions arise—fear, excitement, overwhelm, hope. After listening, write in your Resonance Journal: What collaborative dream stirs my soul? Who would I need to partner with? What would be my unique contribution to this shared vision?

Creating Your Personal Additions: Add songs that represent your biggest dreams or that remind you of successful collaborations you've been part of. Consider how these songs bridge your individual journey with collective impact.

Your symphony awaits—not the solo performance of individual achievement, but the collaborative masterpiece that emerges when authentic voices unite around shared purpose. These songs remind us that our greatest dreams require not just our own gifts, but the courage to invite others into the music we're meant to create together.

FROM SOLO TO SYMPHONY

In this final chapter, we've explored how to transform individual notes into magnificent symphonies of purpose. We've discovered how resonant relationships become vehicles for collaborative creation that far exceeds what we could achieve alone. Through stories of musical collaboration, practical frameworks for building dream teams, and structured approaches to bringing visions to reality, we've uncovered the transformative potential of standing for something bigger than ourselves.

As we transition to the book's conclusion, we carry forward this understanding: that our unique gifts find their fullest expression not in isolation but in harmonious collaboration with others around shared purpose. The Seven Pillars of Resonant Relationships culminate in this final pillar—standing for something bigger—which gives meaning and direction to all the others.

Your journey of resonance doesn't end with creating better relationships. It continues as you discover how these relationships can become instruments in a grand orchestra, playing a symphony dedicated to something greater than yourself.

CONCLUSION

Live Your Song

Music is the space between the notes.

CLAUDE DEBUSSY

THE JOURNEY OF RESONANCE

We began this journey with a simple but profound observation: Despite unprecedented technological connectivity, we've never been more isolated. The loneliness epidemic that sweeps through modern societies isn't just a personal challenge—it's a collective wound that diminishes our health, happiness, and human potential.

Throughout these pages, we've explored the antidote to this disconnection—not through more digital tools or quick-fix solutions, but through the cultivation of resonant relationships: relationships that vibrate with authenticity, that ring with generosity, that hum with deep listening and integrity.

Our path has taken us from understanding the fundamental value of connection, to finding our authentic voice, to striking resonant chords in our closest relationships, to building our band in professional contexts, and finally to sharing our unique song as part of a larger symphony of purpose.

Along the way, we've discovered that the principles of resonance apply universally—across personal and professional domains, in families and organizations, in momentary encounters and lifelong partnerships. We've seen how the seven pillars create a framework not just for better relationships but for a more meaningful and impactful life:

Be Generous of Time and Energy, Be an Offering (the Hands)—Creating a foundation of goodwill through genuine giving.

Listen Deeply and Be Curious (the Ear)—Developing the capacity for presence and understanding.

Be at Integrity in Word and Action (the Tuning Fork)—Aligning your inner truth with your outer behavior.

Add Value Without Expectation of Return (the Horn)—Contributing uniquely to others' lives from authentic generosity.

Find Uncommon Common Ground (the Strings)—Building bridges across differences through shared values.

Create Exponential Opportunities for Connection (the Conductor's Baton)—Facilitating meaningful interactions beyond yourself.

Stand for Something Bigger (the Drum)—Aligning with purpose beyond personal gain.

These pillars aren't isolated tactics but interconnected aspects of a coherent approach to relationships. Together, they create the conditions for that magical quality we've been calling *resonance*—the amplification of connection that occurs when authentic voices align in harmony.

THE ONGOING PRACTICE OF RESONANCE

Relationships are not destinations but continuous practices. Like music that exists only in the playing, resonance emerges through consistent, intentional action. The understanding you've gained through this book becomes valuable not as abstract knowledge but as lived experience—as daily choices that gradually transform how you relate to others and how others experience you.

As with any profound practice, cultivating resonant relationships involves both challenge and reward. There will be moments of dissonance—times when differences create tension, when old patterns reassert themselves, when harmony seems elusive. These moments aren't failures but opportunities for growth, for deepening understanding, for discovering new dimensions of connection.

The journey toward resonance isn't linear but cyclical. We continually revisit and refine the core practices—returning to generosity when scarcity thinking creeps in, recommitting to deep listening when we've slipped into assumption or judgment, realigning with integrity when our words and actions have diverged. Each cycle takes us deeper, expanding our capacity for authentic connection.

This ongoing nature of the practice is cause not for discouragement but for hope. It means that wherever you are in your relationship journey—whether struggling with profound loneliness or already experiencing meaningful connection—the next step is always available to you. Each interaction, each conversation, each moment of attention offers a fresh opportunity to create resonance.

PRACTICAL NEXT STEPS FOR CONTINUED GROWTH

As you continue your journey of resonant relationships, consider the following structured approaches to deepening your practice.

Daily Practices

Small, consistent actions create the foundation for transformation. Consider incorporating these micro practices into your daily routine:

- **Morning intention setting.** Begin each day by identifying one pillar you'll focus on in your interactions.
- **Gratitude reflection.** End each day by acknowledging three moments of connection or resonance you experienced.
- **Presence pauses.** Take three sixty-second breaks throughout your day to center yourself and reconnect with your intention.
- **Generous acts.** Perform one conscious act of generosity daily, however small or simple.

- **Curiosity questions.** Ask one question each day that demonstrates genuine interest in another person's experience.

Monthly Reviews

Regular reflection accelerates learning and growth. Set aside time each month for:

- **Relationship review.** Assess the health and resonance of your key relationships.
- **Pillar assessment.** Evaluate your practice of each pillar, identifying strengths and growth edges.
- **Intention renewal.** Set specific relationship intentions for the coming month.
- **Challenge identification.** Name one relationship challenge you'll address with conscious attention.
- **Celebration.** Acknowledge and celebrate moments of successful resonance and connection.

Quarterly Challenges

Periodic intensity helps break through plateaus and develop new capacities. Each quarter, consider taking on one of these deeper challenges:

- **Difficult conversation challenge.** Initiate a constructive conversation you've been avoiding.
- **New connection challenge.** Build a relationship with someone outside your usual social circle.
- **Deep listening challenge.** Practice extended listening without interruption or judgment.
- **Vulnerability challenge.** Share something authentic that feels risky but potentially connecting.
- **Network weaving challenge.** Connect two people who could benefit from knowing each other.

Annual Retreats

Dedicated time for deeper reflection creates perspective and renewal. Once a year, give yourself the gift of:

- **Relationship mapping.** Visualize your entire relationship ecosystem and its patterns.
- **Value clarification.** Revisit and refine your core relational values.
- **Legacy consideration.** Reflect on the relational legacy you're creating.
- **Vision development.** Create or renew your vision for your most important relationships.
- **Practice commitment.** Commit to specific relationship practices for the coming year.

These structured approaches provide scaffolding for your ongoing development. Adapt them to your specific circumstances, integrating them with existing routines and rituals that support your growth.

CREATING YOUR UNIQUE SYMPHONY OF IMPACT THROUGH RELATIONSHIPS

Your life is a work of art, composed through countless interactions with others. By consciously cultivating resonant relationships—from your closest personal connections to your widest networks of influence—you create not just a beautiful life for yourself but a lasting legacy that continues to resonate long after your individual song has ended.

This legacy isn't measured primarily in achievements, acquisitions, or accolades but in the quality of connection you've fostered, in the growth you've supported in others, in the bridges you've built across difference, in the moments of authentic presence you've offered. In short, your legacy lives in the hearts and lives of those you've touched—a symphony of impact that transcends your individual existence.

As you continue to develop resonant relationships, consider the unique symphony you're creating. What themes characterize your relational music? What distinctive contribution flows through your connections? What particular quality of resonance emerges from your authentic presence?

There is no single "right" way to create this symphony. Some lives are bold and dramatic like Beethoven's Fifth, others intricate and mathematical like Bach's fugues, others improvisational and boundary pushing like Coltrane's explorations. Your relational symphony will reflect your unique gifts, values, and purpose—the particular music that only you can bring to the world.

The question is not whether you're creating a symphony—you already are, in every interaction, every connection, every moment of presence or distraction, generosity or withholding. The question is whether you're creating it consciously, intentionally, in alignment with your deepest values and highest aspirations.

This book has offered tools, practices, and perspectives to help you compose with greater awareness and skill. The seven pillars provide an instrument you can play with increasing mastery. The resonance practices offer ways to tune this instrument and develop your musical capabilities. The frameworks for application show how to adapt your playing to different contexts and relationships.

But the music itself—the particular symphony that emerges from your life—can come only from you. It arises from your authentic voice, your unique perspective, your distinctive blend of experiences and insights. It takes shape through your specific constellation of relationships, through the particular communities and contexts where you live and work and create.

A RETURN TO THE HEART OF RESONANCE

As we conclude our exploration, let's return to where we began—to the heart of resonance itself. Remember that resonance isn't just a technique or strategy but a quality of connection that emerges when certain conditions are present:

- When we show up authentically, sharing our true selves rather than polished performances

- When we extend genuine curiosity toward others, seeking to understand rather than to judge
- When we create generous space for others to be fully themselves, without expectation or demand
- When we align our words and actions with our deepest values, building foundations of trust
- When we contribute our unique gifts without attachment to recognition or return
- When we find points of connection across our differences, building bridges rather than walls
- When we facilitate connection beyond ourselves, creating webs of relationships that sustain communities
- When we dedicate ourselves to purposes larger than personal gain, finding meaning in contribution

In these conditions, something magical happens—a vibration that amplifies, a connection that deepens, a resonance that transforms isolated notes into beautiful music. This resonance isn't just metaphorical; we feel it in our bodies, recognize it in our spirits, experience it in the tangible results of our relationships.

And while the cultivation of resonance requires practice, discipline, and consistent attention, it isn't fundamentally complicated. At its core, it's about showing up fully human in the presence of others, offering the gift of your authentic self, and creating space for others to do the same. It's about recognizing that we are not isolated individuals but interconnected beings, designed for connection, capable of creating something far more beautiful together than we ever could alone.

The world needs your music. Play it with courage, generosity, and joy.

Sources and Further Reading

FOUNDATIONAL RESEARCH

Harvard Study of Adult Development

Waldinger, R. (2015). What makes a good life? Lessons from the longest study on happiness [TED Talk].

Waldinger, R. J., and Schulz, M. S. (2023). *The Good Life: Lessons from the World's Longest Scientific Study of Happiness*. Simon & Schuster.

U.S. Surgeon General's Advisory

Office of the Surgeon General. (2023). *Our epidemic of loneliness and isolation: The U.S. Surgeon General's advisory on the healing effects of social connection and community*. US Department of Health and Human Services.

Social Connection and Mortality

Holt-Lunstad, J., Smith, T. B., and Layton, J. B. (2010). "Social relationships and mortality risk: A meta-analytic review." *PLoS Medicine*, 7(7): e1000316.

Neural Coupling and Communication

Stephens, G. J., Silbert, L. J., and Hasson, U. (2010). "Speaker-listener neural coupling underlies successful communication." *Proceedings of the National*

Academy of Sciences, 107(32): 14425–14430. https://doi.org/10.1073/pnas.1008662107.

Authenticity and Well-Being

Sheldon, K. M., Ryan, R. M., Rawsthorne, L. J., and Ilardi, B. (1997). "Trait self and true self: Cross-role variation in the Big-Five personality traits and its relations with psychological authenticity and subjective well-being." *Journal of Personality and Social Psychology*, 73(6): 1380–1393.

Generosity and Happiness

Aknin, L. B., Barrington-Leigh, C. P., Dunn, et. al. (2013). "Prosocial spending and well-being: Cross-cultural evidence for a psychological universal." *Journal of Personality and Social Psychology*, 104(4): 635–652. https://doi.org/10.1037/a0031578.

Dunn, E. W., Aknin, L. B., and Norton, M. I. (2008). "Spending money on others promotes happiness." *Science*, 319(5870): 1687–1688. https://doi.org/10.1126/science.1150952.

Trust and High-Performance Organizations

Kosfeld, M., Heinrichs, M., Zak, P. J., Fischbacher, U., and Fehr, E. (2005). "Oxytocin increases trust in humans." *Nature*, 435(7042): 673–676. https://doi.org/10.1038/nature03701.

Zak, P. J. (2017). *Trust Factor: The Science of Creating High-Performance Companies*. AMACOM.

BOOKS AND BLOGS

Brooks, D. (2015). *The Road to Character*. Random House.

Brown, B. (2010). *The Gifts of Imperfection: Let Go of Who You Think You're Supposed to Be and Embrace Who You Are*. Hazelden Publishing.

Buettner, D. (2012). *The Blue Zones: 9 Lessons for Living Longer from the People Who've Lived the Longest*. National Geographic.

Dweck, C. (2006). *Mindset: The New Psychology of Success*. Random House.

Ferrazzi, K. (2005). *Never Eat Alone: And Other Secrets to Success, One Relationship at a Time.* Crown Business.

Ferriss, T. (n.d.). The Tim Ferriss Blog. Retrieved from https://tim.blog.

Grant, A. (2013). *Give and Take: A Revolutionary Approach to Success.* Viking.

Mandela, N. (1994). *Long Walk to Freedom: The Autobiography of Nelson Mandela.* Little, Brown and Company.

Nelson Mandela Foundation. (2010). *Nelson Mandela by Himself: The Authorised Book of Quotations.* Macmillan.

INTERVIEWS

Elton John and Bernie Taupin

Grow, K. (2019, May 31). The man behind the Rocketman: Lyricist Bernie Taupin on his 50-year bond with Elton John. *Time.*

Queen/Live Aid

Guitar.com. (2020, November 11). Brian May says Queen first thought their historic Live Aid set was only "kind of OK."

"We Are the World"

Nguyen, B. (Director). (2024). *The greatest night in pop* [Documentary film]. Netflix.

Yo-Yo Ma

Rolling Stone. (2021, October 21). Yo-Yo Ma talks new MasterClass, YouTube cellists and discovering his "own purpose."

Harvard Business Review. (2016, June). Life's work: An interview with Yo-Yo Ma.

Complete citations (more than sixty peer-reviewed studies), extended research, community resources, interactive content, and curated streaming playlists are available at resonance.biz.

Acknowledgments

This book exists because countless individuals shared their stories, wisdom, and hearts with me. Like the resonance it describes, *Resonance* emerged from the beautiful intersection of many voices.

To the indigenous elders whose wisdom flows throughout these pages—you taught me that connection is medicine. To the Harvard researchers and scientists whose rigorous work forms this book's foundation—thank you for illuminating what the heart has always known.

To Rick Chillot and Peter Guzzardi, my editorial partners who helped transform complex ideas into accessible wisdom. To the team at BenBella who believed in this message. To my agent, Jaidree Braddix, for your early belief and guidance.

To the countless individuals who shared their stories of connection and disconnection—your vulnerability became wisdom for others. To my colleagues who understand that changing the world requires first changing how we connect with one another.

To the musicians whose artistry provided the soundtrack for this exploration—from the Beatles to Bill Withers to countless others whose songs capture truths about human connection that science is only beginning to understand.

To my father, for his heart; your music lives on in me. To my mother for her love and fearless advocacy. To my sister and niece for their gracious love. To my family members who trusted me to share our stories, understanding that vulnerability in service of others' healing is among the most generous gifts we can offer.

To the readers who will take these ideas and make them their own—this book is complete only when it becomes action in your life.

The loneliness epidemic is real, but so is our capacity for connection. Every conversation matters. Every moment of authentic presence ripples outward in ways we may never fully comprehend.

Any errors in this work are mine alone. Any wisdom it contains belongs to all of us.

Author's Note

This book represents years of research, personal experience, and reflection on human connection. Several important aspects of how this work was created deserve acknowledgment.

On Scientific Accuracy

All research studies, statistical claims, and academic theories have been rigorously fact-checked and properly cited. The psychological principles, neuroscience findings, and social research are drawn from peer-reviewed sources representing the best current understanding in their fields. Complete sources can be found in the bibliography and at [resonance.biz].

On Personal Stories

The experiences I share are authentic reflections of my journey. However, I have taken creative license to protect privacy and enhance narrative clarity:

"Ananda," the teacher whose wisdom appears throughout the book, is a composite character representing several remarkable individuals who have profoundly influenced my understanding of connection. While the name is fictional, the teachings are drawn from real conversations with multiple mentors over many years.

Names and identifying details have been changed to protect privacy, except for public figures who have given permission. Some anecdotes have been condensed while preserving essential truth and learning.

ON COLLABORATIVE CREATION

While the ideas, framework, and personal insights are entirely my own, this book benefited from collaborative refinement:

Editorial Partnership: Rick Chillot and Peter Guzzardi's expertise helped refine clarity, structure, and impact, ensuring that complex psychological concepts became accessible and actionable.

AI-Assisted Flow: In the spirit of transparency, I utilized artificial intelligence tools for research verification, structural analysis, and language refinement. However, all core concepts, personal stories, frameworks, and conclusions are my own work and reflection.

This reflects my belief that meaningful creation—like meaningful connection—emerges from the intersection of human insight and available resources.

ON TRUTH AND STORYTELLING

Tim O'Brien observed, "A thing may happen and be a total lie; another thing may not happen and be truer than the truth" (O'Brien, 1990). While I have strived for factual accuracy, I recognize that the deepest truths about human connection often live between strict fact and meaningful narrative.

Every story serves the larger truth of our fundamental need for authentic relationship. Where I have taken creative license, it has been to better serve this truth, never to mislead or misrepresent the scientific foundations.

All quoted material falls within fair use guidelines and academic citation standards. Cultural practices have been researched through authoritative sources to ensure respectful representation.

The work of connection—like the work of writing—is never done alone.

About the Author

Michael with his father John in South Africa

In 2013, Michael Trainer received the call every son fears: his father had been diagnosed with dementia. Time, already precious, had just become finite.

Instead of waiting for memory to fade, Michael did something radical. He took his father to South Africa—to track rhinos, watch African sunsets, and create one more adventure that would outlast the disease. In those moments of presence, as his father's mind began to slip, Michael discovered what years of achievement hadn't taught him: true connection transcends memory and circumstance; it's not something we have, it's something we create.

This wasn't an obvious insight for someone who had spent years coordinating billions in commitments from world leaders.

As co-creator of the Global Citizen Festival, Michael helped launch and build a movement that has generated over $40 billion toward ending extreme poverty—working with artists from Beyoncé to Coldplay, leaders from US presidents to UN Secretary Generals, creating an impact that will touch the lives of millions. A Fulbright Scholar and Columbia University graduate fellow, he had every credential and connection.

But backstage at those festivals, between the pitches and performances, Michael kept noticing something: the commitments that moved billions didn't come from perfect presentations. They emerged from authentic relationships. From what he came to call resonance.

This pattern sent him on an unlikely journey—from researching connection science at Columbia University to living with a seventh-generation indigenous healer. From facilitating conversations with President Carter and His Holiness the Dalai Lama to exploring vulnerability with musicians John Mayer and Alicia Keys. He was searching for the science and art behind genuine human connection.

What emerged became the Seven Pillars of Resonance—a framework born from research, ancient wisdom, and the lived experience of creating connection at every scale, from intimate relationships to global movements.

Michael now helps leaders develop the inner capacity for outer impact. He works with executives, entrepreneurs, and change-makers across seven continents, always returning to the same fundamental truth: meaningful work is rooted in meaningful relationships.

Michael believes the loneliness epidemic isn't about lacking people—it's about lacking presence. The Surgeon General has declared disconnection a public health crisis. But a crisis is also an opportunity.

Healing our world begins with healing our capacity to truly see one another. That healing is possible. That healing is practical. That healing starts with resonance.

Resonance is his first book, born from a lifetime of learning how to truly connect.